SHATTERED
Treasure

Springbrook Press

CINDY PATTERSON

For information contact; www.cindypattersonbks.com
Cover design by: Roseanna White Designs
Editor: Charlene Patterson

Published by Springbrook Press, North Carolina

ISBN: 978-1-64669-040-4 Paperback

ISBN: 978-1-64669-041-1 Hardback

ISNB: 978-1-64669-042-8 Ebook

Library of Congress Control Number: 2019918847

Printed in the United States of America.

PRAISE FOR CINDY PATTERSON'S BOOKS

"Author has a gift for emotional description, that pulse-pounding realization that escape is needed, and the physical. Author also gives us rounded settings with plenty of sensory details to add realism, and author brings our attention to some details that can be revealed, while others require our patience for well-crafted story structure. Revelations are very authentic for an injured, fearful character who must unspool slowly, and the author's empathetic writing forms great logic in that." Broken Butterfly~*Writers Digest*

"Broken Butterfly by Cindy Patterson is a well written romance novel with highly developed characters that felt just like real people." Broken Butterfly~*Reader's Favorite*

"A well-crafted and heartwarming cross-cultural tale of first love." Chasing Paradise~Kirkus Reviews

"This lesser known author captured me completely with her words, her complex characters, and a plot line that will blow you away from the start. Her words were captivating, pulling the reader into the heart of the story instantly." Chasing Paradise~Molly Edwards~Reader's Favorite

"Story structure is strong, the pace moves, making readers care about these characters. We get real flutters and our own quickened breathing when author uses realism-building in the story line. Well done." Chasing Paradise~Writer's Digest

"Chasing Paradise is a clean, refreshing romance about forbidden love." ~InD'tale Magazine

PROLOGUE

Mama didn't really want Daddy to die. Addison Morgan was only six, but she was smart enough to know the truth. Mama just couldn't take the pain it caused. She had stayed right by Daddy's side every minute she wasn't working, willing him to live. And when he died anyway even after she'd cried out to God for hours every day, begging him not to take her husband, she'd given up. On life, on love, on everything.

It had all happened so fast. Daddy slipped from this earth within a few months of finding out he was sick.

After Daddy left them, things changed for the worse. Addison tried to comfort Mama, but her love wasn't enough. Mama needed more.

1

The first Monday of April, showers swept across the ocean, driven on the ever-steady breeze. Addison Morgan leaned against the bed's wooden post as she stared through her bedroom window. Rain pelted the glass panes of the older beach house, rattling the loose shutters. Rattling old memories to the forefront of her mind.

Her gut wrenched as the rain stopped and the sun broke between dark clouds as a clear image of her sister faded. *Happy Birthday, Casey.*

Determined to get through the day without crying, Addison grabbed her books and left the safety of her room. The same room her aunt had opened to her and Casey four years ago when Addison started college at the University of North Carolina Wilmington. Twenty-four months before the devastating accident that had taken her sister's life. Pushing one foot in front of the other, Addison hesitated in the hallway. Her boyfriend was standing on the front porch.

On a sharp inhale, Addison stopped and took several slow breaths to regulate her erratic pulse before moving farther into the living room.

Philip opened the storm door, part of his face hidden behind a bouquet of roses. In that moment she caught a glimpse of the boy who had been her rock when she had no one else.

Now his gesture held no feeling or expectation for her. The essence of him remained—the boy who'd spent every summer with her, promising days of fun and laughter, but young love had dissipated little by little until the only feeling remaining almost choked her. She focused on the flowers, the backs of her eyelids burning. "They're beautiful."

"I'll drive you to the school this morning."

"I have a meeting on campus with my professor."

"That's even better. But can you catch a ride home with Taylor? I have practice this afternoon."

Her chest tightened as unspoken truth hurled bullets through her mind. He was only available to her in snippets and only at his convenience. A truth that no longer bothered her. "I can drive."

"Good morning." Aunt Brenda slowed mid-step and surveyed the flowers before entering the living room. "Oh, how beautiful, Philip!"

"They're for you."

Philip instinctively handed Aunt Brenda the vase, and she gave Addison a knowing look. "I love this boy."

Addison took a deep breath to keep from rolling her eyes.

"You kids have a good day. I'll just see to these." Sniffing one of the red blooms, Aunt Brenda disappeared into the kitchen.

Philip nudged Addison closer to the door and stroked her back. Her shoulders loosened as he peered down at her with that unrelenting look that at one time could have melted her heart. "I wanted to spend a few minutes alone with you."

Foolish as it was, she agreed and followed him to his truck. "Are you still going to the frat party tonight?"

Philip cleared his throat and gave a slight nod. "You are, right?"

"I don't know. Today's Casey's birthday."

"I remembered," he said, but he most likely hadn't. He never even remembered hers. "It would be good for you. You need a distraction."

Annoyed at his flippant reply, she squeezed her upper arms. How could a distraction be good? On today of all days? She wanted nothing more than to sleep the day away.

Squinting against the morning rays glistening off the sheen of fresh rain, she settled into the passenger seat and stared through the windshield.

The stereo blared when Philip started the engine. He turned onto the street without lowering the volume. Tuning the screeching heavy metal notes out, she closed her eyes and latched onto her most endearing memories. Only then could she pretend her sister would be coming home this afternoon to celebrate her birthday.

Sliding his fingers between hers, Philip squeezed her hand every few minutes as if that simple action would make up for everything.

"You're so uptight. You should let loose and have a few drinks. It'll make you feel better." He leaned toward her, and the hard lines around his eyes softened. Apprehension squirmed through her middle. "What can it hurt?"

No, she would never make that mistake again. That very demon had taken everything from her. If drinking was the only link that would heal their broken relationship, they were in more trouble than she'd thought. Addison kept her mouth shut. To argue would only lead to a full-blown fight and she didn't have the energy. Not today.

The fifteen-minute ride to school gave her plenty of time to think it through. She needed something normal to keep from getting lost in the spiral of depression threatening to pull her under. The same depression that had taken root two years ago. Maybe it would be enough just being with Philip at the party. Aunt Brenda would be asleep by the time she got home anyway. Same as every other night. Anything would be better than sitting at home alone. Again.

Before Addison could climb from the car, Philip grabbed her arm. "I'll meet you at the party. You may even beat me there. But hey, think about what I said. You deserve a good time. Casey would want that." He shifted the car in reverse and drove away before she could object.

A twinge of uncertainty rushed through her at his admission. Philip was meeting her there. Even though they'd dated for years, she knew none of his new friends.

It wouldn't be so bad if Taylor was going, but she couldn't. Taylor was going on a double date without her. Again.

Shaking off the afflicting thoughts, Addison took the narrow concrete path under the shade trees that blocked the sun. A mist of water sprayed her as a lone bird nestled in the tree soared into the open sky. Wiping the moisture from her arms, she opened the double doors to the three-story education building and stood in the waiting area.

"Miss Morgan? How's everything going?"

"Good." She followed her professor into his office and took a seat facing his desk. "I'm really enjoying the kindergarten class and working with the children."

"I'm glad to hear that. Ms. Stacey has given you nothing but good reviews. Can you give me a few examples of some new things you've included in your teaching time?"

"Yes, sir. I brought a stuffed dog to use as a classroom pet." Her heart swelled at the memory of their excitement over voting for his name. "I give different students the responsibility of feeding and watering him each day. Then the students rotate taking him home to care for over the weekend."

"I like that," he said, as he jotted a few notes. "And easier and probably safer than a live pet."

"Yes, sir. I'm also making anchor charts to use during teaching time. One example is a Good Friends Chart. Because kindergartners are new to the social scene and they all want to make friends, I thought this would be a good way to teach them how to treat others." Addison pulled the binder from her bag and showed him the miniature version. "I'm reading several stories about friendship. One example is, *Be Kind,* by Pat Zietlow Miller, and then added a few items to the chart such as: be kind, share, play together, and help each other. I also let them partic-ipate by adding their own ideas of how to be a friend."

He nodded. "And how do you best deal with their limited attention spans?"

"Kindergarteners, for the most part, are only sixty months old when they start kindergarten. And keeping that perspective, at least for the first few weeks of school, helps me realize they're not much more than babies. And this helps me not to expect more than they're able to give. It's also important to keep them moving. So, I keep the lessons short, no longer than fifteen minutes at a time, and incorporate some movement in between."

"Sixty months old. I've never thought about it that way. It's a great way to look at it," he said, his attention returning to his notebook. "I'm impressed. For the remaining six weeks, Miss Morgan, I need you to record a series of your lessons and I have a list of things I'd like to see."

Within ten minutes, Addison had taken a page full of notes of requirements needed for the videos, intent on each word.

Suddenly, the room swirled within her vision. She stood quickly, regretting the action instantly, and sat back down. After she glanced at the clock, her gaze slowly came back into focus.

"Miss Morgan?"

How long had he been calling her name?

"Are you all right?"

Her gaze shifted to him, at the look of concern etched on his face. "Yes, I'm fine." She latched onto the seat, willing the dizziness into submission. "Sorry, Professor Adams."

"I think that's enough for today." The pity in his eyes welled even deeper. "Bring your video recordings to our next meeting. Let's schedule it for next month, same day and time."

"Yes, sir. Thank you."

Not waiting for a response, Addison stood carefully after finding her bearings and hurried across campus. Anxious to be away from the reminders churning through her head and the dizziness on the verge of recurring, she stopped by the library for a resource book her professor recommended.

The hallway led into a different wing, and she took one of the aisles blindly and paused mid-step to steady herself. She rested a hand against the bookshelf and closed her eyes.

"Whoa, there." A deep voice grunted above her as she stumbled backward knocking a few books to the floor. He caught her by the arm and somehow managed to steady her without dropping his own books.

Eyes dark as chocolate poured over her. His gaze smoldered while she absorbed every inch of his face. Something triggered within her—a full-winged flutter.

"Are you ... all right?"

An apology was on the tip of her tongue, but her throat tightened as any number of sensible words she could've whispered escaped. "Yes," slipped from her lips, the sound cold and dense.

"It looked like you were about to fall."

"I'm fine, really. I'm so sorry."

"Is there someone I can call, do you need—"

"No! No, thank you. I'm much better now. I'm really sorry. Thank you."

Addison raced through the computer lab and didn't stop until she reached the elementary school next door.

Who *was* that?

With her head still whirling and her chest pounding, the dam building inside her burst and tears streamed from her eyes. Because on a day she needed it most, a total stranger had looked at her in a way she would never forget.

Logan Tant stared after the girl. She took off before he had a chance to get her name. Soft blond curls cascaded down her back in waves as she disappeared through the library doors.

Standing in a corner, his eyes flitting to the back entrance of the library, he waited for the precise moment she would walk by. He flexed his fingers, the soft material of her sweater still lingering on his fingertips.

"There you are." His coworker and best friend Matt pressed both hands on his books, startling him from his thoughts. "We're going to be late if you don't come on."

Logan glanced at his watch. He'd been standing there for more than a few minutes.

"What're you doing? Studying the library hall? I thought you were returning those." Matt laughed as he moved toward the front entrance.

An obvious thought occurred. Since she left through the back door, he may catch a glimpse of her outside. "Let's go this way."

Matt stopped. "That's the opposite direction of the parking lot."

Logan moved through the back section of the library. When he opened the door, the cool air blasted against his face, bringing him to his senses. He scanned the area anyway and then like so many times before remembered the pain that ridiculous notions like this could bring. He had wasted his time and now would be late for work.

"You all right?"

"I was looking for something." Sensing Matt wouldn't be content until he gave a better answer, Logan added, "Someone."

Matt's gaze whipped around before settling again on him in a state of full assessment. "Who?"

While walking to the parking lot, he once again envisioned those unforgettable deep blue eyes with a purple tint staring up at him with adorable hesitation.

"Just ... someone." With that, Logan jumped into his truck and drove off toward the police station. Way ahead of Matt, Logan hurried to change into his uniform.

Before Logan could get to his patrol car, Matt climbed into the passenger seat. As soon as Logan started the engine, Matt's chatter was like a cackling hen in his ear. "Who were you looking for?"

"You are worse than any woman I've ever met."

"It was a she?"

Before he knew what was happening, Logan's lips expanded into a smile.

Matt punched the door. "I knew it."

"Hey. Easy on the cruiser."

"Where?"

"She was leaning against a book-case and looked as if she would faint. So, I did the only thing I could. I stopped her from falling. Literally." Logan glanced at Matt. "Before you say anything else, I don't know her name."

"How did you of all people let her go without getting a name?"

"I didn't pull her over, I was just helping her. I'll probably never see her again."

"Of course, you'll see her again."

"Why do you say that?"

"Because you don't miss anything. If she's ever in the same vicinity of you, you'll find her."

Logan wouldn't breathe a word to Matt, but he would definitely be searching.

"Man, I can't believe you didn't get her name."

Matt was almost as excited as he was. But not quite. He could still picture her lips flattened into a thin line. He had been watching her when she tilted forward then back. She had taken full blame as if she'd done something wrong. It was in her unnecessary apologies. It was in the shame written all over her face.

Their very first call of the morning took them across town to assist with a simple traffic stop that had escalated into a vehicle search with several occupants. At their arrival, Logan approached one of the passengers ready to assist in detaining.

He counted fifteen more calls, ranging from domestic violence to public intoxication before he parked the cruiser at the station as their shift ended at four o'clock.

"I just don't get it."

"What's that?"

"All the drugs and alcohol." Logan stared ahead, not bothering to snuff out his irritation. "Three DUIs by noon is ridiculous. I honestly thought there'd be less during daylight hours."

"At least we prevented three potential accidents."

His heart gave a stiff kick. He'd seen enough accidents that weren't prevented and too many involving a mind-altering substance.

"I'll see you later, man." Matt punched his arm. "Good luck finding she."

"Who?"

"She! That girl you've been trying to forget all day."

Logan couldn't help but laugh. It was true. "We still cooking out at your place tomorrow night?"

"Yes, sir. Shelley sent me a text earlier. She's already been to the grocery store."

"Okay, great. I'll bring the usual."

"Maybe you'll find she, so you can bring her." Matt's smug look of satisfaction deepened.

"You need to stop. See you at practice."

Addison stood outside at the end of the day and leaned against the elementary school building; her gaze lifted toward the sky. Clouds shuffled about, obscuring the sun.

Taylor called to her from across the lawn. "My car's over there."

Addison met her in the parking lot. "Thanks for taking me home. Can you share some of that good mood of yours?"

Taylor's gaze softened. "Today's Casey's birthday."

Eyes averted, Addison squirmed, fighting the emotion bubbling in her chest.

"I've been thinking about her all morning."

Addison placed a hand on Taylor's arm. "You're such a good friend."

"I haven't done anything."

"And that's why you're so special. Where're you guys going tonight?"

Taylor tilted her head and frowned. "I don't know yet. I wish you were coming."

"Me too. I'm surprised Philip invited me. He even picked me up this morning and brought me a dozen red roses." It didn't matter that, before she got a good look, he gave them to Aunt Brenda. Still, maybe he was finally coming around. Maybe things could go back to the way they were before.

A tense smile played on Taylor's lips. "That was nice of him. You could come with us and meet him later?"

Addison didn't miss the slight thread of sarcasm. They'd had their share of arguments over Philip. "I wish I could. Maybe next time."

"I need you there. I'm so nervous. What if Michael doesn't show up?"

The idea of feeling nervous about a date with Philip was foreign. It had been years since she'd felt that way.

"Don't worry. I think he really likes you." Addison laced her arm through Taylor's.

"I don't know."

"He does. I see the way Michael looks at you." The same way she longed for someone to look at her. The same way that guy had looked at her this morning making her pulse skip all over the place. Even now.

Taylor's lips twisted into a one-sided smile. "How do you know how he looks at me?"

"You're my best friend. I have to know these things. It's my job."

Taylor's words jumbled into a pile of thoughts of Michael as they walked across the parking lot. Addison didn't understand why they acted so silly. It was only a date. She'd never acted that way over Philip. Well, maybe she had at first. But that seemed so long ago. And it never lasted, at least not that she could remember.

"I ran into someone this morning." Addison's spirit lifted despite the fact she knew nothing about the stranger.

"With Philip's truck?"

"No." A shudder traveled through her middle. *What's wrong with me?* "We bumped into each other. It was more like I fell into him, or he kept me from falling." She couldn't remember exactly what had happened.

"You mean like a guy?"

It was definitely a guy. And she couldn't stop thinking about the way he had looked at her.

"Who was it?"

"I don't know. I've never seen him before."

"What did he look like?"

The perfect kind of gorgeous. "I don't know. He was tall."

"That's it? Come on. You have to give me *something*."

"Okay, okay. He had the darkest brown eyes I've ever seen."

Taylor's eyes brightened. "We have to find him."

"What? No." She shouldn't be encouraging this. Or thinking about this. About him. But she couldn't stop. It was something positive. Something better.

"Are you crazy? This is the first guy you've mentioned since you've been dating that ... jerk." Before Addison could find her tongue, Taylor resumed. "What? My opinions are based only on what you've told me and what I've seen with my own eyes. He treats you like you're his property, not like he should, or you deserve."

Taylor was right. Addison couldn't remember the last time she'd had anything good to say. Until today.

She should've left Philip a long time ago. After the first time she caught him with someone else. After the first time he rough-handled her. But she felt trapped. They had been friends for twelve years, dated for six. He was the only boyfriend she'd ever had. The only one who had been there for her when things were so horrible at home. He promised to never hurt her again, and it had been months since he'd lost his temper.

"Where were you exactly when you fell into this mysterious guy?"

"Taylor, stop. Philip ..."

"Philip, Philip, Philip ... He will not ruin this for me."

"I was in the campus library, but it doesn't matter. I'm giving Philip one more chance."

Incredulous, Taylor exhaled hard.

"I promise. This is the last time."

"Okay. But in the meantime, we *will* find this tall, dark brown-eyed man. Even if we have to camp out at the library."

Warmth kindled at the thought of seeing the guy again. Addison scolded herself. How could she even consider such ridiculous thoughts? She didn't even know him. Besides, Philip showed up this morning with flowers, drove her to class, and invited her to the party. Still, she couldn't shake the image she had so blatantly absorbed this morning. Those dark brown eyes that seemed almost fixated on her. The same look she had longed to see in Philip's eyes for years. Maybe a drink would give her that same feeling toward Philip she'd been fighting all day.

"Why aren't you riding home with Philip?"

"He has practice. I'm meeting him later."

Addison arrived at the fraternity house two hours later than planned. And the nudging rejection that frequented her thoughts lately crept in again. Philip hadn't even bothered to check on her.

People crowded the entryway leading into the house. Unease chiseled at the tender places of her aching heart.

What am I doing here?

She needed this, their relationship needed this, she kept reminding herself. She pushed through the front door and wiggled past the flood of tangled bodies, searching for Philip.

It would do no good to ask if anyone had seen him. The college students surrounding her, most of them rude and obnoxiously drunk, barely noticed her presence. Addison looked through the mass of students, but there were too many to see past the group.

The stench of alcohol, sweating bodies, and the smoky haze that hung in the air produced a coughing spell. If she wasn't careful it could easily convert into a bout of gagging.

Addison pressed through a group laughing near the refreshment table and then she finally spotted a familiar face.

The girl from her public speaking class last year squeezed into the tight space and faced her. "You're the last person I ever expected to see here." She rolled her eyes in a disapproving sort of way. "I'm Amber, by the way."

"I'm Addison." She cast a quick glance behind her, resuming her search. "I'm meeting my boyfriend."

Amber made a spitting sound. "You're dating one of these guys?"

What did she mean by that? Addison staggered backward, bumping into a sweaty body behind her.

"Hello there, baby. What's your name?" Turning, Addison pretended not to hear the guy speaking to her.

"See what I mean? I pictured you with someone ... different ... more reserved ... anyone other than these clowns."

Philip wasn't like these guys. He *was* different. Wasn't he? Instead of dwelling on the girl's questions, Addison asked her own, "What're you doing here?"

"My roommate wanted to come for a few minutes. I'm making sure she stays out of trouble."

Desperate to escape Amber's intimidating gaze and ease her scratchy throat with something cool and wet, Addison grabbed a cup and filled it with red liquid from the punch bowl.

Taking a long sip, Addison felt immediate relief and glanced at the balcony above her.

She'd been here only five minutes, including the time it took to get inside. And already she wanted to give up and leave. She should've never come.

"You drink?"

"No." She never imagined the girl she barely knew would be so judgmental. It was irritating. Especially since she still hadn't found Philip. "He must've already left."

Gulping another mouthful, she searched upstairs again.

"If you're not used to drinking, you should—"

Addison took another sip relishing the soothing sensation as the liquid traveled down her throat. Then Philip walked from a room upstairs, tucking in his shirt.

"The punch is spiked."

Amber's warning fell on partially deaf ears as a blonde followed Philip from a room and pressed against him. Bile rose in the back of Addison's throat mixing with the liquid contents she'd just forced into her body.

Addison gaped at the two of them, standing together, too close. Philip twisted and faced the girl, then tugged at the tail of her shirt before pressing his mouth against hers.

The room spun as white dots flashed before Addison's eyes. She thrust the cup onto the table and the remaining liquid splashed onto her hand. Not looking back, Addison pushed her way toward the front door.

"Where're you going?" Amber's voice carried over the clatter of music, slurred speech, her racing pulse.

Addison hurried through the front door, blood rushing to her head, the cool air jolting as she reached the front lawn.

Running toward her car, resounding questions detonated through her head. How could he? Why hadn't she broken up with him already? Taylor was right.

Tears blurring her vision, she slammed the car into drive and sped away. She drove unaware of her surroundings, alert only to the tormenting voices in her head. Harsh wails lunged from her throat, the sound deafening to even her. She could end this all right now. To never see Philip again, to never have to face the questioning, judgmental glances of her peers. Their accusations that somehow, someway, she should've been able to stop Casey from losing her life to a drunk driver. The driver she should've stopped her sister from leaving with.

All the loose ends of her life spiraled into a dusty haze. The images played through her mind out of order, and she tried to categorize them. Casey chasing her through the snow. Young summer love promising the world. Dark brown eyes threatening to swallow her whole on a face she would never forget.

The wooziness grew worse and fear gripped her. She was losing control. Addison pressed the brake, but it was too late. Grabbing the steering wheel with both hands, she wavered as darkness seized her.

Addison opened her eyes, her head pounding. The seat belt pinned her against the seat as the stench of the airbag's powder filled the car, burning her lungs.

Trees surrounded her car, and a murky fog filled the night air. Sirens blared and lights flashed from every direction as rescue vehicles pulled to a stop in front of her car. Her stomach lurched.

How long had she been sitting here?

Smoke drifted from a white car wrapped around a light post. "Oh no!" she screamed.

A fireman yanked on her door until it opened. "Are you all right?"

Addison touched her face, feeling a wet warmth oozing around her ear. She pulled her hand away, the sight of blood, the smells, the sounds nauseating her. Staring ahead, she was unable to force an audible answer.

"Can you hear me, miss?" He yelled across the field. "Davis, I need help over here." The fireman wiggled her seatbelt until it unsnapped, and the leather band slipped into place, the sound oddly loud. "Does anything feel broken?"

"I don't know." She closed her eyes a moment, hoping to clear the blurred haze. Blinking, she braced herself for the next bout of dizziness. "I don't feel good."

Another fireman and two EMTs appeared, one carrying a white board. "She's conscious?"

"Yes," he told the others before returning his attention to her. "Just relax, honey, we're going to lift you onto the gurney."

The first man strapped something against her neck and pulled the seat back. In one fluid motion, they lifted her from the car. She stared into the inky night sky trying to remember how this happened.

Two officers arrived and searched her car while the EMTs pushed her toward the ambulance's blinking, bright lights. They were searching for evidence, she assumed, but there was none. She'd only taken a couple of sips. Her pulse raced. The spiked punch. Had that been enough to impair her? Something had happened—something terrible. She'd blacked out.

The right side of her car was crammed inward, her windshield busted. And the other car; it was nearly unrecognizable.

An uncomfortable twist squeezed her belly. This was her fault.

The EMT stared down at her. "How're you feeling?"

"Dizzy and nauseated." Her voice sounded husky, like she hadn't spoken in days.

Her tears fell unwillingly as she glanced again toward the wreckage splayed out in front of her. The only sound she could muster was a broken hiccup.

Addison searched the area for a sign of the other driver. Long, blonde hair spilled over another stretcher's rim. A woman crying hysterically stood over the girl.

The girl hadn't moved. Addison closed her eyes against the flashing lights, the broken girl, and the woman crying as stark pain seared through her head.

2

L ogan parked at his apartment just before midnight and leaned against the leather seat, exhausted.

A yawn escaped as he stared up at the balcony leading to his front door. His cell phone beeped. Feeling around the floorboard, Logan retrieved it. Three missed calls. All from his mother. He must've dropped it earlier and, with the radio blaring, hadn't heard it ringing.

At the sound of her frantic voice, heaviness settled in his stomach.

She spilled only a few minor details. Logan listened as she told him where to come when he arrived at the hospital.

"What happened?" He wanted more information … some reassurance, but she didn't budge.

"I'll tell you everything when you get here. Please drive carefully."

Before Logan could take a deep breath, a text from his best friend materialized. *Call me immediately.*

Dazed, he grabbed his car keys and restarted the engine. The speakers erupted with screeching notes from a Led Zeppelin song and, with a quick twist, he silenced the volume, then called his best friend. "Matt?"

"There was an accident. Ami—"

"How bad is it?"

"You should get to the hospital."

"I'm already on the way. What happened?"

"I wasn't there. Captain asked me to call you but didn't have any details."

Fifteen minutes later, Logan stepped into the emergency room and headed straight for the receptionist. The stench of the waiting room, the sight of patients and their companions slumped in chairs, nauseated him. He reached the receptionist's desk and pressed his hands against the counter. "Ami Tant?"

The woman studied the computer screen, never making eye contact. "I'll call someone out here to meet you. Have a seat. It'll be a few minutes."

Logan paced in front of the glass doors leading down a long hallway. People crowded the area, lost in their own thoughts, perhaps lost in prayer. He had prayed from the moment he spoke to his mom, but his jumbled words fell flat, didn't seem strong enough. His gaze veered from the glass doors as he closed his eyes, but just as they opened, his mother walked through. He rushed toward her, and his pulse raced as fresh tears leaked from her eyes and she collapsed into his arms.

"She's banged up really bad. A broken arm, and a few fractured ribs. And they're keeping her in a medically induced comma because of some swelling on the brain."

His mind absorbed the new information and what it might mean. "What happened? What kind of accident?"

"The car ..." His mother paused. "I was following her. If only I'd insisted we ride together. It scared me so bad." Sobs garbled her words. Logan's mind raced as he tried to follow. "The car came out of nowhere and merged into our lane at the same moment Ami reached the car. It all happened so fast. It was horrible."

"A head-on collision?"

"Not quite. It slammed into the front corner of Ami's car," she explained.

"Did the doctor say anything else about how long they have to keep her induced?"

"No, but they should know more in the next few hours."

He led her to a seat near the back of the waiting area and helped her sit. He desperately wanted to go to Ami, but his mother needed a moment. She had witnessed the whole thing.

When they finally entered Ami's brightly lit room, his breath caught in his throat. Ami slept in the hospital bed, tubes connecting her to the machines, her face covered with cuts and dried blood. A neck brace holding her head in place. Reaching for her hand, he rested his arm against the cold bar separating them.

Logan stared at his baby sister lying helpless and allowed his mind to escape to another day only three years ago when he stood in this very position. He closed his eyes against the images that threatened to unravel him.

Addison woke and her head spun. The dim lights, the soft hum of the machines, and the familiar smell caused her heart to leap.

"Casey?"

A nurse walked through the door just as she whispered the name of her sister. Addison pushed herself back against the pillow.

"Where am I?"

"You're in the hospital, sweetheart." The nurse's voice was soft, kind.

"What happened?"

"You don't remember?" She pressed a button, causing the machine to beep.

Addison tried but could only remember one thing—staring as the men lowered the box holding her sister into the ground.

The nurse waited for her response, but Addison couldn't breathe. A garbled sob escaped as her mind whirled in a haze. The memory of the accident suddenly came crashing back.

Aunt Brenda was slumped in a corner recliner, her head tilted in an odd angle. "How're you feeling?"

"I'm okay," Addison answered, fighting the pain shooting through her head. How would she explain this to Aunt Brenda after all she'd done for her?

Addison sat up and loosened the stiff white sheets tucked securely around her. "There was a girl in the other car. Is she okay?"

"I don't know, honey."

The nurse reached for her. "You need to lie back."

As Addison pushed one foot over the edge of the bed, her head spun with the sudden motion. "Do you know what happened to the girl?"

"Hold on, young lady."

"I need to find her. I need to know she's all right." Hot tears burned the backs of her eyelids as blonde hair glaring against the emergency lights slammed against her memory.

The nurse situated her pillow a little higher. "I'll see what I can find out. But for now, lay back and try to calm down." The nurse moved to the sink and washed her hands. "Do you use drugs or drink alcohol?"

No, but she had tonight. Something she'd planned to do. And because of that, she was responsible for hurting another person. Another family. "Not usually, but I did have a little tonight."

Aunt Brenda surged to her feet and came toward her, disappointment evident in her expression.

"I'm sorry, Aunt Brenda."

The nurse fitted the blood pressure cuff around Addison's arm. "Do you feel dizzy or nauseated?"

"Both."

There was silence as the nurse waited for the results of her pressure. "90 over 55. Is that usual for you?"

"I don't know."

Aunt Brenda took her free hand as Addison leaned heavily against the pillow. What had happened? Had she really had enough alcohol to cause her to blackout?

After the doctor came in, evaluated her, and asked more questions, the nurse returned with another bag of fluid.

"We're going to get some fluids in you and hopefully get you feeling back to normal." The doctor focused on Aunt Brenda. "Low blood pressure and dehydration are most likely the reasons this young lady blacked out."

Addison should've felt relief after hearing the doctor's assessment. That maybe alcohol in her system wasn't the reason she'd crashed into the other car, but she didn't.

Throughout the night, Addison dozed in and out, unable to rest fully. When she awoke the next morning, her gaze roamed the small room until it fell on Aunt Brenda. The soft hum of her snore hindered Addison from waking her.

Instead, her mind raced. She needed answers about the other driver, something to ease her guilt.

The doctor returned the next morning. "How are we feeling this morning?"

"Better."

"That's good. Your vitals are looking better but we're going to keep you for observation for another day or two." He turned his focus on Aunt Brenda as she leaned forward wiping strands of damp hair away from her cheek. "Are you her mother?"

"Her aunt. She's staying with me while she's in college."

"Can I speak with you for a moment outside?"

"Of course."

As they exited her room, Taylor stepped through the door holding two cups of coffee. "How're you feeling?"

"Thank you, girl." Addison rose up on an elbow, relieved her dizziness had weakened, and reached for a cup. "I'm feeling better."

"What happened?" Taylor's voice was comforting.

"I blacked out."

"While you were driving?"

"Yes, as I was leaving the party."

"Philip was with you?"

"No, I never even spoke to him." She steeled herself for Taylor's tongue-lashing.

Taylor grunted and lowered herself to the edge of the bed. "What did he do?"

Addison finished her explanation while ignoring her friend's question. Somewhere hidden in the trenches of her heart, Addison knew she had planned to drink, hoping to relax and salvage her connection to Philip. It only deepened her guilt.

Suddenly, her bottled-up tears flowed freely, her chest swelling and falling in a harsh rhythm. What happened to the girl? She wouldn't relax until she knew she was all right.

Logan was staring at the lines gliding across the monitor's screen, displaying Ami's heart rate, when his mother walked in carrying a box she'd brought from home.

He took it from her and placed it on the table near Ami's bed. "What's all this?"

She pulled a room freshener from the top and set it on the counter. "I thought it would be nice for Ami to wake to the smell of home."

"Good idea." He pulled out Ami's pink blanket. "Where's Dad?"

"He had to stop by the office for a few minutes."

"You never told me exactly what happened." He broached the subject hoping to get some answers.

Mom unpacked a teddy bear from the box. "It all happened so fast." She positioned the bear on the table and then covered Ami with her pink blanket. "The car swerved into Ami's lane at the last minute. There was no time to react."

"Why did the driver merge into Ami's lane?" A tight knot wrenched through Logan's stomach. He needed to know the reason and his heart and mind were already spiraling in the direction that it had to be something that could've been avoided. His baby sister shouldn't be suffering because of someone else's inability to drive.

His phone vibrated and he glanced at the message he'd been waiting for from Matt. *The officer thought the other driver had been drinking. But they're not sure to what extent.*

All thoughts of coherency were lost with the sentences that changed everything.

The rest of Mom's words were void of sound as rage swept through him. "I'll be right back." He hurried through the door to escape the suffocation squeezing his lungs.

Logan balled his fists as the doctor slipped through the door past him. A drunk driver. *Who did this to my sister?*

He walked outside, unable to catch his breath. The next text made his chest ache. *You know you can't get involved in this case. The less you know, the better.*

He didn't respond. He had nothing more to say. There was nothing he could do.

Except be by Ami's side when she woke up, so he returned to her room.

"Logan, there you are. Where did you disappear to?" Mom tucked the blanket around Ami's chin.

"I had to get some air."

"The doctor plans to keep her a few more days. But they're confident she's going to be all right," Mom finished, her voice breaking. He reached for her and held her tight.

Logan forced himself to stay calm.

It didn't matter that he was a law enforcement officer, that he was prohibited from working on this case.

Logan wouldn't rest until the guy responsible paid for this.

3

A ddison stared through the passenger window as Aunt Brenda drove her home, her headache finally fading. The older beach house was located on the sound side of Wilmington, North Carolina.

Aunt Brenda had revealed to her a different kind of life—one where a woman didn't have to depend on a man. Her aunt, a beautiful woman, had never married and had done just fine. Aunt Brenda worked hard, managed her own funds, and never allowed her to pay rent. All Aunt Brenda expected from her was decent grades, a part-time job to pay for her own gas, and a little help around the house.

In her aunt's house, Addison could talk about her father, her aunt's brother. She didn't have to pretend he never existed. She could keep her only framed photo of him by her bed.

Philip and his betrayal at the party were like shards of glass nicking at her wounded heart. She had given him everything, yet still he wasn't faithful. She would never be enough. But it didn't matter.

When Aunt Brenda veered the car onto their street, Country Lane, and down the path beside a row of American elms, she breathed a sigh of relief. Philip's car wasn't at their house.

"You need to call your mama."

"You didn't tell them about the accident, did you?"

"No, but she would want to know."

No, she wouldn't. "I'll call her later."

Once inside, Addison sat on the wooden bench at her familiar keyboard, losing herself in the soft music as she played. Music had become her escape … an effort to keep her pain at bay. The notes to *Claire de Lune* hummed through the room as her fingers soared across the keys.

She had discovered nothing about the blond girl's well-being, and it wasn't until Taylor retrieved the accident report from the police department that she learned the girl's name.

Grateful to Taylor for getting the information, she'd stored it in her memory.

Ami Tant.

She thought about the questions from the police officer and how she wasn't found guilty because she had blacked out. It wasn't fair. It wasn't enough. The doctor confirmed that she'd passed out suffering from dehydration and low blood pressure and even stress, when Aunt Brenda told the doctor it was her sister's birthday. But her responsibility in the collision, her responsibility in harming another person afflicted her without ceasing. It was her fault. She had taken a drink and had almost killed the girl—just like drinking and driving had killed Casey.

Within a week and a half, Ami was able to go home. Logan turned into the familiar neighborhood and swerved his truck to the right past the brick wall separating the park from the houses.

He grabbed his overnight bag after helping his dad get Ami settled. Each day he traveled the twenty-minute drive to UNCW and on his off days, spent his evenings at his Mom's studying.

It had been almost a week and though she was still sore, she was improving.

He was studying for a test when his dad sat across from him in the living room. "How's work?"

"Good."

Dad leaned back in the chair. "I'm surprised you didn't take some time off."

"Do you need me to?"

"No, I just thought you'd need some time."

"I thought it would help, keeping busy."

"Ami's better. I think it's best you get back to your normal routine. You don't want to do something that will jeopardize your grades and job. You've taken on a lot, working the streets your senior year of college."

"It's not so bad." Although truthfully, the long hours of school, work, and baseball with very little sleep were catching up to him.

"We really appreciate you staying here and helping with Ami, but you should get back to your life. You have so much going on. We can handle things."

His dad was right. Logan had been fumbling through all his duties in vain. His schoolwork had suffered, and he'd been little help to Ami or his mother with his non-pursuit of the drunk driver weighing on him. But could he just forgive and forget?

A week after the accident, Addison's phone held five messages from Philip. On his latest attempt, she answered ready to settle things. "Hello."

"Why haven't you returned my calls? I've been going crazy."

"There's nothing to say. It's over, Philip."

"What? How can you say that after all we've been through?"

"I just can't do this anymore. Too much has happened."

"What do you mean? Everything was good. Better than ever."

"Things haven't been good in a very long time. I have to go."

"No." His voice rose, and she pulled the phone away from her ear. "Do not hang up, Addison."

Images of him walking from the room, tucking in his shirt, pervaded her mind. Philip kissing the blonde would forever be burned in her memory. It would do no good to argue with him though. He would have the last word.

"I just can't deal with this anymore." Her stomach clenched with tightly wound knots. "I really need to go. I've got lesson plans to do."

"I'm coming over."

Her pulse raced. "No, Philip. I don't want to see you anymore."

"It's not over between us. It will never be over. I love you."

Addison ended the call, his false affection making her physically sick. The combination of Philip and the haunting images of the girl in the accident overshadowed everything else.

She had called the hospital last week to check if Ami Tant had been released. Unable to stomach hearing that the girl had to stay longer, she waited. Until this morning. Today they informed her there was no one registered by that name.

Addison's stomach twisted with additional knots. She had no idea how long the Tant girl had been home, but she couldn't wait another day to visit. Nothing would stop her, not even the nervous flutters of facing the blond girl and her mom raging through her stomach.

There was only one problem. Aunt Brenda knew nothing of her plans.

"Good morning, honey."

"Morning. Can I borrow your car? I have a few errands to run. I'll only be gone a few hours."

"You sure you feel up to driving?"

"Yes, ma'am. I'm fine."

"Okay."

Addison kissed her aunt's cheek; thankful she hadn't asked more questions.

"Don't you want to at least eat first?"

Giving Aunt Brenda a backward glance, Addison opened the door. "Will you save me a plate so I can eat later?"

"Sure, baby girl."

Dark clouds hovered beneath the afternoon sun. With shaking hands, she pressed the map app on her phone with the Tant's address from the accident report once she was settled inside the car.

Only a seven-minute drive.

She jumped and slammed her knee into the steering wheel when someone knocked on the window. Dropping her phone, her hand flew to her pounding chest.

"Philip, you scared me to death. What are you doing here?" As the window eased down, she crammed her violently shaking hands beneath her legs.

Leaning inside the car, he stopped her from leaving. "I had to come. I had to see you."

"No, Philip. I'm leaving."

"Where're you going? I thought you were doing lesson plans."

"Something came up. I've got to go."

A few raindrops fell, and she pressed the window button. The way Philip looked at her made her ill at ease. It was the same way he always looked when he talked her into giving him another chance. He would not worm his way back into her life. But he wouldn't give up easily.

The map app's automated voice led her through town and into a neighborhood she wasn't familiar with. After eight minutes of glancing sporadically through the rearview mirror to make sure Philip hadn't followed, Addison pulled the car in front of the designated house.

The two-story brick home had a manicured lawn with perfectly spaced Leyland Cyprus lining the driveway and a small garden of vibrant flowers of every imaginable color.

Addison parked the car across the street as if by doing so they'd feel her presence and come out to tell her it was okay—that they didn't blame her.

Her chest collapsed with a disconcerted sigh as another spout of remorse hacked at her hesitancy. Had she made the right decision coming here?

After five minutes of telling herself to drive away and return home, she climbed from the car. With slow, unsteady steps, she ambled to the front door, through a row of bushes bordering the sidewalk. She was trembling so hard, she had to press the doorbell twice before the sound of music streamed from inside the house.

A beautiful woman wearing a navy-blue jogging suit answered the door. "Hello." The lady searched Addison's face, wiping her hands on her pink-striped apron. "May I help you?"

Addison withdrew a step, widening their proximity. "Yes, ma'am. I'm so sorry to bother you. My name is Addison. I ... I wanted to see how your daughter is feeling?"

Her large, rounded eyes brightened. "You're a friend of Ami's?"

Refusing to surrender to the awkwardness of the moment, she pressed on. "No, ma'am." She inhaled. "I just wanted to check on her."

Addison waited in anticipation of the woman's reaction just as the sky opened and heavy raindrops drenched the earth.

"Come on in. Let me get you a towel." The woman closed the door and disappeared down a long hallway.

From the entrance, Addison studied a picture hanging above the fireplace in the living room. She couldn't make out the faces standing so far away, but there were five people in the photograph. The long blond hair of the shortest person in the photo held her attention. She wanted to take a step closer but stopped herself.

"Here you go." The lady handed her a warm, thick towel. "It's unseasonably cool today. I hope you won't catch a cold."

"I'm so sorry to bother you like this. I ... well, I've been thinking of your daughter since the accident, and I wanted to make sure she was going to be okay," Addison managed, the shock of the situation filling her all over again. The image of the girl being hauled away on the stretcher had replayed itself time and time again since the accident.

"It's so nice of you to check on her. She's still sore, but everyday she's feeling better. How do you know Ami?"

"I don't." The lady shook her head, not understanding her purpose for coming, still waiting for an explanation. "I was the other driver."

"Mama?" They both turned at the sound of the voice coming from upstairs.

"Oh, well, it was considerate of you to stop by."

Mrs. Tant regarded her with uncertainty, validating her doubt. It had been a mistake to come here.

"Mama, who is it?"

"I should go." A downward glance and Addison realized she still held the towel. She handed it to Mrs. Tant, uneasiness demanding her attention. "I'm so sorry. I hope she'll be okay."

Mrs. Tant hesitated for several seconds. "Would you like to see her?"

Sweat mixed with the raindrops clinging to her skin. "No, I don't want to impose."

"You've come all this way to check on her. Ami will never forgive me." She turned to walk toward the stairs, allowing no argument. With a brief glance over her shoulder, Mrs. Tant made sure Addison followed behind, her cautious smile softening.

Addison reluctantly followed the woman upstairs and into the vibrantly colored bedroom, the scent of a candle mixed with a fruity body spray clinging to the air. "Ami, this is Addison. She came to see how you're feeling."

With one single look at the young girl sitting up in bed, remorse ripped through her with a brutal wave. Bandages covered the girl's face, her blond hair peeking from underneath the wrap on her head, covering part of her cheek.

"Do I know you?"

Addison crumbled inside. She didn't want to announce to this girl that she was the one responsible for her pain.

When Addison hesitated, Ami's mother stepped forward. "She was the other driver in the accident and stopped by to make sure you were all right."

Ami pulled herself up. "Oh? Are you okay? Were you hurt?"

A sheet of moisture swelled in Addison's eyes, and she blinked, hoping to clear her vision. How could she have come here?

Ami's mother wrapped her arm around Addison. "God was truly looking out for you girls that day."

She could do no more than whimper at the woman's affection. How could this mother be so receptive knowing she'd been the cause of her daughter's pain? Addison lowered her chin in brief, silent appreciation of the woman's empathy.

Ami's cheerful voice brought Addison back to the present. "How old are you?"

Addison's uneasiness was trumped by compassion and she cleared her throat as she moved to the edge of Ami's bed. "I'm twenty-two. What about you?"

"Almost eighteen." Ami's brown eyes sparkled. "My birthday's in one month. My twin brothers, Logan and Nathan, are twenty-two."

Addison's shoulders loosened for the first time since she'd arrived. "How cool to have twin brothers. Do y'all get along?"

"They're way too protective, especially Logan. They're both in college, but Nathan's at NC State, so he doesn't hover as much. Are you in college?"

Addison glanced at Mrs. Tant, who shared an earnest smile. "I'll leave you girls for a few minutes."

Mrs. Tant walked away as Addison answered Ami's question. "I'm at UNC Wilmington."

"So is Logan. Do you live here? Do you have any brothers or sisters?"

"I have a sister. She died two years ago." She wobbled with an eruption of emotions ... disbelief, guilt, and unforgiving grief.

Ami sat up straighter. "I'm so sorry. How old was she?"

Addison perched on the edge of Ami's bed, careful to keep a safe distance, but needing to be closer. "She would've been eighteen this year. Same as you." Talking to a stranger about Casey should've been impossible. But this felt normal, like everyday conversation.

"What happened to her?" Ami asked, her face a mask of sorrow.

Sorrow bled through Addison's middle too, as if in that moment she was finding her sister all over again. She couldn't tell Ami the truth. She hadn't been able to tell anyone. And then suddenly her silence registered. "There was an accident."

"I'm so sorry. I can't imagine how it would feel to lose one of my brothers."

Addison looked past Ami toward the door and for a moment thought about bolting, until she remembered the reason she'd come.

"Did your sister look like you?"

33

"No, not at all. She had red hair and green eyes."

"You're really pretty."

"You're so sweet." Her gaze stumbled past Ami and rested on a framed photo of Ami and a young man. "That's enough about me. What school do you go to?"

"I'm homeschooled and will be a senior this year."

"Really? How do you like homeschooling?"

"I like it. Most of the time." A strained silence fell between the two girls, and Ami's eyelids shuttered. "I'm in my fifth year of high school. I'm taking a few dual enrollment classes at the community college."

Addison stood. "I better go so you can rest."

"Will you come back?"

The idea was almost laughable. Surely, she'd misunderstood. "You want me to come back?"

"Yes. And I'm really glad you're okay." Ami's smile faltered, but only a moment before she beamed again. "Will you bring a picture of your sister when you come?"

"Sure. Feel better soon." Addison spun to leave, but Ami's sluggish voice stopped her.

"Wait. Leave your number." Ami reached for a tablet on the table.

"I got it." Addison's brain worked overtime as she scribbled her number onto a pink notepad lying on the bedside table. The girl couldn't have known what she was saying. Heart in her throat at the girl's unconditional acceptance, she reached for Ami's hand and squeezed it. "It was so nice to meet you, Ami. Take care," Addison told her while conjuring the things that had brought her here. As Addison walked toward the door, Ami's eyes finally relaxed, and she drifted off to sleep.

"Mrs. Tant," Addison whispered as she walked down the stairs leading to the front door.

"Everything okay?"

"Yes, ma'am. Thank you for allowing me to meet her. She's so sweet." It was time to go. She'd overstayed her welcome.

"Thank you, Addison. I can't express how much I appreciate you coming to check on her. I know Ami does. Can I fix you something to drink before you leave?"

"Thank you, but I really have to go. You've been so kind." Addison wanted to reach for her, to weep in her arms, to beg for her forgiveness. Instead, she turned, swiping at an errant tear.

"You take care of yourself."

"Yes, ma'am, thank you," she managed through the swelling sob. "I'll continue to pray for her." Addison stepped onto the front porch, evading Mrs. Tant's gaze.

When Addison reached her car, she saw Mrs. Tant still standing at the front door. The lady waved and smiled when Addison met her gaze. Addison's hands trembled as she started the engine and drove down the street. As she took several slow, deep breaths, her shoulders loosened, and her breathing settled into a steady pace as her thoughts drifted back in time.

"This is your new daddy." Mama lifted a cigarette to her lips and scrunched her eyes like she always did as she lit it.

Addison glanced up at the man standing there. He was much older than Daddy. The man cocked his head, peered at her through wrinkled, half-closed lids, and lifted a weak smile.

"Give him a hug," Mama said, blowing out a string of smoke.

Addison looked nervously at her mama but obeyed. It was the fastest hug she'd ever given. She didn't need a new daddy. She already had one. Her daddy was just waiting for her in heaven.

"That's my good girl." Her voice was tired but gentle. Mama hadn't gotten enough sleep. Her puffy eyes were proof. She sucked in hard, her cigarette still hanging between her lips.

"Don't you worry, little girl. I will take good care of you and your mama." He lifted a shaking hand and removed the cigarette from between Mama's lips. "And the first thing we're going to do is get your mama to quit smoking."

Mama's eyelids lifted before she rolled her eyes. "Whatever you say."

35

He put his hand on Mama's waist, pulled her closer, and kissed her right on the mouth, the same way Daddy used to do.

It was the look on Mama's face that made Addison pause. It was a look of happiness. A look she hadn't seen since her daddy died. It didn't matter how Addison felt. Her mama needed him.

It was over.

She'd done what she'd longed to do since the accident and, knowing Ami would be all right, maybe she could put this all behind her.

Philip's car sat in the driveway when she arrived home from the Tants. It was too late to keep going. He jogged out to meet her before she could climb from the car. "What are you still doing here?"

"You said we could talk, so I waited."

"You've been here the whole time?"

"Yeah, I talked to your aunt. Why? That's okay, isn't it?"

Addison leaned against the driver's door. "You shouldn't have come."

Philip took her hand and led her to his truck. "Come with me. We haven't spent a day together in so long."

After the emotional overhaul she'd just experienced, she had no energy left for a fight.

"I thought we could go to dinner and catch an early movie tonight?"

Her mind whirled. "I told you I'm not doing this anymore."

"Doing what?" He drummed his tan fingers against her arm.

She snatched her arm back. "Stop it."

"You're so beautiful when you're angry."

Addison's instinct was to walk away and leave him standing there. With each breath, he would only add more promises, more lies. She had to settle this. Now. "I'm not angry. I just don't want to be with you anymore. Go out with that girl from the party."

"What girl?"

"The one who couldn't keep her hands off you."

He took her hand. "Oh, her?"

She wrenched her fingers from his grip. "I was two hours late. The first thing I saw was you ... with her, and I left."

"Addison, I was waiting for you. She wouldn't leave me alone."

She ignored his blatant lie. "You didn't even bother checking on me." She twisted away, her jaw clenching. "You didn't even call."

"I've been trying to call you for days."

"You just expect me to pretend nothing happened."

"Nothing happened. I was only talking to her. You act like I'm not supposed to talk to anyone but you."

"You can talk to whoever you want. You can kiss whoever you want. It's over between us."

"I didn't kiss her."

"I saw you. You can't lie your way out of it this time."

"I'm not lying. She kissed me. I guess you conveniently missed me pushing her off."

His anger was escalating, but she didn't care. "The only thing you were pushing was your shirt back into your pants."

"Because she yanked it out. I don't even know her. She was drunk as—"

"Just stop. I'm not doing this."

"Why don't you chill out? You're too serious. If you would loosen up and—"

"Don't you dare turn this around on me."

"I'm not." He eased his arms around her waist and pulled her closer. "We haven't had a day together in so long." He lifted her chin. "We've known each other for how long? You should know me better than that. I would never do anything to hurt you, Addison."

"What am I supposed to think when I keep catching you with other girls?"

"Have you ever seen me out with someone else on a date?"

"No, but Taylor has."

"Taylor hates me. You can't believe what she says."

"I can't believe what you say." Addison pulled away from him. "It doesn't matter. I can't do this anymore."

He leaned across and pressed his lips against hers.

Addison snatched from his grip. "Don't do that."

"You can think whatever you want, but I'm not going anywhere." With a look of satisfaction, he left her standing there as he climbed into his truck.

As he pulled from the driveway, the irony of it all churned through her mind. That's exactly what he was doing. Leaving. But only after he'd said everything he wanted. Leaving her without accomplishing her goal: bringing their relationship to a definite end. But to her it didn't matter. It was over.

No matter what he said, or how he promised to never hurt her, she would never trust him again.

4

———————————

Three days later, Logan arrived at his Mom's house surprised to find his brother standing in Ami's room.

"When did you get here?"

"A few minutes ago." Nathan yanked at the blanket tucked around Ami. "Let's go, young lady. Time to get some fresh air." Not waiting for a response, Nathan lifted her into his arms and carried her from the room.

Shaking his head, Logan lingered for only a moment before charging toward the door after them.

"Nathan, put me down. I can walk."

Nathan grunted. "Can you grab the door?"

Logan's jealousy flared. He would never be able to carry his sister down a flight of stairs. "He's just showing off, Ami."

He and Nathan were twins, but the only thing that was even remotely similar was they looked too much alike. While Logan spent more of his time studying, Nathan spent more hours at the gym. The width of his arms and the broadness of his chest were proof of that.

"How long are you here for?"

"Just the weekend, I have an eight-thirty class Monday morning."

Logan's harsh thoughts crumbled. His smaller muscles bulged as he pulled the door shut. There wasn't that much difference.

Nathan sat Ami on the swing next to Mom and headed to the kitchen. "Ami's doing so much better."

Logan followed him. "She's a fighter."

"Are you coming by tomorrow? I haven't had one of your cheeseburgers in months."

"Yeah, we could cook out." Maybe it would lift his mood to do something normal … something they hadn't done since the accident.

After many nights of unrest, Addison had thought seeing Ami would satisfy the agony of not knowing how badly the girl had been hurt and she'd finally be able to sleep. But every day since her visit to the Tants', her nights were dominated by restlessness.

She slept late on Saturday, hoping to make up for lost sleep in the early morning hours. Her cell phone vibrated across her nightstand and she squeezed her eyes shut, willing the invasion to dissipate.

Philip had called every day this week and had even shown up outside the elementary school where she did her student teaching. If it was him calling, she would let the final few rings play out and then curl deeper into her warm sheets and go back to sleep. Lifting her phone, she focused on the number. A local number appeared on the screen and Addison stared at the seven digits. It wasn't him. But she didn't recognize the number either.

Curiosity nudged harder than her resistance to ignore the call, and on the fifth ring she answered, "Hello?"

"Addison. It's Ami … Ami Tant."

Ami? Addison sat up; her breath caught in her throat. "Ami, hi." She pushed her blanket away and scooted to the edge of the bed, suddenly embarrassed for still lying there. "How are you?"

"I'm great. I know it's really short notice, but do you have plans today?"

"Plans?" She glanced at her pajamas and then at the clock. 9:55. "No, I have nothing going on today."

"I was hoping you could come over?"

"You want me to come over?"

"Yes, I was hoping to show you something the last time you were here, but I fell asleep."

"Oh?" Addison had already moved to her closet, searching blindly for something to wear. "Is it all right with your mom?"

"Yes, of course."

"Okay. I'll be there in about an hour."

"Great. See you then."

Addison took a shower, analyzing their conversation as the hot, steaming water woke her fully. She couldn't believe Ami invited her to come back. Why would she? What could she want to show her?

After dressing, she walked toward the kitchen and her phone rang again. Philip's name flashed across the screen. She pressed the mute button and dropped it into her purse.

Aunt Brenda was sitting on the couch watching the TV screen, though she didn't seem interested. "What're you up to today?"

"Nothing much. But I need to run out for a while. Can I borrow your car?"

"Sure. I'm not planning to leave." Aunt Brenda lowered the TV's volume. "Are you meeting Philip? He's stopped by a couple of times looking for you."

"No ..." *I broke up with him.* "Not today."

Her stomach tensed as she filled a cup with orange juice. She hadn't explained about Philip yet. It would be best to wait until she got through to him first.

"Where are you off to, then?"

"Ami's." Addison didn't feel like answering questions about why she would be going to her house again. Aunt Brenda was shocked when Addison had told her about showing up to apologize last week, though she seemed proud of her choice.

Aunt Brenda stood and came toward her. "You mean the Tant girl?"

Addison nodded, keeping her mouth occupied with her cup.

"Why would you be going there again? I thought you told me it was the hardest thing you've ever had to do."

"I forgot to mention that as I was leaving, Ami asked for my number. I'd forgotten all about it, but she called me this morning and asked me to come."

"Okay, but honey, you shouldn't feel like you have to do this. You shouldn't let your guilt guide your motives."

"That isn't it. I don't know, maybe Ami just enjoyed my company or something." Addison was just as baffled that the girl had called her. Though guilt may play a big part in her decision to accept the invite, it was more curiosity than anything. "It's just something I feel I have to do."

"If you're sure, I won't talk you out of it. It's honorable for you to visit her. But you can't keep blaming yourself. You had no control over blacking out."

Addison always cherished these moments with her aunt. If only her mama could be more like her sister-in-law. But they were completely different.

This wasn't the first time Aunt Brenda had questioned her guilt over the accident with Ami. Aunt Brenda only wanted to ease her pain … to somehow take the responsibility from her, but no matter how Addison tried, she blamed herself.

5

Addison stood on Ami's porch. That ever-present sting of guilt over her choice to drive that night loomed and stole her breath as footsteps drew near. Then the door opened. The guy who appeared in the door frame observed her with wide, vigilant eyes. Her hand flew to her mouth. It was him. The guy from the library.

"Hi, can I help you?"

"I'm here to see Ami."

He reached out to take her hand. "Oh, you must be Addison. I'm Nathan, Ami's brother."

Despite the familiarity of his face, those dark eyes set apart at just the right distance, the straight nose, the smooth skin, there was something different.

He tipped his head, motioning for her to go first. She entered the Tants' trying to remain calm. Could the guy from the library be his twin brother?

"Addison," Ami squealed from the kitchen.

"Hey." Addison's throat swelled and she felt the need to bow her head in shame.

"I see you met Nathan. He's only here for the weekend. Addison's your age, Nathan. She's at UNC Wilmington," Ami added.

"No, kidding." Nathan was staring at her in unbelief as Addison lifted her head with a shake. "So is Logan."

"I told her."

Logan. Logan Tant. How on earth was it possible that he ... *he* the one she couldn't stop dreaming about, could be the brother of the girl she almost killed?

They were talking, but thankfully her response wasn't necessary, not with the lump in her throat thickening with each mention of Logan. So, she smiled and nodded at the appropriate times.

The subject of the accident never entered their conversation. And that fact alone loosened her shoulders.

Someone bounded down the stairs, and it wasn't until she got a good look at the older gentleman that she blew out the breath she'd been holding.

"Hi, I'm Alan Tant, Ami's dad." He offered his hand. "You must be Addison."

She took his outstretched hand and relaxed under the warmth of his eyes. "Yes, sir."

"Well, it's certainly nice to meet you. I hope you'll join us tonight. We're barbecuing out."

"Thank you, sir, but I have to work tonight."

"That's too bad. Maybe next time," he said as he disappeared around the corner.

Nathan moved into the small space next to her. "Have you met Logan?"

She swallowed hard. "No, not yet."

"She's only been here once."

Nathan shrugged. "I didn't know. I thought you had been friends awhile."

Again, her response wasn't needed, but they were treading dangerously close to the topic she dreaded.

An hour later, Addison had decided that Nathan and Ami Tant were angels sent by God to minister to her though she had been the one seeking forgiveness. When she finally said her goodbyes, Nathan walked her to the door, but she kept silent, awed by the acceptance this family had shown her.

Ami was disappointed that Addison had to leave before her other brother arrived, but Addison promised to stop by after her classes one day next week.

It dawned on her as she turned onto the main highway headed for home that Ami had never showed her anything.

Images of Ami lying in the emergency room filled Logan's mind and without warning he slammed his fist against the steering wheel. There were no charges pressed against the other driver. The scum would never pay enough, not for what he'd done … drinking and driving and slamming into his sister. An unhealthy shot of adrenaline rushed through him every time he thought of the guy.

Ami was standing in the foyer when he walked inside his mom's house and punched him playfully. "If you were here a few minutes earlier, you could've met Addison."

"Addison?" He said the name out loud. Ami had never mentioned anyone named Addison. It had to be someone from her home school group. "I've never heard you talk about her."

"Of course, you haven't? I just met her."

"Who is she?"

"A friend of mine. She was here earlier. She met Nathan." She sighed. "I was hoping you would get here before she left."

"Sorry."

"It's okay. She'll be back. I can't wait for you to meet her."

"She must be something special to get you all worked up like this."

"Oh, she is and she's so pretty. You're going to like her."

The thought of his sister finding a new friend made him smile.

"She felt so bad after the accident that she wanted to check on me."

Ami's words confused Logan at first, because anyone would feel bad about the accident.

"I couldn't believe she actually came. Most people wouldn't even care, but there were tears in her eyes when she saw me."

Logan decided Ami must be talking out of her head. Nothing she said made any sense. The thought troubled him—what if she'd suffered brain damage? "What do you mean, most people wouldn't care?" He leaned against the stair banister. "Everyone cares about you."

"I'm talking about when someone causes the accident. But she came last week and then I invited her to come over today." Ami stood straighter. "And she came."

Logan's blood ran cold. Surely, she didn't mean Addison was the same person who caused the accident. The drunk driver. Before he could respond, Ami threw her arms around him. "I know you're going to love her," she said with delight.

Ami pulled back and Logan stared in horror as Ami slipped the wrap from her head. "What're you doing?"

"I'm taking off the bandage. I wanted to show you how good it's looking."

He looked at her cut, the long slash starting at her crown and weaving a curved line past her eyebrow, just above her eye. The cut that broke his heart. It was so close to her eye—too close.

"Doesn't it look better?"

"It does," Logan told her, giving it another quick glance. "Are you still rubbing cream over it?"

"Every day, three times a day," Ami said, securing the bandage back in place. "Just one more day until I can take this aggravating wrap off."

Logan's mind whirled in anguish. The driver was responsible for the cut that would leave a scar, a scar that would never fade completely.

He still hadn't found any answers concerning the drunk driver, but he couldn't talk to Ami about it. She was too young to understand. He had to wait and talk to his mom as soon as he could get her alone.

How could Mom allow that monster in this house? Maybe Mom was just as upset but wouldn't have said anything to Ami, not wanting to upset her. He bit his tongue, revulsion seeping into his veins.

Nathan was walking toward them, so Logan rushed to the kitchen to speak with his mother.

"Ami was telling me someone named Addison came over."

"Yes. It really took me by surprise. I wasn't sure what to think, but it was nice of her to check on Ami. I couldn't believe she agreed to come again today when Ami called her."

At his mother's words, bile rose in the back of his throat. He'd thought the driver was a guy. For one moment, his hatred eased. A girl? That had to be different, right?

No, it didn't matter.

It changed nothing. The girl still made the decision to drink and drive. She nearly killed his sister. A new realization hit him as he pondered his mother's words. She had come twice. What was she trying to do, get away with what she'd done? Trying to suck up to his sister, hoping to redeem herself? Well, he wouldn't stand for it. This would stop right now.

"That girl shouldn't be coming here."

His mother faced the sink, wiping the counters. "What? What do you mean?"

Nathan entered the kitchen, interrupting their conversation. "What did I miss?"

"You missed nothing, honey. We were just discussing Addison."

Nathan's lips curved into a crooked smile. "What about her?"

Logan's fists tightened. "What do you mean, what about her? She nearly killed our sister and you just invite her into our home like she's a friend of the family?"

Mom and Nathan faced him, their eyes bulging, but he continued, "What? I'm not the one who's done something wrong here. She's only using you to get out of what she's done. Well, she can't. She will pay for what she did to Ami. You need to press charges." The harsh tone of his voice surprised even him.

"Logan Tant, what on earth has gotten into you?"

Nathan said nothing, only stared at him in disbelief.

Logan swallowed the growl caught in his throat and turned to walk away.

47

"I've never seen him so mad," his brother said as Logan walked through the front door, letting it slam behind him.

The girl had already pulled the wool over their eyes.

6

Wearing her uniform and a damp head of hair, Addison sat on the front porch steps awaiting her ride.

When Taylor parked at the curb, Addison ran out to meet her.

Addison secured her seat belt before leaning back against the seat. "Student teaching and then waiting tables five nights a week is wearing me out."

"I bet." Taylor turned to face her, in no hurry. "I have to talk to you, and you have to listen to me."

Addison's stomach sank. "What is it?"

Taylor took a deep breath. "Michael took me downtown to this off-the-wall restaurant. There was some party and I saw Philip."

The rush of emptiness deepened. "So? Philip parties all the time. You know that."

"He wasn't alone."

Addison wasn't surprised. That had been the reason she ended things. Lately her emotions were on a roller coaster ride. She rolled her eyes at the irony of it all. "I know, Taylor. I caught him at the party, remember?"

"Yes, but he denied it. And you keep letting him get away with it."

"I'm not letting him get away with it. I told him it was over, remember?"

"I'm tired of him hurting you."

"I appreciate what you're trying to do, but I'm handling it the best way I know how."

"I'm sorry, Addison. I hate seeing him do this to you."

"I'm okay, really. I no longer care what he does. How did your date with Michael go?"

"Not so good."

Addison turned to face her. "Why not?"

"I was so worried about you, I was getting on his nerves."

She glanced at her friend. The truest friend she'd ever had.

"Someone will come along one day and sweep you off your feet. Laugh all you want to, but your true love is out there somewhere."

Love was something Addison knew nothing about and neither did her mama.

"Do you love him?"

"What kind of question is that for a nine-year-old?"

"Do you? Do you love him the same as you did Daddy?"

"You know better than to talk about him."

Yes, she knew it only made Mama worse, but she couldn't help it.

Maybe talking about Daddy would help Mama feel better. "I remember—"

Mama snatched her by the arm, making Addison stumble into her. "Don't." The hate that emerged in Mama's eyes scared her. "He left us. He doesn't deserve our memories."

Several days later, Addison walked up the familiar steps with slow and steady breaths and rang the Tants' doorbell. She had only stepped inside a moment when the door behind her opened again.

Addison turned and took an awkward step back as Ami's other brother entered.

Blinking up at Logan Tant, she inhaled hard while reprimanding herself for not maintaining control. A glimmer of recognition filled his eyes, just before Ami burst into the front entryway, their mom following behind.

"You're here. Both of you. "Ami grabbed Logan from behind.

"Ami." The words left his lips as smoothly as if he was more than used to Ami's hug attacks.

"I'm so happy you came. I've been wanting you to meet Addison." Ami turned and faced her. "Addison, this is my brother, Logan."

The creases around his lips tightened, and his lack of response ignited regret within her middle.

It had all happened so quickly, Addison told herself it was only her imagination. She'd been so worried what this family would think of her. Nathan seemed to like her. And though deep down she knew she didn't belong here; she'd thought she was doing the right thing by befriending them.

But she was wrong.

———

It's her. Logan recognized her the moment their eyes met. For several seconds, all he could do was stare. Her slight smile exposed a hidden glow.

Tearing his gaze away, he turned toward Ami, breaking the trance.

Addison. He had thought of her often, since that day in the library, and had hoped to see her again. That she was here standing in his parents' living room confounded him. Yet here she stood, staring up at him with those guilty eyes.

She averted her gaze for several brief moments and Logan once again took full advantage by drinking in every feature of her unblemished face. She was strikingly beautiful. The kind of beauty that demanded his attention, the kind that made it hard to look away.

But something in her eyes captured him even more. Something hidden beneath the midnight blue. Something—

He refused to stare another second to prevent his heart from softening. Who was he fooling? It had already softened.

How could she be the same girl? He'd never seen her out partying, drinking, or at any of the hang outs the college students frequented. Still, she was the one responsible for nearly killing his sister. As that detail rotted into his core, his pleasure shifted from yearning to mounting anger. And beneath it, an even deeper resentment. One he'd buried. One that hadn't surfaced for over three years.

Her smile quivered, then faded completely. He'd made her uncomfortable. Good. She wasn't welcome here. She should leave and never come back.

Ami's whining voice jerked him back to the present. "Logan, aren't you going to say hello?"

Logan glanced at his mother, hoping for an escape, but her eyebrows creased with a look of warning. What did she expect him to do? He couldn't just stand here and pretend there was nothing abnormal about this. Addison was responsible for hurting his sister, almost killing her. Logan looked into Ami's face, the cut on her forehead a pale red from the newness, her puzzlement of his silence obvious on her face.

He unchained a burst of air from his tight lips, consenting only for Ami's sake. "I'm Logan." The acrid bitter taste of his anger seeped into his short stern introduction.

The girl rewarded his effort with a conjured smile, but quickly fixed her eyes on Ami.

Ami's laughter broke the tension. "Logan? What's wrong with your voice? It sounded other-worldly."

A grunt of laughter gripped him but, rebelling against it, he cleared his throat and curled his lips into a weak smile.

Addison's soft, delicate voice approached him with regret. "It's so nice to finally meet you, Logan. I've heard so much about you." She reached for his hand and wrapped it inside both of hers, the warmth of her fingers placating his anger, restoring his sanity. "Your sister ... she's been so sweet to me."

After another glance at her face, Logan's remorse swelled as moisture glazed her eyes.

As her hands slipped away from his, her meek frown deepened. "I'm so sorry, Ami, but I can't stay."

"What? You just got here."

"I know. I'm so sorry. I forgot about something I was supposed to do."

"Are you sure it can't wait?"

Addison was already going through the front door, fresh tears leaking onto her cheeks. "I'm so sorry, I can't."

"Don't forget about our plans Sunday afternoon."

With one timid glance in his direction, Addison grinned, but it was as if his response had bruised her heart. And he was the one who couldn't look away.

"I don't know. Maybe it would be better if I didn't."

"Logan?" There were hundreds of questions in Ami's frantic stare.

"Of course, you should come." At Nathan's words, Logan spun to face him. "Right, Logan?"

Logan seethed yet marveled over Nathan's reaction to the girl. "What plans?"

"Nothing specific." Ami skipped past him and looped her arm through Addison's. "I just invited her over."

His gaze darted away from Ami and settled again on Addison. Hesitancy played across her face, and impulsively he gave in. "You should come." It wasn't until his agreement was out that the weight of what he'd done settled over him.

He'd just gave his consent for Ami to have her over again, the girl who almost killed her.

Ami cheered and hugged Addison. "See, you have to now."

Logan took deliberate steps to the kitchen, the scowl on his lips twitching. It was as if she was part of their family now. As if she had bewitched them. Bewitched him.

Ami carried on without taking a breath about the girl once Addison walked away. He would have to keep his opinions to himself. At least for now. His sister had been through enough. He wouldn't be responsible for causing her further heartache.

But Logan wasn't finished. He wouldn't rest until Addison paid for what she did to his sister. He didn't have to wait very long. Addison was coming on Sunday and he planned to be here no matter what.

Silence and emptiness encased Addison as she reached her car and drove away from Ami's house. She wiped at the tears now pouring from her eyes.

She was a fool.

As hard as she struggled to thrust the image from her mind, Logan's glaring eyes seeping with revulsion burned in her memory. There was no mistaking his feelings.

He hated her.

Swelling tears obstructed her vision, but she blinked through them and drove mile after mile, afflicted that her acceptance into the Tant's perfect family had been shattered.

At home, she entered the house quietly and made her way to her bedroom, avoiding Aunt Brenda. She would have too many questions, especially with mascara and eyeliner now staining Addison's cheeks.

Agony uncoiled in her chest as each defeat, one by one, registered with deep conviction. Losing her sister, the accident, Philip, and the hate she'd felt from Ami's brother. The same brother she had been dreaming about since that day in the library.

Her grief thickened as she lay on her bed, turning her world black and sweeping her into an exhausted sleep.

"I'm leaving, I'll be back in a few minutes."

Addison startled and sat straight up, her eyes focusing on the clock. 6:00. How long had she been sleeping? Clearing her throat, she croaked, "Okay." Wretched thoughts fought their way back into her conscious.

She got up and stared into the mirror wiping away all evidence of grief smeared across her face.

Logan had every right to hate her. She'd been responsible for hurting his sister. But because of her guilt, because she truly cared for Ami, Addison couldn't let Logan Tant hinder her relationship with his sister.

No matter how much he hated her.

7

Guilt stabbed Logan's conscience as he left the church. For days he had anticipated retaliating against the drunk driver until the sermon this morning resonated. A message that shattered his reasoning. A verse that he couldn't stop repeating. *Get rid of all bitterness, rage and anger, brawling and slander, along with every form of malice. Ephesians 4:31*

Bitterness. Logan shook his head. Bitter. He wasn't bitter. This was different. He had a right to be angry.

Every right.

He wasn't only doing this for himself, but for them, for Ami. Anyone who chose to ignore the consequences of drinking and driving deserved to be punished. Since he was the only one not blinded by her attempt to redeem herself, it was his obligation to see this through. And he was anxious to make Addison regret that very decision.

The wait was short. He arrived just before she did, and he held the door as she stepped onto the front porch.

"Addison." He drew her name out, his tone chastising. One hand stuffed in his pocket, the other squeezing the knob, he waited for her reaction, though he refused to look at her.

"Logan, it's so nice to see you again." His stab at a warning did nothing to rattle her. Instead her voice was warm and inviting. It bubbled with compassion. "I ran into you not too long ago on campus. In the library." Her remark lowered his gaze to hers. Her smile widened and held nothing back. Within the span of two short breaths, she trapped him with her eyes.

Again.

Addison didn't give him a chance to reply. "Maybe it wasn't you."

Before he could react, she was already moving away from him and toward Ami.

He had planned to stare at the girl, waiting for the perfect opportunity to crush her, but instead he studied her subtle motions, the way her dimple deepened with the slightest movement of her lips, the way her eyes darkened with concern with every glance at Ami. She was beautiful.

And he couldn't look away.

"Ami tells me you're student teaching a kindergarten class," his mom asked Addison.

"Yes, ma'am."

As Addison went into detail of her daily routine, of how much she loved the children, Logan seethed over the fact that his family was warming up to her even more. Then she told her mom how most of the class came from lower income families, how there were some who were only fed when at school—how it broke her heart. There was so much compassion in her voice, her expression, it softened his resolve to see her punished.

Over the next hour, Addison's conversation with his family grew faint as something within him surrendered and welcomed her presence.

Every time Addison glanced in his direction, his eyes aligned with hers, hers begging for affirmation. But to his disappointment after only twice she wouldn't glance in his direction again, not even when he spoke trying to get her attention.

What was he doing? He would not give into this. He could not let her get away with this.

Logan stood. "I'm out of here. Let me know when things get back to normal."

Nathan followed him into the kitchen, a scowl tightening his face.

"Don't look at me like that."

"What's wrong with you? I've never seen you treat anyone that way."

Logan had only barely kept to his original plan. "What do you expect me to do?" He slammed his hat onto his head. "That girl you keep inviting over here almost killed our sister."

"People have accidents every day, Logan. That's all it was. An accident."

"An accident that would've never happened if she hadn't decided to drink and drive." His own declaration pricked his conscience.

"Is this about Carrie?"

A coldblooded laugh resounded in his throat. "Don't ..."

"Logan, it's been over three years. You can't blame Addison for what happened to Carrie."

Logan snarled. "This has nothing to do with Carrie. But I see no one else to blame for the permanent scar my sister will live with the rest of her life." He walked through the entryway but stopped when he found Addison standing there.

She'd heard him.

He rubbed his jaw as another blow of remorse darkened his determination. She stood near the door, seeking an escape.

Because of him.

Shame distorted the perfect smile she'd worn earlier. And his resentment bound his tongue as he stepped through the front door.

Sorrow slowly slithered back onto the surface of Addison's heart when Logan walked past her and out the front door.

"Addison?" Nathan led her into the kitchen. As soon as they were alone, he took both of her hands. "Please don't let Logan bother you. He doesn't mean any harm."

"It's okay. I understand how he feels. He's right. The accident was my fault. I don't belong here."

"Ami loves you and she's the one that matters. I haven't seen her this happy in months." He barreled on, leaving no room for her objection. "Hey, cheer up. He's gone. Now you can finally relax." Still holding one of her hands, Nathan escorted her to the living room.

The chair where Logan had sat was now vacant. She took a deep breath and instructed herself to maintain her composure instead of going after him. To apologize for intruding on his family.

She shouldn't be here. Not instead of him. It was wrong. But she wanted this. More than anything. The Tants made her feel she belonged, like she was a part of their family. Something she'd never had.

When she arrived home, Philip was waiting in the yard.

He rose from the front porch and met her halfway. "Where've you been?"

"With a friend."

He spat in the dirt, shot her a backward glance, but kept walking toward his truck. "Taylor?"

"No, you don't know her."

"Can we go somewhere to talk?"

Her stomach recoiled at the thought of all she needed to say. "Yes, we need to talk."

"Where do you want to go?"

Somewhere they could talk but wouldn't be alone. "How about the boardwalk at Carolina Beach?"

When they reached the pier, she absorbed her surroundings with awareness. She welcomed the crowd, the bright lights.

He took her hand as soon as they stepped onto the wooden planks. She snatched it away, cringing against his touch, and gripped her hands tight to her waist. "Don't."

"Don't what? I thought you wanted this."

"You wanted to talk, so talk."

"We have a lot of making up to do. I'm going to grab a beer. I'll be right back." He didn't wait for a response.

As soon as it was in his hand, he popped off the top and sucked down two-thirds of the bottle as he made his way back to her. How was she supposed to get home? What had possessed her to come all the way out here with him?

She would have to call Taylor. Again.

Teeth clenched, she scowled. "You can't survive one night without drinking?"

He leaned closer, the stench of alcohol offensive. "I'm celebrating."

"Celebrating what?"

"You and me." He guzzled the remaining liquid.

Philip had never been one to get excited about anything. Especially anything concerning her. His drinking would only complicate everything. "Philip, I'm being serious. You're not listening to me." Every instinct told her to call Taylor and leave now.

Playing the devoted boyfriend, he cupped her elbow and led her to a bench.

Before she could form her thoughts into words, Philip threw his empty beer into the trash, slipped his hands beneath her shirt, and grabbed her bare waist. "I'm listening, baby. You have my full attention."

She laid both hands flat against his chest and pushed, but it did no good. He was solid, unmoving. "Let go of me."

His hands drifted way below her comfort level. In a desperate attempt to free herself, she twisted from his grip and he pushed her back, the bench cutting her leg as she went down.

A set of different hands grabbed her upper arms and secured her into his own, before she hit the wooden floor. "Whoa, there." The voice she recognized instantly, and her pulse raced in a disturbing rhythm, causing her legs to wobble.

"Logan, my man. You'll have to excuse my girlfriend." Philip chuckled crudely. "She's had too much to drink."

Logan's pools of dark brown pored over her as she rested against him, the weight of his gaze crushing her airway. Time seemed to slow as Logan held her, but then just as suddenly, he helped her stand on her own and let go. "Sorry to interrupt. See you at practice."

Practice? Baseball. Logan and Philip were teammates? Logan didn't even speak to her. Or acknowledge that he knew her.

The shuffle of Logan's boots was the only indication of his departure.

At the end of the next day, Addison stopped by the university to drop off some books she'd borrowed from the library. She walked across campus, her mind cloaked with defeat. It was impossible to carry on a firm conversation with Philip—especially after he drained three more beers within twenty minutes.

A gentle tug kept nudging her to tell someone. It would be easy to ignore some of Philip's deceit, but she could no longer ignore his violence.

Even though Logan said nothing last night, she could easily imagine what he was thinking. His telling gaze said more than enough. It didn't help that every time she looked at him, she nearly swooned.

"Addison? Wait."

She risked a brief glance over her shoulder.

Logan? Her breath caught in her throat as she slowed. Their last encounter was still scrambling to the forefront of her mind. How she fell into him. How he caught her. How Philip accused her of being drunk. How Logan looked at her.

He caught up to her and stretched out his fingers. "You left these on the hood of your car."

"Oh, my gosh. I just got my car back and already I'm losing my keys." Why had she said that? It was a reminder of the accident, a reminder of his hate of her. "I'm sorry. Thank you so much." She balanced the books so she could take the keys, but the books tumbled to the ground. Heart leaping to an unrecognizable beat, Addison bent to retrieve them.

Logan lifted the books before she could and settled them in the crook of his arm. "These are the kind of college books I need."

She laughed as she reached for them. "Activity books for my kindergarten class."

61

"I've got it."

"You don't have to carry them."

"You should never argue with a man trying to be a gentleman."

The intensity of his gaze lingering on her shattered any remaining fight within her.

Still struggling to believe Logan Tant was walking with her to the library, she savored the hope that stirred within. Stomach fluttering when they reached the library, Addison turned and started to retrieve her things. "Thank you."

"It *was* me."

"It was you?" Needing more space, she shuffled backward. "It was you, what?" A tremble shook her fingers as she reached for the books. Chills slithered down her arms as her hand brushed against his rough palm, his fingers almost twice the size of hers.

"In the library that day."

"Oh." She felt every element of that moment as if it was happening all over again. "I knew it was you." Her words came on a whisper. Maybe he didn't recognize her last night.

"So, you and Philip, huh?"

Or maybe not. Heat stung her face.

His gaze shifted to her leg before she could respond. He'd taken a step closer, then looked straight at her, his gaze softer. Polite. Confusing. "You're bleeding."

"What?" Addison glanced at the deep red trickling down her calf, below her skirt. Shifting her scraped leg from his view, she swallowed hard. "Just a little scratch."

He bent to get a closer look. "That is not a little scratch. What happened?"

In the distance she spotted Philip walking toward them. Instinctively, she snatched her leg from Logan's touch.

"Let me get something for that."

"No, really. It's fine. I can grab a paper towel from the library restroom."

"There you go again trying to keep me from being a gentleman."

"Thank you so much, Logan, but I've really got to go." She rushed inside before he could say anything more, her cheeks flaming, her pulse racing.

Watching her hurry inside, an ache filled his chest. With one last glance, she offered a smile. Not a formal, forced smile, but one that brightened the blue of her eyes.

She was dating Philip Thomas. The centerfielder for the Seahawks. He would've never imagined them together. But how was he any different? He'd been horrible to her.

Sitting in class, he pulled out his Criminal Law notebook, but the color was wrong.

Purple.

He stared at the cover, enchanted. Addison's name drawn with a black marker, a heart dotting the i.

Resisting the urge to open it, he placed it to the side. The professor started his lecture, but Logan's attention was diverted. The effect Addison had on him, the way she had distracted him so fully, surprised him. And he couldn't help but smile.

"What are you smiling about? I've never been so bored in my life."

Logan's best friend, Matt, spoke releasing him from his thoughts. "I was thinking about something."

"Tell me, I need something to think about other than this boring lecture concerning this Italian guy. Does it have something to do with *she*?"

Logan had spoken without thinking and now was expected to share his thoughts.

He couldn't.

He wasn't even sure what happened to cause such a drastic change in him. Maybe it wasn't so drastic, after all. He had been unable to stop thinking of Addison since they'd met in the library. But things were different now.

The professor spoke, presenting an escape. "Matt, could you please come to the front?"

Logan held his laughter. Maybe he would tell him later.

But what would he say? How would he explain she was the same she who had caused Ami's accident?

Logan placed his paper on the desk, the purple notebook catching his eye. What if she needed it right now? Was it for her kindergarten class? He couldn't tell from the cover. Only her name drawn creatively adorned the jacket. Logan traced each letter before slipping his finger beneath the cover and opening it.

He skimmed through the pages filled with her neat handwriting. But still he hadn't discovered what it was used for. He flipped back to the front page, hoping to find an answer as he read the first page.

The bell ringing startled Logan. Closing her notebook, he stood fumbling with his books when Matt's voice reached his ear. "What're you doing with a purple notebook, man? Or is it a shade of blue I've never seen?"

"It isn't mine. I picked it up by accident."

Matt snatched it from his grasp. He scanned the cover. "Addison?"

Logan grabbed it, cramming it between his books.

"Who's Addison? Is it her?"

Logan tried to come up with an excuse. A lie. But none came. "Yes, it's hers. She dropped it."

"You mean you saw her again? Her name is Addison?"

It would be so easy to say no, but his voice didn't cooperate. "Yes. Her name is Addison. She dropped it on the way to the library."

Matt's grin stretched from cheek to cheek. "The library? She spends a lot of time there. Good job, buddy, finally getting her name."

"Don't get any bright ideas." Logan took off in a sprint. "I've got to go. I'll catch up with you later."

"Sure, you do …" Matt called after him, but Logan missed the last part. It was for the best. He had a hard-enough time coming to terms with his feeling for Addison without Matt's help. Right now, he had something more important to do—to see if her car was still parked beside his.

Something about Matt's reaction wormed into the marrow of his bones as he sprinted to the parking lot.

Logan was asking for trouble.

He turned the corner, a touch of dread replacing his skepticism. The space next to his stood empty. Addison had already left. Before he realized what he was doing, he whipped out his phone and searched his contacts for Ami—his direct line to Addison.

Ask Addison to come over.

Ami's reply was fast and just as expected. *Why?*

Don't worry about that. Just make sure she comes.

It was too late. He was already in trouble.

8

As soon as she returned the books, Addison hurried across campus to her car. And inspected Logan's truck so she'd recognize it the next time.

Blood still trickled down her leg and onto her ankle. The saturated napkin was no longer working.

A large bandage would fix her leg, but what was she supposed to do about Logan Tant? One minute he was arrogant, seething in her presence, accusing her of something he had no one else to blame. The next he was charming, looking at her in a way that made her feel cherished, beautiful, a way no one had ever looked at her.

Apparently, the way she'd looked at him had been obvious. The minute Logan Tant was out of hearing, Philip accused her of embarrassing him. He then called Logan arrogant. A drunk sleaze who had a different girl every week.

Arrogant, maybe. Drinking, she couldn't picture. She'd been around alcohol her whole life. Something she could identify immediately. Something she'd never choose for her remaining years.

Different girls? She'd seen no evidence, but they'd had only a couple of encounters. So, it was possible. But something deep down rejected that fragment of information.

As the distance between her car and the school grew, that annoying tug nudged her again. Maybe she needed to tell someone about last night. How Philip had reacted to her before and after Logan appeared. How a prickle of unease squirmed through her middle until Taylor showed up to drive her home. How even today, in their brief encounter, he held her arm with more force than necessary. Even after she'd made it clear she wanted nothing more to do with him.

Philip only revealed his anger when drinking, but she wasn't going to put up with it. Not ever again.

Reflecting on her newfound freedom, she lowered the volume of the car stereo. Things were going to be so different now that she no longer had a boyfriend. Going straight home to take a short nap before her shift tonight was just what she needed. It would be nice to have a few hours to herself.

That all changed when Ami called begging her to take her to the mall.

Ami's bubbly voice always brightened Addison's mood. Instead of taking a left that would take her home, she took a right and drove straight to Ami's.

The thudding of Addison's pulse gave her hesitance. She was doing this for the right reasons. Guilt demanded she comply with Ami's every wish. Still, she enjoyed Ami's company. Had come to think of her as a close friend, that the accident had been a blessing. One that had brought them together. One that had given her a peek inside the kind of family she'd always longed for. A family who seemed to truly care for each other. For her.

Then she thought of Logan. She couldn't deny her hope that she'd see him again. Her thoughts fluttered to their chance meetings and she flushed from the memories. He'd been so kind. Had even smiled. His irresistible lips curled into a pleasant semicircle still lingered in the tender places of her memory.

She arrived at the Tants' and walked toward the front door. Addison pressed the now-familiar doorbell, inspecting the white wicker furniture adorning the covered entrance. The blue green cushions beckoned her to sit and relax. Did the Tants ever sit out here?

"Hello, beautiful."

Butterflies invaded her stomach at the deep sound of Ami's brother's voice. Turning quickly, she found Nathan standing in the doorway, staring at her. She allowed the breath she'd held to escape. He and Logan sounded just alike.

"Hi. I wasn't expecting to see you."

"I'm heading back tonight." Nathan slipped his arm through Addison's. "We've been waiting for you to get here."

Ami stuck her head around the corner. "Do you care if he goes to the mall with us?"

"I'm craving one of those pretzels," Nathan said. "Well, two pretzels. One with salt and one with cinnamon and sugar. They're better together." Nathan's smile was so infectious, it was impossible not to join in. "I'll share."

The playfulness she detected in his voice was comforting. It was like she belonged here. Like she always had.

Logan pulled his truck in front of his mother's house two hours later, searching for Addison's car. It was parked beside Nathan's truck.

He still had Addison's notebook and it wasn't likely he'd run into her again on campus. He had looked for her constantly, after bumping into her at the library, but never saw her ... until today.

The scene last night between her and Philip had replayed hundreds of times through his mind today. He hated himself for not taking up for her. But it wasn't his place. Addison was dating Philip.

He wanted to see her brought to justice, but there was also something about her that fascinated him. And he wanted to know more. Some of that information he held in his fingertips. In her purple notebook.

It wasn't used for a subject. It was her journal. He couldn't justify reading anymore. It was wrong. Logan had learned more about Addison in those first few pages than seemed possible.

The sun setting just beyond the tall pines shaded the front yard early. The wind had blown over a vase that now leaned against one of the patio chairs, and he reached to position it back on its base.

Soft notes from the piano played through the bay window. Ami. She'd taken lessons and could play anything. He thought he'd heard all Ami's songs, but this one didn't sound familiar. Still, it was beautiful. Walking through the front door, he headed straight to the piano.

Nathan stood by the baby grand, blocking his view. "What're you doing here?"

"I was about to ask you the same question."

The music stopped abruptly. And then he saw her. Addison faced the piano, her fingers resting on the keys.

"Logan," Ami said in a sing song voice. "Addison's playing for us. He loves the piano. Don't you, Logan?"

"I do. Please don't stop on my account." He turned, heading toward the kitchen, needing a moment to gather his thoughts. How would he get an opportunity to talk to Addison if Nathan lingered the entire time?

The sound of soft music played again, but this time it was Ami. She was playing her favorite song.

Nathan followed him into the kitchen and the moment was interrupted. "Please tell me you're not still …"

Logan cut him off. "What're you doing here?"

"I took the day off. I'm heading back tonight." Nathan said, yanking Logan into a hug.

Logan adjusted his ball cap and caught sight of Nathan's neck outstretched toward the living room—toward Addison. "We went to the mall earlier."

"Who?"

"Me, Addison, and Ami."

Unwelcomed envy slithered into his thoughts. "Why would you go with them?"

"Nothing wrong with spending time with my little sister. I'm the lucky one that Addison didn't mind me tagging along."

Nathan was moving in on Addison? No! He couldn't be.

"We're planning to go to the beach this weekend. The temperature's supposed to be in the mid-seventies. You should come."

He had to be mistaken. But Nathan didn't have a girlfriend. "Yeah, sure. What time?"

"Early afternoon, around one. You could cook some cheeseburgers afterward. Unless you already have plans?" Nathan cast a crooked smile in his direction. "Addison's coming."

Why does he insist on torturing me? Logan thought about telling him he wasn't free, but that would be lying. He had to work a twelve-hour shift Friday night from 7:00 p.m. to 7:00 a.m., but he wouldn't miss their beach trip. "I'm free."

The same notes from earlier hummed through the house, yet softer. He peeked around the corner. Addison sat motionless on the bench, her back facing him. He imagined the deep creases in her forehead as she concentrated on each note. Ami sat by her side, swaying to the melody.

A grin split Nathan's face before he moved back into the living room and stood next to Addison, almost hovering over her. What were Nathan's intentions?

What were his?

Deep down, he wanted to be the one standing next to Addison—to slide into the space next to her. Close enough to inhale her sweet, clean fragrance that had dissipated hours ago. Not standing here, watching from a distance, like an outsider.

Nathan stayed on one side of Addison, Ami on the other. Nathan looped his arm so that his was touching Addison's and a deeper bout of jealousy flared through Logan. It drove him crazy watching Nathan flirt with Addison. But what bothered him most was observing how uncomfortable Addison seemed. He could blame no one but himself.

Because of her unease, Nathan tried harder.

The purple notebook in his truck would give him the perfect excuse to speak to her—to direct her attention away from Nathan. There was no reason to hold onto it.

Except he just wasn't ready to let it go.

9

Friday night, Logan parked at the local coffee shop on his lunch break as subtle calls from his radio faded in and out. He reached for the purple notebook from his backpack. Allowing his finger to run down the spiral wire that held the pages intact, he couldn't help but wonder what other information he would find hidden within.

It was wrong. He should've given it back already.

But holding it, though he'd promised himself not to read another word, felt like he held a piece of Addison ... a reason to talk to her again.

This is crazy.

He opened it anyway and hovered his flashlight over the now-familiar handwriting of her name, reminding himself that he'd already read the first page. It couldn't hurt to read it again. Before he could talk himself out of it, he opened the purple cover and explored the beginning as if it was his first time reading and then devoured three more pages before he stopped.

Reading the words in class had the same effect they were having now, including a new disturbing reaction.

Shock.

Addison was the same girl he'd been praying for every day for two years. He'd heard at the station about a local girl losing her life to an accident involving alcohol, leaving behind her older sister, a student on campus. Not knowing the sister's identity hadn't mattered. He felt an urging immediately to pray for the girl. And he had. Every day.

He had seen more than enough drug overdoses and the grave effects of alcohol in the two short years he had patrolled the streets of Wilmington.

Flipping through the notebook, he found the pages nearly full, but he closed it. The pain that ripped through him reading her handwritten words again gave him a strange desire to comfort the girl.

But he had at his fingertips evidence of the night of Ami's accident. He could lay to rest forever his suspicions. He could read for himself if she'd written anything about it. About him. How serious she and Philip were. He had no doubt it would all be there. He could tell by her first entries. The details she revealed. Addison wrote from somewhere deep within. Her feelings bled onto each page.

But his guilt escalated, and he closed the cover.

He slid it back inside his backpack, then searched the area surrounding him. A couple walked by his cruiser, glancing inside briefly as they passed. He nodded with a smile. They disappeared inside the Waffle House and he relaxed against the head rest.

Addison's chin quivering when he ran into her today stirred in his memory as did the gentle curve of her neck. He'd been careless with her feelings, but rightfully so. His empathy now wrestled with his attempt to see her punished. Better to commit to active prayer for your enemies than to accommodate bitterness.

Attaching her name, her face, to his daily prayer for her, he lifted his heart to God in the last few minutes before his lunch break ended. It was impossible to hoard anger for a person while praying for them.

The loving way she spoke of her kindergarten children, the sincere display of friendship she offered his sister, and the genuine warmth that almost seeped from her, pervaded his thoughts as he pulled out of the parking lot.

After his shift, he took a three-hour nap before showering and driving to his parents' house. He glanced at the notebook lying in the passenger seat before getting out. Playing scenarios over and over in his mind regarding how to handle it, he opted for the easy route.

A tiny white lie.

How else could he explain keeping it so long? Mending all the wrongs he'd added together since they'd met already seemed impossible.

He didn't want to add to her list of good reasons to avoid him.

Exhaling a deep breath, he left the notebook in his truck and walked around back. Chattering voices filled the yard. Addison was standing by the fence, laughing at something with Nathan. A person would think the sight of her allowing Nathan to flirt—the way she looked at Nathan with admiration—would cause him to look away. But even with the ominous thoughts latching on like a leech, it wasn't enough to thwart his gaze.

When he watched for several more seconds, the truth materialized before his eyes. Addison wasn't flirting with Nathan. People naturally flocked to her.

"Logan, you're here," Ami screamed from across the yard causing all heads to turn. "We can go to the beach now."

He glanced in Addison's direction. She looked up and fastened her gaze on him.

He had to find a few moments alone with her today. A few hours. He'd thought of nothing else since yesterday. But with Nathan's presence, Logan would be lucky if he found any chance to speak to her alone.

It would be a waste of time to expect anything more anyway. She had a boyfriend.

It didn't matter that the guy didn't deserve her.

Nathan walked toward him and opened the gate. Addison followed Ami to Nathan's truck.

The ten-minute drive to the ocean gave him plenty of time to think. Why did he keep doing this to himself? Hadn't he learned anything? Beautiful women were nothing but complicated distractions that would do more harm than good. One minute they would give a man security in their affection, and the next seek the attention of someone else.

Leaving the parking lot, Nathan and Ami walked ahead with Addison, leaving him behind. Despite his efforts, fumes of envy stirred within him. Slipping his slides off, Logan allowed the texture of the warm sand to penetrate his toes, hoping to distract his unwarranted thoughts. He wanted to be the one walking next to Addison, making her feel comfortable. Not his brother.

Addison glanced back and caught him staring. Her dimple deepened with her slight smile, and she slowed, allowing him to catch up to her.

"Hi." She continued, giving him no chance to reply. "I'm so glad for the break this week."

"Yeah, me too." He had been waiting for this moment. "This year has flown by."

"It has. Ami told me you are working for the police department. Will you continue working there after graduation?"

His strength quivered beneath a steady torrent of pleasure. "Yes, but hoping to get off the streets. I've applied for a detective position. What about you? Will you continue teaching at Middleton Elementary?"

"I would love to stay there, but all their permanent positions for this fall are taken."

"Do you want to keep teaching kindergarten?" He knew so little of her but stored what little he'd learned in his memory. He wanted to know everything about her. Not quickly, but slowly. Very slowly, memorizing every detail, one by one, intimately. He mentally slapped his luring thoughts back into submission.

"Yes, I absolutely love that age. They're eager to learn and they're so precious." The deep smile that covered every inch of her face said more than any words ever could.

"Sounds to me like you're going to make a great teacher."

"I don't know about that, but I sure would love the chance."

"Are you applying to other elementary schools here in Wilmington?"

"Several of them. And a few out of town." When her gaze returned to his, his heart gave in another notch. "But hopefully I'll be able stay in Wilmington."

"I hope it works out for you." And he meant every word.

The gritty feel of sand pressed against Addison's feet as they walked toward the water, but Logan's presence overshadowed her every thought. As their conversation came to an uncomfortable halt, she slung her beach bag over her shoulder and focused on the small waves crashing onto the shore.

Children played along the edge, running and kicking sand, building sandcastles, and dodging swelling waves. Ami stopped at an umbrella near the pier and helped Nathan set the chairs out after dropping their towels and bags into one pile.

"Put your stuff next to my chair, Addison." Ami threw her stuff in the middle chair and took off for the water.

Addison dropped her bag into the chair next to Ami's and slipped out of her cover top. She started to sit, but Nathan grabbed her arm and pulled her to the water's edge. The chilly water enhanced the chill bumps spreading across her arms and legs. She turned just as Logan set his chair next to hers.

When Nathan pulled at her again, she lost her balance. She fell to her knees as a wave crashed above her shoulders. Nathan stood over her, laughing. Ami slapped him on the back, and he laughed even harder. Sinking deeper, she looked toward Logan, but he wasn't watching.

Trying to relax, trying to forget that Logan sat just a few yards from them, she stood and walked deeper into the water, but her body's temperature wasn't acclimating to the cold water and she shivered almost uncontrollably as she gave up and staggered to the chairs.

"It is way too cold to play in the water. I'm fr-e-e-e-e-zing."

"Nathan shouldn't have ..."

"No-o-o-o, it's oka-a-ay. Really."

"Here, use this." Logan spread the thick, full-sized blanket of warmth across her legs.

Immediately, she pulled it to her middle, stopping herself from inhaling his scent clinging to the blanket, and tucked it around her body. "Thank you so much. That feels like heaven."

As they sat quietly side by side, Addison replayed their earlier conversation over and over. It had been going well and even ended well. But somewhere along the way, his attitude changed, briefly, as if he was fighting against something.

Forcing him into a conversation hadn't been her intention. She'd felt uncomfortable in his presence from the moment she met him in the living room. She wanted to resolve any tension between them, but what if he didn't want to let go? What if he couldn't forgive her?

Never finding the nerve to stand up again, Addison stayed in her seat even when Logan, Nathan, and Ami threw a frisbee at the shore's edge.

When Logan returned to his chair, Addison lifted his towel from around her, the edges and middle soaked through.

"No, you keep it. I'm good, but you were right, the water is freezing." He paused only a minute and leaned toward her. "Oh, and by the way, I paid Nathan back for you."

"I saw that."

His vigorous laugh resonated somewhere deep within her and drew her even closer before she realized it. A burning sensation filled her cheeks and she stared at the distant waves crashing.

"Logan, I wanted you to know that my intentions for visiting Ami, for coming even that first time—I was so worried about your sister." Addison twisted in her seat and met his gaze. "It was my fault. All my fault. I was at a party and did take a few sips of ... something. I never should've left or driven. I never drink. And I would never drink and drive. That night I was just—" she shook her head. "It was a stupid decision."

For a long moment, Logan only stared at her.

"I didn't mean for it to happen, and I'm so thankful Ami's okay." With a rapid release of breath, she added, "I just wanted you to know."

He nodded, his gaze softening as if pondering her words. "I'm thankful you are both all right."

They stayed only an hour before leaving, and once they reached the Tants', Nathan pulled her to the side. "Don't worry. Logan likes you." She hadn't expected those words and her neck flamed. "He's just weird." He flashed a mischievous grin.

Addison exhaled an exaggerated breath. "I better go."

Ami grabbed her arm. "We wanted you to stay for dinner."

"I really ..."

"Logan will be disappointed. He's grilling his famous cheese-burgers."

With all of them nudging her, emotion expanded in her chest and her eyes glazed over with a sheet of moisture. "Y'all have been so nice to me. I know it was under terrible circumstances, but I'm so thankful to have met you all."

"So, you'll stay?"

"How can I say no to you?" Battling the disturbing sensations raging through her chest, she glanced at Logan across the yard and swallowed hard. "I can't wait to taste Logan's cheeseburger."

Addison and Ami unfolded the red-and-white tablecloth and stretched it across the table. After setting out plates and napkins, Addison helped Ami fill cups with ice from the cooler. Mr. Tant, finally home from work, lit two lanterns filled with citronella oil and placed them on the center of the table. The strong scent swirled from the wicks, blending with the fragrant charcoal fumes.

Addison followed Ami to the patio and took a seat on the wooden swing next to her.

"I should've invited Zach." Ami stared across the yard, looking over the tall picket fence.

"Zach? Is he your boyfriend?" Addison studied her hands and feet instead of looking in the direction of the grill.

"He's my next-door neighbor. And no, we're just friends."

Mrs. Tant opened the kitchen door. "Ami, can you help me a minute?"

Ami stood. "I'll be right back."

Nathan immediately took Ami's place.

"Are you having fun?"

"Yes, I love spending time with you guys."

Amusement illuminated his eyes. "Even Logan?"

At the mention of his name, she glanced in Logan's direction. When Logan's face rose and he met her gaze, it displayed none of the irritation she'd expected to find. Instead kindness materialized in his smile.

Nathan leaned against her. Startled, she glanced at him. She'd never answered his question and he was still waiting.

Addison exhausted every inch of lawn along the fence line while desperately avoiding glances toward Logan standing across the yard.

Not until he pulled the cheeseburgers off the grill, did she take a seat at the table next to Ami. Not expecting Logan to take the seat on her other side, she straightened, trying to appear at ease. She suspected she was failing miserably. Her pulse spiked and her lungs refused air.

"Honey, will you bless the food?" Mrs. Tant asked her husband as Ami grabbed Addison's hand.

Logan's gaze flicked to Addison as he reached under the table and wrapped his fingers around her other hand. "It's a family tradition."

The sensation of his skin against hers was immediate and widespread. Starting at her fingers and sweeping through her body with intangible speed, the warmth of his touch penetrated every fiber.

Thank goodness she could close her eyes.

A persistent thudding resounded in her ears, and she was unable to concentrate on Mr. Tant's prayer. When the blessing ended, Logan squeezed her hand softly before releasing it. Or had she only imagined that?

Waiting a few seconds, Addison swallowed a small bite of the burger, her throat expelling her decision. A lump lodged in her throat, so big she had a hard time breathing, much less swallowing. Unable to take another bite without risking an embarrassing display of choking in front of this family, especially the Tant sitting next to her, she pushed around her chips hoping no one noticed.

"You don't like the burger?" Tone deflated, Logan stared at her plate.

Addison eased her gaze in his direction. "It's delicious."

It was a shame to not be able to enjoy the food fully. The perfectly balanced seasonings that flavored the burger were mouthwatering. She wanted to tell him, but her brain and mouth wouldn't cooperate. Especially with her mouthwatering for reasons that had nothing to do with the burger, but everything to do with the cook.

After they ate, Logan followed Nathan into the kitchen. He'd been waiting all afternoon to get his brother alone. "What're you doing, Nathan?"

"What're you talking about, little brother?"

Nathan knew just what to say to ruffle his feathers. "I'm not your little brother, Nathan. We're twins."

Nathan slapped him hard on the back. "What's wrong with you today? You seem so uptight."

"Have you got a thing for Addison?"

Nathan crossed his arms and leaned against the counter. "What?"

"You're flirting with her."

"So?" Though the kitchen light was dim compared to the brightness of the sun outside, Logan didn't miss Nathan's crooked grin as he looked through the kitchen window, his eyes focused on Addison. "Why do you care?"

What could he say? Stop flirting with Addison? There was no sensible reason for telling him to leave Addison alone, especially when he himself had barely spoken two words to her since dinner. "She isn't your type."

"I think she's great. I really like her."

Logan's hair stood on end at the smirk on Nathan's mouth.

"It wouldn't matter whether I wanted her anyway ... She's in love with someone else."

Logan's blood ran cold. *Philip.*

The back door creaked open and Addison entered the kitchen. Logan thought she had changed her mind when she started to turn, but she stopped instead. "I'm sorry, I don't mean to interrupt. Your mom sent me in for the brownies."

Nathan wasted no time walking toward her, but then slipped by her and flashed a mischievous grin toward him. "Logan will be glad to help you."

"Yeah, they're here somewhere," Logan said as though her standing only a few feet from him wasn't intoxicating. He scanned inside the refrigerator but found nothing. "I have no clue ..." He turned toward her. She held the platter in her hands. "Oh? You found them?"

"They're still warm."

Logan's gaze fell to her mouth as her lips curled into an uneven line. "I guess we need some plates." His mind raced as he pulled the plates from the cabinet. He ached to be alone with her, to get to know her. He wanted to somehow make up for his earlier behavior. But what did it matter? She was in love with Philip.

Had she told Nathan about him? Of course, she did. How else would Nathan have known?

"We may need a few more napkins too."

They reached for the package at the same time. His hand brushed against hers and she pulled away quickly, her cheeks a stunning shade of pink.

"Thank you." She rested her hand on his arm. "Your cheeseburger was really good."

"I'm glad you liked it. Maybe we'll do this again soon." His words held a lighthearted tone, matching the weightlessness of being this close to her.

Her hand slipped away from his arm. "We better get these out there."

"You have the most beautiful eyes I have ever seen."

"Wow. That's the sweetest thing anyone's ever said to me."

Bewitched, he lost focus, so consumed by her thick lashes surrounding those violet orbs, breaking him piece by piece from the inside out. Without restraint, his gaze wandered slowly, carefully, to the curve of her mouth. Her enchanted smile weakened, then faded completely.

He tore his gaze from hers. Finding no other excuse to keep standing there, he opened the door to let her pass as he salvaged what little focus remained.

But she stopped—in the doorway, leaving only inches between them, her gaze affixed to him. Her smile curved in a way that unleashed his pent-up desires all at once, quickly, leaving him breathless. "Thank you, Logan."

His laugh came naturally, and he savored the sudden swell of relief as he followed Addison into the yard.

Sitting around the table with his family, Logan stared with ease even when Addison looked in his direction. A soft laugh escaped her lips, the sweet sound wrapping him in warmth. Nathan was right. She was great. And he couldn't stop thinking about all she had said. How she wanted him to understand it had never been her intention to drink and drive. How it mattered to her that he knew the truth. She said nothing about blacking out, the actual cause of the accident, according to the report. And that still left unanswered questions. But all she had said made more sense than her partying and drinking and driving. There was nothing about her that would even remotely fit that description.

Looking at her now, watching her interact with his family, something within him stirred. She was a loving, goodhearted person, and the rest of his family had seen that from the very beginning. Logan listened with only one ear to the ongoing conversations the rest of the afternoon, his concentration absorbed with the girl. Until Ami invited her to the ballgame.

"Please come. It's Monday at seven. Right Logan?"

My ballgame?

"I would love to. I haven't been to a game this season." Addison turned and faced him fully. "I'm anxious to see this pitcher I keep hearing about."

Throat constricting, he coughed. "Trust me. There's nothing special about him."

Her breathtaking smile scrambled his thoughts. "I'll be the judge of that." She was flirting. Definitely flirting. "Thank y'all so much for having me and for the delicious dinner. It's getting late, so I better get going."

"I'll walk you out." The words tumbled from Logan's mouth without his consent, but he had no choice. He couldn't put off returning her notebook any longer. He closed the fence gate gently behind them. Addison's curls bounced with each motion as they walked toward the front yard.

Logan stopped when he reached his truck.

She faced him and pulled her fingers through her hair, brushing the stray strands from her face. "How do you do it all?"

"What?"

"You're a police officer. But you're also taking college classes and playing college baseball."

"Oh, that." He could stand here all night talking to her. "There definitely isn't much free time. So, I really enjoy times like this."

"I bet." Then she rested her hand on his arm. "Thank you again, Logan."

The brief, unexpected touch imprinted her mark onto him even deeper. "Oh, I have something of yours." Turning, Logan opened the passenger door and reached into his truck.

When he revealed the notebook, uncertainty washed across her face as she gasped.

"I picked it up by accident."

Addison stared at her journal, seemingly speechless. What was he thinking? He should've never kept it this long. Especially after realizing what it was used for.

"I'm sorry," he added, handing it to her. "It got mixed in with my books that day. The day we walked to the library."

Her mortified gaze lifted to him, then returned quickly to her book. "I've been looking everywhere."

"Addison, I—"

Her mobile ring tone blared through the moment.

She pulled her phone from her purse, glancing at the ID. Her brow furrowed before she pressed mute and dropped it back into her purse. He knew it was Philip. His name had flashed across the screen. A mixture of guilt and embarrassment splayed across her face. She belonged to someone else. Even though Philip didn't deserve her, she was committed to him.

He hated that.

"I'm so glad you found this." Her words didn't match the edge in her voice. He'd read part of her journal and she knew it. "I better go." She glanced over her shoulder with a strained smile. "I'll see you later."

Logan took her words for what they were. A brush-off. He had betrayed her. Not intentionally, but he had. And nothing he could say or do would change that.

11

On Monday, Addison reached the Seahawks baseball stadium and searched for a seat near the front, but deep from center-field's view. It didn't matter, Philip had already zeroed in on her. With an arrogant swagger, he crossed the short space separating the dugout from the stands at the same time Logan stepped onto the mound.

Philip getting the wrong impression hadn't crossed her mind.

Until now.

That unleashed a whole new category of regret. Philip seeing her with Logan's sister would complicate things even more. And she had never attended a Seahawks ballgame. Though blood drained from her face, she braced herself for the accusations he would hurl at her.

"What're you doing here?" Philip slipped his fingers through the fence, his tone neither condemning nor welcoming. It was reserved and held tension. His smile rigid and detached.

"I'm not here to see you, Philip." With a detached gaze, she edged deeper into the stadium seat. "But good luck."

"I'm glad you're here, baby. I needed my girl here today." He winked, but there was no change in his demeanor. He remained aloof. "Wait for me after the game."

It was a demand, not a request. She should've seen that coming.

Addison mentally chastised herself. What was she thinking coming here? Of course, Philip would think she came for him. Was spending a few moments with Logan Tant from a distance worth the trouble she'd have undoing this mess she just created with Philip?

Her gaze stumbled past Philip as he departed and settled on the pitcher's mound. The white uniform lined with navy blue stood out against Logan's naturally tan skin. His dark brown hair curled out from underneath his ball cap. His movements were controlled, polished from throwing that little white ball thousands of times.

Her pulse tripled when she found Logan's gaze on her. A thousand sensations rushed through her all at once, and his gentle smile caused her stomach to quiver in response. Within the safety of her unruly thoughts, Addison envisioned him coming over to her.

"You came?"

The soft whisper from Addison's right seized her full attention and her neck flamed from the thoughts still dancing around her brain. Ami's sweet, compassionate demeanor always gave her a feeling of warmth. "Of course, I did."

"Good, Logan's leading off. I was hoping you'd get to see him throw. He's amazing," Ami added, her eyes gleaming with pride.

Addison's focus returned to Ami's brother. He was no longer facing her, but turned at an angle, with one foot up before he released his first live pitch.

"Strike," the umpire yelled as he stretched his arm toward first base.

Ball after ball flew across home plate as batters swung, missed, and returned to the dugout.

"He just struck out all three of them." Addison was saying the words more to herself, but Ami joined in, though her enthusiasm seemed minor compared to Addison's shock.

"I told you he was good."

"Yeah, I know. But I wasn't expecting all that," she teased, though in truth, she had scrutinized his every motion, expecting nothing less. Logan walked toward the dugout and, after waving at Ami, met Addison's gaze and awarded her a gentle smile. The weightless flutter that tickled her middle nearly took her breath.

"Logan can be aggravating, but he's something special. And I'm not just saying that because he's my brother. You just have to give him a chance and get to know him."

Addison laughed not only at Ami's comment, but at the pleasure still flowing through her veins. She wanted nothing more than to get to know Logan better.

Coming here today was definitely worth it.

At the bottom of the eighth, Logan sat in the dugout, struggling to stay focused on the game. Adrenaline had driven each pitch, every inning, knowing Addison was there.

Philip had stood behind him in center field, but it wasn't Philip she was watching … it was him.

Addison sat on the bleachers to his right, in his perfect view and Philip leaned against the fence just a few feet from him. Philip shifted, though his eyes never moved. Even though they were nearly hidden beneath the ball cap, Logan saw the creases that seemed permanently etched across his forehead. Philip looked agitated.

If Logan were the one dating Addison Morgan, he would be smiling from the inside out, not fuming because Addison might ruin things with the blonde Philip was all over before the game—before Addison arrived.

Logan knew he wasn't the main reason Addison had come. But when he made a point to look her way after each inning and found that same smile aimed at him, he hoped he was part of the reason.

Especially when their gazes met, and she wasn't the first one to look away.

Not once.

He finished the game, the full nine innings, with only 105 pitches, eleven strikeouts, and ending with a shutout.

After the coaches finished their post-game talk, Philip lingered in the dugout. Was he waiting for the blonde? How could Philip do that with Addison right here?

He wanted a reason to pursue Addison and had hoped Philip would mess up. But he didn't want to see Addison hurt. It didn't matter whether Philip got caught; his intentions were less than honorable. And Addison Morgan deserved better than him.

Logan stepped out, eager to see her, but couldn't approach her. Not with her boyfriend coming out any minute. Her uneasiness was evident, and Logan stood by the fence where he could see her clearly.

He had no choice but to wait and observe her reaction to Philip. And that's exactly what he aimed to do.

When Philip approached the blonde, Addison kept her eyes on Ami. But inside she cheered. She was wrong. He was finally moving on.

Her gaze instinctively roamed her surroundings. Where was Logan? She had hoped to speak to him before leaving. To tell him how much she enjoyed the game.

To congratulate him on the win.

Who was she kidding? She could tell him all those things, but in truth, she only wanted to be near him.

Heat rushed to her cheeks when her gaze wandered toward the dugout and caught Logan leaning against the fence, watching her.

"Addison," Philip called from thirty feet away.

If she didn't go to him, he would come to her. It was better to comply. "I'll be right back, Ami." She felt guilty for not including her but didn't want to introduce Logan's sister to Philip.

"Baby, I'm glad you came." He glanced over her head as he placed a hand on her shoulder. "I've got to take one of the guys home tonight."

She wanted to tell him it didn't matter. That nothing had changed. But it would do no good to bring that up now. She'd made it clear already.

"Who's your friend?" Philip asked, glancing in Ami's direction. "Wait. Isn't that Tant's sister?"

Addison looked in that direction just as Logan approached Ami. "It is." She didn't have to explain why she'd been spending time with Ami … with her family. It was none of his business.

"What are you doing here with her?" A scathing huff blew from his mouth. "Are you trying to embarrass me?"

Under her breath, she said, "Why don't you go back to your girl-friend?" Addison turned, annoyed that she'd made the mistake of coming over here. Philip yanked her arm, shifting her back toward him, and squeezed her wrist. "Let go. You're hurting me."

"You're here to see Tant? I should've known you little—" He pulled her closer. "You will not make me look like a fool in front of my team."

"Me and my friends have nothing to do with you," she snapped, but his white-knuckled grip tightened, expanding the fear bleeding through her veins. "You're only embarrassing yourself. Go take your buddy home and leave me alone."

With another jerk of her arm, he leaned in near her ear and whispered, "I wish I had never met you."

Eyes misting, she tried to shrug him off, but Philip clutched her closer. "I'm sorry. I didn't mean that." He pressed his lips hard against hers, holding the back of her head. Releasing his grip, he stepped back. "I'll see you later, baby." His voice climbed a whole octave. "I love you."

Pain ricocheted up her arm when Philip turned and walked away as if nothing had just happened.

Addison hesitated, her chest pounding. She took a deep breath, turned, and searched for Ami, searched the place where Logan had been standing. He was no longer there.

Ami rushed to her side. "Is he your boyfriend?"

"No, not anymore."

"Oh, I'm sorry. It was your idea to break up?"

Suddenly exhausted and fighting back a new layer of tears threatening to spill, Addison clutched her stomach. "Definitely."

Ami's eyes twinkled. "He must still love you to kiss you like that."

"You saw that, huh?"

"Yeah, so did Logan. He didn't like it too much."

Chills prickled her arms. She suspected Philip wanted to confirm his claim on her, for Logan's sake. But she hadn't thought Logan witnessed Philip's twisted display of affection. How much did he see? How much did everyone see? "Why do you say that?"

"As soon as your boyfriend kissed you, Logan grunted and walked off."

12

On Tuesday night, Logan drove toward Olive Garden for the date he'd made last night, right after the game. The girl had followed him on Instagram weeks ago and kept messaging him about getting together. So, he gave in last night, still fuming over seeing Philip kissing Addison ... and Addison letting him.

Addison was off-limits and he needed to stop this nonsense of imagining what he wanted to happen. His gut had told him it was the best thing to do.

Now he had second thoughts. He knew nothing about the girl he was meeting except she was persistent.

He needed to get his head and heart focused on something else. Anything other than those midnight blue eyes that were driving him mad.

It had been a long time since he'd been on a date. Exactly three years.

Shoving his hands into his pockets, he walked to the front entrance and toward the hostess. He put his name on the list hoping the wait wouldn't be too long. What if he had nothing in common with this girl?

He stepped back outside and sat on an empty bench to wait.

A young couple walked from the restaurant, capturing his attention. Their backs facing him, he imagined strolling hand in hand with—

"Logan." The high-pitched voice behind him made his head swivel in the opposite direction.

"Meredith?" The significant differences comparing her now to her profile picture and the few others of her he'd glanced at astonished him as he moved toward her. Was she the same girl?

Her dark green eyes flashed. "That's me." She moved into the space next to him. Too close.

Logan fumbled with the vibrating device as it hummed and he turned quickly, putting more distance between them. "Wow, that was fast. They said it would be ten to fifteen minutes."

He stood and led her to the door but lingered behind as she approached the front desk.

The hostess led them to a corner booth, and he waited until Meredith sat before taking his seat.

"Matt's told me all about you."

"Matt?"

"Your best friend."

Slow comprehension draped over him. Matt had put her up to this?

"You play baseball, right?"

"Yeah. I uh ..." he stammered, still wrapping his mind around Matt's involvement.

"I'd love to watch you play. When's your next game?"

He wasn't sure how to reply. Meredith wanted to come to his game, but what if ... What if nothing. *Addison's dating Philip.* "We play—"

"Hi, welcome to Olive Garden," the waitress interrupted. The familiar voice heightened his pulse from a slow tread to a bolt of lightning.

Addison?

"I'll be serving you tonight." Lines of strain settled across Addison's forehead as she lifted the bottle of wine she held. Had she noticed him? "Can I interest you in a—"

"I'll have a Diet Coke," Meredith interjected before Addison could finish, her demanding voice causing a sharp whip of his head in Meredith's direction.

Addison turned slightly and faced him. "What would you like?" Addison's soft voice held more compassion than disappointment, but still she wouldn't look directly at him. She was completely focused on removing the two wine glasses from the table.

"Iced tea," Logan said, training his gaze on Addison, waiting for the precise moment when she would give in and glance at him. When she finally did, a tiny but confident smile broke free, her beauty leaving him breathless. She gave no hint that she knew him, and, regarding her, he returned her smile.

"Can I start you off with an appetizer?" She stated a few items to choose from, but her words fell on deaf ears. He studied her hands, the hint of clear nail polish glistening against the soft light. Her delicate fingers curled tight around the goblets.

"Can you give us a minute? We just sat down."

"Yes, of course. I'll be right back with your drinks." Turning her attention fully on Logan, Addison asked, "Would you like lemon?" Her voice was softer and quivering with emotion, reminding him of that first day at his house. She bit her lip while waiting for his answer.

"Yes, I would love lemon. Thank you." Logan stopped himself before saying her name. He worried familiarity would spill from him, and he would give into his yearning to reach for her trembling fingers.

It wasn't Meredith's fault Logan was distracted. And his responsibility in providing a nice date for this girl, if only for tonight, could not be ignored. Logan surrendered to the pledge he'd made and focused on Meredith as she spoke. Wrestling to keep his gaze from zooming to the same door where Addison had disappeared took all his effort.

From the corner of his eye, he caught sight of Addison walking toward them and lost the battle to keep his attention on Meredith. His glance in Addison's direction was rewarded with a warm smile from her, but then it faded completely. Meredith burst into laughter, breaking his trance.

Logan's smile came naturally, knowing Addison was returning to their table, but still his brow crinkled at Meredith's amusement. "What's so funny?"

Another wisp of laughter fell from her lips. "I'm sorry, I shouldn't. The waitress is coming with our drinks." She reached across the table, placing her hand over his. "I'll tell you when she leaves."

Logan slipped his hand out from underneath Meredith's and leaned back. When Addison reached across him to place the glass on his beverage napkin, he inhaled, catching a trace of her scent. "Thank you."

Addison's expression tensed, like she wanted to make sure he wouldn't tell his date that they knew each other. "You're welcome."

"This is not diet," Meredith rebuked, spouting her lips in a spitting motion as she pushed the glass toward Addison. "I asked for diet." Her harsh tone sliced through the moment.

Addison's eyebrows slanted inward. "I'm so sorry. I'll be right back."

"Can you believe that?" Meredith's somber voice thickened as her eyes darkened.

Logan leaned forward, squaring his shoulders. "Are you diabetic?"

"Who, me? Of course not." She leaned back, her innocent expression returning. "It just took me completely by surprise when I tasted it. You would think she would pay more attention. Especially if she's expecting a tip."

He didn't even have time to blink before she continued.

"I can't wait to come to one of your games. What position do you play?"

Logan was now sure he didn't want Meredith sitting in the stands cheering for him. He wanted someone else, and that someone else was heading back to their table now. It no longer mattered that Philip held her heart. Being Addison's friend would be better than nothing. "Our next few games are out of town."

Addison placed Meredith's drink in front of her and waited while Meredith took a sip. "Is that better?"

"Yes, now that I had to wait for it."

Logan took a sip of his drink, too embarrassed to look at Addison.

He'd agreed to this date with Meredith despite knowing nothing about her and was paying for his mistake.

"I'm so sorry about that. Are you ready to order?" Addison's voice was certain, confident. She ignored Meredith's bickering, and Logan's chest swelled with pride.

"Yes, we are," Meredith snapped. Logan cringed. "I'll have the lasagna and, on my salad, I don't want any olives or peppers and please make sure you get it right this time."

Insecurity wrinkled Addison's forehead when she glanced at Logan.

"Aren't you going to write it down?"

It was as if Meredith tried even harder when her quarrelsome tongue didn't offend Addison.

"I'll remember." Addison licked her lips and frowned.

The unflattering sound that spewed from Meredith's lip startled him yet infuriated him further. "I'll have the Tour of Italy and I don't want the soup or salad." Logan wanted to make it as simple as possible. But then in the last second, he changed his mind. "Actually, I'm sorry. I would like a salad, if you could bring me a separate one."

"Oh, well, we can share." The unmistakable regret in Meredith's voice made him squirm.

"If you don't mind, I'll take everything, just as it comes," he rushed on, ignoring Meredith's remark. "But I'd like ranch dressing, please. Thank you, Addison." He glanced at her name tag, but his tongue embraced her name with full recognition and affection.

13

Glancing at her watch two hours later, Addison felt her shoulders loosen. Finally. The long hour of Logan's visit had kept her on edge. Every visit to their booth, every comment, every minute, she'd expected something to go wrong. Tears had threatened to spill several times throughout the night. Determined not to cry in front of Logan or his arrogant girlfriend, she'd held them back. With her section now cleaned and money turned in, all that waited was a long, hot bath and her warm bed.

Her body aching from hours of constricting every muscle, she stepped outside into the moonless night. Its eerie darkness raised her awareness as she turned the corner toward the parking lot. Every sound intensified, and her breath quickened. Regretting her decision to leave before the other girls, she stole a glance at the restaurant, hoping to see one of the other waitresses. In such a hurry, she hadn't thought about walking outside alone—something she never did.

A truck faced her car in the opposite parking lot. An icy shiver slithered down her arms when she thought about the sleazy guys she'd had at one of her tables. They had left an hour ago, but what if they were still here waiting? Keeping her head down, Addison sauntered forward. It was too late to turn around now. She was almost there.

A door slamming rattled her, the noise shoving her forward, faster as she held to her keys with a white-knuckled grip. Breaking out in a cold sweat, she glanced over her shoulder. No one was there.

Chattering voices forced her attention on a couple climbing into their car parked several spaces down from hers. There was nothing to worry about. Nobody was waiting. The heightened rate of her pulse pounded as she took the last few steps to her car.

"Addison?"

She stumbled, her hand flying to her chest as she caught herself, her keys slipping from her grasp. Logan reached for them as a relieved breath swooshed from her lungs. "Logan, what on earth are you doing here? You scared the daylights out of me."

"I'm so sorry. I should've waited inside."

He was waiting for her?

Even though he didn't say it, the stabbing realization hit her ... the extra twenty dollars he'd left on the table. "Oh, your change, I was going to give it to Ami when I saw her."

Logan's ready smile materialized, easing the tension through her middle. "That was your tip."

"No, I mean the extra twenty on the table." Addison fumbled through the bills in her apron.

"I know."

"That's too much."

He touched her arm, stopping her—leaving behind a tingling sensation on her elbow.

"It's yours. I wanted you to have it."

As she bit her lip to stifle her embarrassed smile, her gaze traveled to his chin and then farther down to the hands that had just touched her. "What're you doing here?"

His knuckles whitened as he squeezed his fists. "I saw those drunks at the table behind me. I waited until they left but wanted to make sure they didn't come back."

An unexpected longing rose within her and she blinked before once again meeting his gaze. His dark pools of brown affixed to hers with such intensity left her breathless.

"Where's your girlfriend?" Her voice sounded calm, though her heart still pounded against her chest. She focused on the soft hum of leaves whistling in the wind.

"She isn't my girlfriend. It was a first and last date. We drove separately." His eyebrows dipped. "I thought I would follow you home, if that's okay?"

He wanted to follow her home? He came back to make sure she was safe? Addison drank air into her lungs, fighting the urge to throw her arms around him.

"Or wherever you're going," he added.

She smiled at the huskiness seeping into his voice. "I'm going home." His presence, his consideration, eclipsed all her common sense and a stupid, embarrassing question came flying out of her mouth. "How did you know they were bothering me?"

"I was listening."

He took a step back when someone called her from across the lot.

"Addison, are you all right?" One of the waiters was walking toward them. "You know that guy?"

"Yes." Her cheeks flamed in response. "Thanks, Tony. I'm fine."

"Cool, see you later."

Addison wiped her sweaty hands across her apron. "I never walk out by myself. I always wait for someone else."

"That's definitely a good idea." The feel of Logan's fingers surprised her when he cupped her hand into his and gently placed the keys into her palm.

The awareness of his fingers filled her with a strange sensation. He took a step closer, his breath warm against her skin. The nearness made her dizzy, and she fumbled with the keys, the jingle of metal breaking through the awkward silence.

"It was all your fault she left."

"What?" she queried with an injured gasp but then discovered the teasing gleam in his eyes. "I was not making her happy. But I really tried to take good care of you ... and her."

"You did a great job. Nothing would've made her happy." Logan's smile widened as he opened her door and waited as she settled into the driver's seat. "I didn't know you worked here." He paused as if he wanted to say more but stopped.

"It's a good job. I love meeting new people." Most of them anyway.

She could use that twenty dollars for buying extra snacks for the little boy in her class whose parents never packed him anything. It broke her heart watching all the kids surrounding him eating crackers, cakes and cookies while he looked on, his eyes glazing with hunger. She grasped the steering wheel and lifted her gaze toward him. "Thank you, Logan."

He propped a hand against her hood. "How many nights a week do you work here?"

"Four to five."

"So, you stay busy too?" He glanced over his shoulder. "Working and student teaching?"

A few of the other girls were walking out in a group and she waved when they glanced in their direction.

"It pays for my gas." Addison tilted her face up to him. "My aunt has been so good to me letting me stay with her. And even though she doesn't expect it, I still try to help with groceries and stuff like that."

Logan spread his feet apart, lowering himself to where she could see him more clearly. "It has to be hard waiting on people who deliberately try to make it difficult. By the way, I'm really sorry about that."

"It's not your fault."

"Well, you're very good at it. And I'm not just saying that because I have a crush on you." A teasing smile played at one corner of his mouth.

She laughed out loud.

"It's easy to see why my family adores you."

She clutched her hands together in her lap. "I adore them." *And you.*

"I'm going to let you get out of here. Be careful." He thrummed a few beats with his fingertips on her hood. "Goodnight, Addison," he said right before closing her door.

As he returned to his truck and pulled in behind her, his words lingered, her mind whirling in confusion.

Logan's headlights gave Addison an incredible sense of security. She shook her head in wonder. He'd waited to follow her home because of those guys harassing her.

His unexpected kindness made her hope skitter all over the place.

Her attraction to Logan Tant growing with every encounter was nothing but trouble and would surely lead to her broken heart.

That, she could not afford.

14

It had been two days since Logan had seen Addison. His chances of seeing her in time to invite her to the game tonight were growing slimmer by the hour.

Why hadn't he asked her Friday night?

He'd stalked the vicinity of the parking lot the same time of day he had run into her before. But she was nowhere to be seen.

"Logan?" Matt called from across the parking lot, the look in his eyes full of disappointment. "What happened the other night, man?"

Logan's gut clenched. He hadn't thought another moment about that girl. "Didn't Meredith tell you? Since you've been talking to her."

"Not in so many words. She only said you were a jerk. What did you do to her? Were you flirting with the waitress?"

A rush of heat coursed up his neck. "Addison was our waitress."

"*The* Addison? Oh man. My bad. I had told Meredith about you way before you ran into Addison."

"Good reason to mind your own business where my love life's concerned."

"She's a friend, well, more of an acquaintance of Shelley's. You know how Shelley is. She just wants you to be happy and was only trying to help."

"It's all right. No harm done. In the end, it actually worked out to my favor." Logan's gaze shifted across campus and he caught a glimpse of Addison walking toward Leutze Hall, across from Morton Hall—the same direction he was headed. He wasn't about to pass up his opportunity to talk to her. "Hey, I got to go. See you later, Matt."

"Where're you going?"

"Got to go," he turned, jogging backward, unable to hide his enthusiasm. "See you at the game."

Logan cut across the manicured section of lawn, desperate to catch her.

Just before she reached the door, Logan gripped the handle, stopping her from pulling it open.

She turned, startled, her face a lovely shade of pink. The dimple in her right cheek emerged as a soft smile played across her lips. "Logan Tant." Something about the way she spoke his full name sounded good and right, and he wanted to hear her say it again and again.

"Hi." His voice was barely a whisper. Out of breath, he refueled with a lungful of air, her clean, fresh scent mingling with it. "You smell really good."

The pink deepened, saturating the flesh of her cheek bones. "That is the last thing I expected you to say."

"I have a huge issue with speaking before thinking."

She laughed out loud, the sound comforting. He wanted to move closer, to tread in that narrow space separating them. He didn't want to blurt out his reason for approaching her, suddenly remembering that her boyfriend played center field. The silence stretched.

Addison looked at her watch. "Do you have a class in this building?"

"No, I'm headed to Morton Hall. What are you doing here?"

"I have a meeting with my professor. I'm a little early," she said, locking her gaze with his. "Did you take a full schedule this semester?"

"No, but it feels like it. Playing ball, working, and keeping up with my classes takes so much time, especially when we're out of town for games."

"Are you playing today?"

The question caught him off guard even though it had been his main reason for stopping her.

Although her boyfriend played for the Seahawks, Logan knew Philip didn't want her there. He was too busy flirting with whoever paid him any attention.

None of that mattered. Logan wanted her there and she'd given him the perfect excuse to ask.

"Our last home game is tonight. I hope you can come. I'm sure Ami would love to see you." *So, would I.*

Addison glanced at him, her sunglasses hiding those violet blue eyes. "Are you pitching?" A tiny hint of caution broke her smile. It was so faint, he almost missed it.

"I'm scheduled to."

"That would definitely help determine my decision. You're sure Ami's going?"

Logan wanted to question her about her sudden unease but instead answered with confidence, "She always comes."

Of course, she was cautious. She was dating Philip. He shouldn't be talking to her this way, feeling this way. But it was too late.

"Addison?"

Repulsion swelled within Logan at the sound of his voice. Philip was walking toward them. He needed to leave. Now. But a hidden force kept his feet planted. "I need to tell your boyfriend he should wait for you after work."

Addison pulled her glasses off. "No, please don't." Logan didn't miss how quickly Addison's smile diminished. And would never forget the fear that flittered across her features. "I better go."

Logan wanted to reach out and grab Addison's hand, to stop her from going to Philip, but instead he took a step back. "I'll see you later."

Philip never acknowledged his presence, just jogged past him and reached Addison before she slipped inside.

"Hey, baby. I'm glad I caught you. You're coming to the game tonight, right? I need my good-luck charm there cheering for me."

Logan had walked too far away to hear her reply. Good, let Philip ask her to come too. She would definitely be there now.

His mind raced with anguish, mixed with affection. He wanted to protect her, but it wasn't his place. It was Philip's. Even more reason to keep his distance. He just had to figure out a way to convince his heart.

Addison recognized the jealousy in Philip's eyes the moment he caught her speaking to Logan.

He crossed the short distance between them, stopping only an arm's length away. "Why is he talking to you?"

The coil that had been released in her chest rewound, tightening the air longing for escape. "I'm not supposed to talk to him?"

"I don't like it." He grabbed her wrist.

She snatched her hand from his grip, her pulse picking up speed. "I don't care what you like."

"What has gotten into you?"

"We broke up, Philip. Or were you too drunk to remember?" Every lie, every mental and physical attack he'd inflicted on her resurfaced, searing those fresh wounds all over again. "Why don't you leave me alone?"

"You belong to me, and he knows it. Him moving in on you is nothing but a game. I'm not going to let him win."

He ignored everything she'd just said. Why had she expected anything different? "You're being ridiculous. I'm friends with his sister. He's going to speak to me when he sees me."

"Stay away from him and his sister."

"No." The thought of never seeing them again caused her physical pain. "You can't tell me what to do anymore."

Students started filling the area around them, some leaning against the railing, some trying to walk past them—their presence a blessing.

Philip seemed to physically unwind. "Are you coming to the game?"

It didn't matter to her that people were all around them. Fury shimmied straight through her and flew from her mouth without restraint. "Am I coming to the game? You've been playing ball for the Seahawks for four years and have never invited me until today."

"That was stupid of me." His tone simmered to a whisper. "I didn't think you would enjoy it. But things are different now. I want things to be different between us."

"There's nothing left between us." She opened the door to the building not caring if it slammed behind her.

She was only asking for another confrontation with Philip, but she would let nothing stop her from watching Logan's last ballgame.

15

Addison pulled on a pair of white shorts and a sleeveless brown top. Not backing down from Philip today had increased her confidence. But all too familiar with the gravity of Philip's temper, she reconsidered her decision. And anxiety attempted to steal her joy. That was something she would not allow.

Not today.

Right now, her main priority was being on time. She wanted to enjoy every moment of the Seahawks' baseball game. Slipping on her flip-flops, she rushed out the door.

At the ballpark, Addison found a seat, the pitcher's mound directly in her view. Her dark sunglasses hid the object of her focus from anyone sitting around her. Ami hadn't arrived yet, but her brother had just stepped onto the mound to warm up and Addison's pulse tripled.

She was in more trouble than she'd thought.

Logan paused, his eyes taking her in before the catcher called out to him. The way he looked at her unwound a whole new set of emotions. Warmth, longing, a deep-rooted ache.

Logan made her world more vibrant, more stunning, less frightening. And she wanted more of whatever was happening between them.

The smile behind her raging emotions mushroomed and it was

impossible to hide. She lifted her bag onto her lap, searching for something, anything to distract her thoughts. Nothing worked.

After searching for several seconds, and only after her enthusiasm weakened enough to control her expression, she looked up to find Philip standing at the fence.

Blood heated her cheeks.

How long had he been standing there? She stared at him, praying he wouldn't make a scene.

"Come here, baby."

"No." She'd spent the afternoon preparing for this exact moment. The only way to get through to Philip would be persistence. She couldn't give in. No matter what.

"I'm not leaving until you do."

If she spoke to him now, maybe she wouldn't have to after the game. Addison took the two steps to meet him at the fence.

Philip instinctively slipped his fingers through the fence grabbing hers. She cringed.

"I knew you would come. Wait for me after the game. I have something for you."

"No, Philip. I can't."

"Don't leave until I come out."

He didn't give her a chance to respond. And she couldn't scream at him across the field. More important than being civil, she must remain firm. She rolled her eyes at his false affection. Her longing to be loved had left her vulnerable to years of suffering his verbal and physical abuse.

No more.

She wanted nothing else to do with Philip, but he wouldn't make it easy. Why did she keep allowing him to dictate her choices? She no longer felt anything for him.

Not even pity.

Logan glanced in Addison's direction at the end of every inning longing for a chance to speak to her.

After the game, he peeked around the dugout, hoping Addison hadn't left. She stood by the bleachers talking to Philip. Ami stepped around the corner.

"Hey, li'l sis."

"You were great." Ami beamed, giving Logan a hug.

He nodded quickly. Compliments made him uncomfortable. "You're getting ready to leave?"

"I'm waiting for Addison. She wanted to walk with me to the parking lot, but that guy stopped her before we could walk away. Something's wrong with her. She's acting different."

"Like how?"

"She's nervous. Like more than usual."

Logan knew exactly what Ami meant. Addison never relaxed in his presence.

"Do you think something's wrong? Should I ask her?"

"Maybe it has something to do with her boyfriend," he said, more to himself.

"He's not her boyfriend. They broke up a while back."

They broke up? Why was she always talking to him, then? He wanted to ask more questions, but Addison was already walking in their direction.

An uneven smile crossed Addison's lips as she approached them. "I have to go, but thank you for sitting with me, Ami." She glanced his way, but her gaze missed his by a millimeter. "Great game, Logan," she said, her voice trembling.

"Thanks." He'd been so excited to see her. So full of plans to spend a few minutes talking to her. From the moment she spoke to Ami, and her urgency to leave, Logan knew something was wrong.

"I'll see you later."

Ami rushed to her side. "Wait. I'll walk with you."

Glancing over her shoulder, Addison nibbled on her lip. "Okay."

He didn't miss Addison swiping away an errant tear that sparkled under the fading sunlight. Automatically he walked faster to keep up but still maintaining a safe distance.

Ami handed her an envelope. "This is for you."

Addison slowed her pace, but only a little. "What is it?"

"My débuette presentation ball is this Saturday night. I want you to come."

"Me?"

"Yes, you."

Logan had kept his distance until Philip's car sped out of the parking lot. It was as if Addison noticed his departure at the same time, and she seemed to physically unwind.

Logan quickened his steps. He wanted to hear Addison's response. She stopped and took the envelope, her gaze fixed on her name.

When she pulled her fingers through her hair, her blond curls bounced across her shoulders and she slowed to a stop. "I would love to, Ami. I feel so honored."

Logan watched her, a heap of satisfaction expanding in his chest at her response.

"What should I wear? What're you wearing?"

"The freshmen and seniors are presented during the first part, so I have to wear a formal gown, but there's a dance afterwards."

"So, a dress for me?"

From where he stood a few feet away, he listened to their conversation. He already knew Ami's plan.

"Anything you wear will be beautiful. I was hoping we could spend the day together getting ready. We could get our hair done and a pedicure."

"That would be fun." Addison glanced at her feet, her smile thinning into a straight line. "Oh, wait. I forgot. My aunt has to borrow my car Saturday."

Logan took a step closer. "I'll swing by and pick you up." The words were out before Logan could reel them back in. He'd have to share her with his whole family Saturday. Riding together would give him a few minutes alone with her.

"You don't have to do that."

"I don't mind." He cut her off, but then softened his tone. "I want to."

Addison stared at him, a hundred questions in her distracted gaze. "Thank you, Logan." She agreed, though her response dripped with apprehension, and she seemed so unsettled. "I'll see y'all later."

He had to find out why.

Waving at Ami and her brother, unable to voice another syllable, Addison hurried to her car, hoping to hide the heaving motion in her chest.

"Addison, wait."

She turned and gave Logan time to catch up. Instead of his face, she focused on his damp hair curled beneath his ball cap, his neck glistening with sweat, his white Seahawks T-shirt. Prayed the tears building in her eyes wouldn't escape.

He said nothing at first but walked along beside her until they reached her car. "What's wrong?"

Throat constricting, she met his gaze. "Nothing, why?"

"You seem upset."

He was too gentle, too compassionate, too handsome for any of this to be real. "I'm fine."

"So, you usually cry for no reason?"

Regaining a trace of control, she smirked. "Actually, I do. Sometimes."

"Well, that sucks." The lightness in his expression instantly shriveled the dejection wrestling for her attention. "I don't like seeing you cry."

Changing the subject would be her only escape from falling into him and never returning. "I'm so glad I came. It was a really good game." Her hand involuntarily reached for his arm. "You're really good, Logan."

It was a bad habit. Touching him. But she couldn't help herself. Addison looked away from his scrutinizing gaze.

"Is ten okay?"

"Ten?"

"Saturday morning?"

"Oh, sorry. Yes, ten is great." Addison glanced at the invitation.

"It starts at six."

"So, I should plan to be gone most of the day?"

"Is that okay?" Logan shifted, closing some of the space between them. "Will your aunt be okay with that?"

"Yes, she made an appointment to get her car worked on this Saturday. So as long as she can use mine ..."

His expression softened with confused interest.

The last thing she needed was for Philip's other teammates to tell him she was standing in the parking lot with Logan. But somehow, at this very moment, she didn't care. And none of what happened when Philip approached her as soon as the game ended mattered. Not now. Her complete focus had shifted to this time with Logan. And she clung to the moment as if her life depended on it.

"Lucky for me."

"What?"

"Because of her appointment, I have a good excuse for picking you up Saturday."

Keeping silent, she ground down on the overzealous smile pleading to burst through.

"Either way, I would've figured it out ... siphon out your gas, something."

With that, she lost control and her smile raced upward and mushroomed into a full-blown laugh.

He joined her in laughter, and even though they had reached her car, he made no move to open her car door. And neither did she.

"I'm looking forward to Saturday. I love your sister." She relaxed into a grateful smile. "I love your whole family."

"The feeling's definitely mutual. I'm glad you came to the game."

"They didn't have a chance. Not with you on the mound."

He smiled, though she could tell he was fighting against it. His humbleness was completely adorable.

"I hate I missed the rest of the season. I really enjoyed watching you ... the Seahawks ... play. And now it's over."

Her statement didn't seem to affect him, because they stood in silence for several seconds. But then he straightened his ball cap and something in his expression changed.

"Can I ask a personal question?"

Oh no! A vision of her journal between his hands clouded her concentration. Had he read any of it?

"Ami said you and Philip broke up."

"Yes. It's been over awhile."

"You were crying before. Did he do something?"

"No," she lied. She wouldn't drag Logan into her problems. He and Philip were teammates and she didn't want to cause adversity between them. There had to be a way to handle Philip herself. Logan's sincerity moved her. Then a whole new batch of tears spilled over onto her cheeks. "Oh my gosh. What is wrong with me?"

"What is it? What happened?"

"Nothing. See, I told you I cry for no reason." With no warning, more emotion welled up in her chest. "Sometimes ... I get over-whelmed with—"

Before she knew what was happening, Logan pulled her against him and wrapped one arm around her, his other hand resting softly against her head. He kept silent while securing her in his embrace.

After a full minute of bawling for no one reason, she pulled back. "I cannot believe I just did that. I am so embarrassed."

"No, please don't be. I'm glad you feel comfortable with me."

"I wouldn't go so far as to say that." She feared her tense laugh revealed her discomfort. "I mean, look at me. I'm a nervous wreck around you." She was talking way too much.

"Me? Really?" Logan lost that look of confidence.

She pressed the invisible wrinkles from her top, until she realized she was drawing unwanted attention to her trembling fingers. "Yes, but at the same time, I feel like ... I don't know. Ami's right. You're some-thing special." In his presence she rambled with no restraint. She could talk to him forever.

He leaned backward, his arms outstretched. "Now I'm worried. I hope that's a compliment."

"Most definitely a compliment." Addison lifted onto her tiptoes and kissed him on the cheek. Both of his hands rested on her arms. That simple motion balanced her yet comforted her at the same time. When both of her feet were once again planted on the ground, a tremor traveled down her spine.

I kissed him.

Her action was forward. But there was no ounce of disapproval in his expression; instead she found unmasked affection. Shocked pleasure traveled through her veins at a rapid pace.

"I better go," she said.

When she settled in the driver's seat, Logan leaned inside the car, propping his arm on the back of her seat. "I'll see you Saturday at ten."

It wasn't until he walked away that she scanned the parking lot to see how many of his teammates saw them. There were no other vehicles. Only Logan's truck.

How long had they been talking? Time seemed to stand still in his presence.

16

Friday morning, Addison called Taylor. It had been too long since they'd spent time together aside from work, and Addison needed her help.

Taylor agreed to meet her at a secondhand store across town. This had nothing to do with Logan, Addison reminded herself. It was all about Ami. But each thought of him triggered new emotions. One in particular she could do without.

Queasiness.

Looking through the window of the shop, she admired a black cocktail dress with shimmering beads across the neckline, wondering if Logan would like this on her.

This was not the time to fall for someone, but her heart wasn't cooperating. Last night, Logan never once glanced into the stands during the inning. But as soon as the last out was called, his eyes searched the bleachers and didn't retreat until his gaze connected with hers.

Images of Logan throwing strike after strike from the mound infused every inch of her thoughts. His long, strong body slinging every ball with all his effort, his whole being revealing his strength. A strength that didn't take advantage of a weaker species but a strength that exposed a rare power. A strength that wouldn't dissipate. Even when a batter got a hit, or when a runner stole bases, Logan handled the setback with impressive composure.

The exact opposite of Philip who threatened and punished when he didn't get his way.

She drifted into a shadowy daze, and Addison wasn't sure when her thoughts merged from reality to daydreams.

"That would look beautiful on you."

Addison turned to find Taylor leaning over her shoulder. "Don't do that."

"What's this all about?"

Addison drew her lips into an exaggerated line. "Ami's débuette dance."

Taylor propped her hands on her hips. "Logan Tant's sister?"

Flames of heat rushed up Addison's neck.

"That's interesting." Crossing her arms, Taylor tilted her head. "And what's this about you going to two ballgames without me?"

"I know. You don't know how close I came to make you come with me, but I didn't want to drag you into all the drama with Philip."

"Philip?"

"Yes, Taylor. He plays for the Seahawks too."

"I know that. I was just making sure he wasn't the reason you went."

Addison avoided anything deeper than a friendly chat. "Stop teasing me. I'm already a nervous wreck."

"I want to hear every detail." Taylor narrowed her eyebrows.

Addison inhaled an exaggerated breath. She adored her friend and wanted nothing more than to spill her heart. "I'm going for Ami."

"But he'll be there."

A wistful smile curved Addison's lips. "Yes, he'll be there. He's picking me up."

"*He* as in *Logan*?" Taylor's words came out slowly, matching her shocked stare.

"I told Ami I wouldn't have a car and he offered."

Taylor grabbed her arm. "So, you and Logan will be alone?"

A flutter tickled her stomach and she gave into her laugh, feeling lighter than she had in months. "Yeah, for a total of ten minutes."

"Not if he drives really slow."

Addison's boisterous laugh turned all heads their way. She wasn't sure whether to look forward to or dread that sixth of an hour.

Over the next few hours, they skimmed through a dozen different choices, while Addison told her all about Logan showing up at her table with a date, then waiting for her after work, and their talk yesterday after the game.

Choosing the first original black cocktail dress hanging in the window, Addison approached the register.

"Have you talked to Philip?"

"I told you, I officially broke things off with him." Taylor didn't voice her opinion. But Addison knew more than anyone how Taylor felt. "I know what you're thinking, but things used to be different. He wasn't always ..." She paused, choosing her words carefully. "Like this." Shame almost strangled her for once again defending him and discounting her own fear.

"You did the right thing. I'm so proud of you." Taylor moved around so they were standing face-to-face. "Hey, stay firm in your decision. You've given that boy more than enough chances. He'll have to give up eventually."

Addison swept her into a hug praying she was right. "I haven't seen or heard from him since the last game," she said, talking to herself more than Taylor. Maybe he had already given up. "Thanks for coming, Taylor. You're the best."

"I can't wait to hear all about your night dancing with Logan."

Addison rolled her eyes. "Yeah, right. That will never happen." But that didn't stop her heart from fluttering at the possibility.

Saturday morning, Logan was early. But only by a few minutes. He hadn't been able to wait any longer to drive to her house.

And now he was here. His awareness heightened when Addison

stood from the rocker on the front porch as soon as he pulled into the drive. He parked and jumped from the truck, hurrying to take her things.

"Good morning."

A shadow of a smile spilled over her lips as she accepted his offer. "Hi."

He extended his arm and tossed her lightweight bag over his shoulder. "Is this everything?"

The brilliant violet color of her eyes sparkled. "Yes, but you don't have to carry my things."

He sighed. "I'm trying to be a gentleman."

"I haven't met many of them." Addison's hand flew to her mouth. "I'm sorry, I shouldn't have said that."

"Don't be." He wanted to say more but stopped. He could only imagine how rude Philip could be. But it made him wonder about her father. Had she been referring to him as well?

They rode in silence for a few minutes when he could think of nothing sensible to say, but his time alone with her was running out. Ami would snatch her away as soon as they arrived. This was his only chance and he was wasting time.

"How long have you lived in Wilmington?"

Logan could feel her sudden movement. He'd startled her. He glanced over to find her looking at him. Her presence did strange things to him, things he'd never experienced, things he could get used to.

"I moved in with my aunt when I started college. What about you? Have you always lived here?"

"My whole life. It's a shame we've both been at the same college for four years but are only now meeting."

She smiled but it was restrained, wounded. And he was certain it had everything to do with the accident.

Of course, his attempt at flirting would backfire. He wasn't sure what to say but needed to say something. "What about your parents? Where are they?"

"My Mom and Stepdad live in Raleigh. Me and my sister moved in with my aunt when I started college. My sister was still in high school, but it was better ... she didn't want me to leave without her, so my aunt took us both in. Then my sister was killed in a car accident two years ago."

"I'm so sorry."

He pulled his truck onto his mother's street. His time was almost up, but this isn't how he'd expected their conversation to end. Addison said nothing for several seconds and the silence was deafening. "Someone at the station told me about the accident, and then our preacher mentioned it. But I didn't realize it was your sister until Ami told me and I put the two together. I had just lost a ... friend and was still hurting, so when I heard about the accident, I know this is going to sound crazy, but I prayed for you, every day. Even before I knew you."

She said nothing for several long moments. "I don't know what to say. That's the sweetest thing anyone has ever done for me."

The slight break in her voice brought his gaze to hers and after parking his truck, he turned to fully face her.

She focused on her feet. "Thank you, Logan. I'm so sorry about your sister, for—"

He ached for her and instinctively took her hand. "I'm sorry for the way I treated you."

A soft sigh escaped, and her dimple flashed within her tender smile.

Logan wanted to pull her to him, to hold her in his arms. "There were so many things wrong with the way I treated you. But if it's okay with you, I would love to start over?" He gently squeezed her hand. He wanted to caress the softness of her skin but stopped himself, though he didn't let go. "I'm Logan Tant. Will you save me a dance tonight?"

17

"It was a good idea to save this for last," Addison announced, leaning back in the cushioned massage chair, her feet soaking in warm bubbling water. She held the pink polish embedded with glitter.

Would Logan like this color, or would he like something more natural? It didn't matter. He wouldn't be staring at her toes.

"Zach's coming. I invited him."

Addison shook her thoughts away. This day was for Ami. "Zach? The guy who most definitely isn't your boyfriend?"

"Yeah, we're just friends." Ami unleashed a grin. "But I've had a crush on him since he moved in next door."

A crush. The same thing Logan had teased her about. Warmth spread through the cold recesses of her heart at the memory.

Brimming with anticipation, Addison shifted to look at her. Ami was adorable with a few strands of her golden locks pulled back with a single bobby pin. "Does he know?"

"No, he's a dufus." Ami's smile swiveled into a frown.

Addison bit her lip to hide her own smile. "But you still like him?"

"We're really good friends, but that's all."

Addison tipped her head, suddenly eager to meet this young man. "Maybe he likes you too."

"Nope. He's never asked me out and is constantly telling me about his girlfriend problems. If only he'd see what's right in front of him, I'd solve all his girlfriend problems."

Addison's much-too-loud snicker turned several heads in their direction. Addison couldn't remember having more fun.

After her toenails were painted, she wobbled to the manicure table with Styrofoam dividers between her toes. The young man looked at her for instruction, holding the nail polish toward her.

"No color."

He nodded and started on her unpolished nails. Ami sat next to her wearing a crooked grin.

"How old is Zach?"

"My age. We're both graduating this year."

"What? Why are you smiling?"

"Logan."

Her stomach fluttered. "What about Logan?"

"He asked me a stupid question."

Addison waited. There was no room in her shattered heart for stupid notions.

"He asked me what kind of music you liked."

"Really?" she asked, remembering the music she hadn't expected to hear playing in his truck.

"I told him anything classical."

The laughter that escaped her lips traveled to the depths of her soul, making her feel lighter than she had in months.

Hours later, when they arrived back at Ami's, Logan's truck was no longer parked in the same place. Maybe it was best that he wasn't here. It would give her time to restore her sanity.

Nathan met them at the front door. "Look at you two."

"Thank you." Ami gave a curtsy as she walked past him. "Come on, Addison, we have to hurry and get our dresses on."

They reached her bedroom and Addison removed the plastic from the dress, slipped from her sweat suit, and pulled the dress over her head. The silky material was cold against her warm skin.

Ami returned to the bedroom moments later, wearing her white formal dress.

Addison stared at the flowing white material sparkling in the sunlight. "You're so beautiful."

"Logan is going to flip when he sees you." Ami peeked in the mirror, adjusting her strap.

Addison smiled, glancing in the mirror. How many times would she have to remind herself that Logan was out of reach? Ami was only making her wandering heart gain false hope.

She slipped on her black heels and sat on the bed, the throw pillows shuffling from the motion. "What exactly is débuette's?"

"It's a club for high school girls. We're required to give a certain number of hours to charity work each year. We can pick and choose some of the charities but some we do as a group, depending on what year we are."

"Really? That sounds awesome."

"I like doing the charities, but Mom wanted me to get into it for social reasons. You know, since I'm homeschooled, and people have preconceptions about homeschoolers not getting enough social interaction."

"I'm going to be honest. If you hadn't told me you were home-schooled, I would've thought you were the most popular girl in your class."

"She is the most popular girl in her class," Mrs. Tant said as she peeked into the room. "And she's also the smartest."

They all laughed.

"Just thought I'd check on you girls and make sure you didn't need my help with anything."

"Thanks, Mom, but we're good," Ami said, giving her mom a side hug.

"I can see that. See you downstairs. You both look gorgeous," Mrs. Tant added as she walked away.

A flutter of nerves raged war within her as her mind spun with Logan's final question to her. *Will you save me a dance?* The possibility of swaying to music tucked safely within his arms whirled through her mind. Standing, she paced back and forth until Ami stopped her.

"What are you doing?"

"Thinking. How come you invited me over all your other friends?"

Ami turned to face her. "I know this is going to sound weird, because we haven't known each other long, but you're like a sister to me. I feel like I can tell you anything, and I like spending time with you."

Tears burned the back of her eyelids. "That's so sweet."

"It's the truth and don't start crying or you'll ruin your makeup." Ami's endearing tug on her arm pulled her forward. "Come on. They're waiting for us."

"I can hardly wait to meet your Zach."

They descended the stairs, Ami first. Her white sleeveless dress swished back and forth with each step. Addison followed holding the rail to steady her stride in her three-inch heels. She didn't notice Logan standing at the bottom of the stairs until she'd taken the last step. He leaned against the wall, holding his black jacket. She focused on his white shirt against the black vest of his suit. Her stomach stirred as his gaze shifted from her dress to her face. Her gaze involuntarily fell to the floor, a smile filling her face.

He reached for her hand as she took the last step. "Wow! You're so beautiful."

An instantaneous blaze heated her from the inside out. With no attempt to suppress the flame, Addison savored the warmth. "You're sweet and you look pretty good yourself."

He released her hand, leaving in its wake a pleasant spark of hope. Just being near him drove her to insanity. When he said nothing more, she walked past him, following Ami into the living room.

"We're ready for pictures," Ami announced to her mom and everything was set into motion.

Ami took her place in front of the fireplace for the portrait session to begin. Ami looked like a princess awaiting her knight in shining armor. The doorbell rang on cue and Nathan answered it.

A nice-looking young man stepped into the foyer and Ami walked toward him, showing no indication of her excitement.

"You're late," Ami scolded him.

"You're beautiful."

Ami smiled. "You're forgiven."

They shared a friendly hug before Mrs. Tant ordered them both to stand in front of the fireplace for more pictures.

Addison soaked in everything. She loved this family, everything about them. Nathan teased Ami while Mrs. Tant coordinated more poses.

Logan sat in the corner, his shoulders leaning forward, his forearms propped on his knees, his head tilted down.

When his face finally rose, his gaze locked with hers, his expression revealing a deeper layer of warmth.

Then he stood and moved across the room, his smile brightening with each step that brought them closer. "My family's a little ..."

"They're wonderful." Flustered by his heart-stopping smile, her words came on a rushed exhale. "You're so lucky to have them."

"Yeah, I guess you're right." Logan rubbed his jaw. "Would I happen to be included in that *wonderful* description of yours?"

Addison held his gaze though the fluttering in her stomach nearly took her breath. "Maybe." Her fingers sifted through several strands of her hair. Not only was he wonderful, he had somehow stolen her heart when she wasn't paying attention.

Mrs. Tant was suddenly standing beside her. "Okay, it's your turn."

Addison looked around. "Me?"

"Us. And by the way, you really are absolutely gorgeous." Logan whispered close to her ear. His voice was tender, confident, and his warm breath tickled her senses.

Addison allowed Mrs. Tant to show her where to stand and Logan moved next to Addison in front of the mantel.

"Put your arm around her, Logan. She isn't going to bite," Ami scolded, her voice teasing.

"If you don't, I will," Nathan said.

Logan rested his hand gently against her waist, pulled her even closer, and squeezed her softly. Mrs. Tant only snapped a few, but it wasn't until Logan released her that she took a breath.

Addison moved to the corner of the room and fidgeted with a home and garden magazine for only a second before Logan rejoined her.

"Do you mind riding with me? Everyone else is riding together, but I thought—"

"I would love to ride with you." A stout burst of laughter exposed her nerves, but in that same moment, a glint of delight radiated from his eyes.

Addison's brain searched for something coherent to say. "You have to drive me home anyway, unless you want me to get your mom to."

"No, I'll drive you."

Addison turned, her heart thumping in her chest, when Mrs. Tant rescued her from her thoughts.

"Let's go, or we'll be the last ones to arrive."

Addison stepped outside first and pulled the briny air deep into her lungs. The sun had dipped just over the horizon leaving shadows of light across the Tants' yard.

"We'll meet you there," Logan called over his shoulder from right behind her.

He opened the passenger door, and she took a careful step up, his hand lifting her gently. She inhaled the familiar scent of his truck as she scooted onto the seat. He waited while she gathered her skirt before closing the door. She kept her eyes locked on the silky material until his dark form rounded the truck and in anticipation, she smiled.

"Did you have fun this morning?"

"It was so much fun."

"What did you girls do?"

"One of her friends did our hair and makeup, then we got a manicure and pedicure, grabbed a salad and came back here to dress. You know, girl stuff." Without realizing it, Addison leaned toward him. "What did you do all day?"

"Just a bunch of guy stuff."

The feelings he stirred complicated her efforts to maintain a safe restraint against false hope. "What kind of *guy* stuff?"

"Played ball for a couple of hours."

"You had a game today?"

"No. A few guys from our baseball team get together one Saturday a month to play ball with a group of kids and adults that have mental disabilities."

Addison shifted in her seat to look at him. "Really? You play against them?"

"Actually, we each team up with one guy and play catch for a while. Then go to a position with them to help make the plays. And when they're batting, we help them hit and run bases with them."

"That is so nice." The more Logan Tant talked, the more she liked him. "I bet they love that."

"It's a lot of fun."

"You had a busy morning."

"I also ran, showered, shaved, and studied for a Criminal Law test for an hour while waiting for the girl I picked up this morning to come downstairs." Logan shot a long glance in her direction. "I started missing her as soon as she got out of my truck this morning."

She mentally shuffled through every moment since they'd first met, attempting to pinpoint the exact moment she'd fallen in love with Logan Tant.

It was impossible.

Twenty minutes later, they stood at the front entrance of McPhearson Center for the Arts. A mixture of students, parents, and friends stood in the main lobby. Logan's hand gently pressed the small of her back with each step forward. Her stomach quivered in response, every single time.

It was impossible to concentrate on the discussion going on right in front of her while beside her the man she was falling in love with stayed close, not once leaving her side.

She glanced at her watch right before they reached the steps, hating herself that she'd waited until now. "I should go to the ladies' room before it starts."

"I'll wait for you."

"No, that's all right. I'll find you. I'll only be a minute."

Emotions trickled through her as the memory of his last words on the way to the auditorium spun webs of bliss through her brain. *Don't forget about our dance.*

She stared at her reflection in disbelief of how the day, how the past month had unfolded. And now she would be joining Ami's family as she was presented. The honor of being invited still lingered.

After drying her hands, she turned the corner leading out to the open space. All those feelings dissipated when she spotted Philip standing across the room.

Stopping abruptly, she quickly turned to the safety of the restroom. She hurried, her pulse tripling with each step. But she was too late. He was right behind her. And they were the only two left in the lobby.

"Addison, what're you doing here?"

She took several, slow deep breaths before facing him. "I'm here for a friend. She's graduating this year."

"Oh." He said nothing more, and she hoped he wouldn't ask more questions.

"I better find them."

"I came with a friend too." He chuckled as he took her hand. "She has a crush on me and begged me to come."

Addison's stomach recoiled in response. How could she have wasted so many years with him? Turning, she shook off his hand, keeping her unpleasant thoughts to herself. "Have fun."

He grabbed her arm. "I'm not finished."

"Let go of me." She tried pulling away, but he peered down on her, gratification creeping into his smile at his strength over her. Philip had never been one for violence, in the beginning. Instead he used manipulation, exploiting her own weaknesses against her. It wasn't until he sensed her fear that he altered his attacks with a mixture of insults and strikes. "What do you want? They're waiting for me."

"Don't you mean he's waiting for you?" His voice dropped and he hovered over her. "Logan Tant. Isn't he the real reason you're here?"

Her brows creased and she looked away, panic shrinking her composure. There was no one to help her, protect her. She was alone. And he knew it.

Why did she let him do this to her? She tried turning, but Philip tightened his grip causing her to stumble in her heels. A burning sensation stretched through her ankle as she righted herself. "Let go of me."

His eyes bore into hers. "You will not do this to me."

"I'm not doing anything to you. Just leave me alone." She tried prying her arm away, but he pressed deeper. The cutting of his nails digging into her flesh wasn't painful enough to hinder another attempt at escape.

"Is everything all right over here?"

Addison glanced at the man speaking to them. Her tears threatened to escape just as Philip released his hold on her.

"She tripped." Philip laughed. "I was trying to keep her from falling."

Philip was a blur through her tears as she stared at him in horror.

One arm reclaimed her shoulder as if he expected her to stagger and he was preparing for her rescue.

When the man left, Philip spoke softly yet harshly against her ear. "Keep on humiliating me. You're only hurting yourself. No one will come between us. I promise you that."

With a confidence she didn't fully trust, she frantically wiggled from underneath the heaviness of his arm and raced toward the stairway, her ankle stinging with each step.

"No one, Addison," he called after her. "Especially Tant."

She shuddered with relief as she stepped through the rear auditorium doors within the safety of hundreds of others surrounding her. Before moving forward, she took several seconds to catch her breath.

While she scanned the audience, Addison's pulse raced as Philip's threats unlocked one by one like a massive wave ready to break over her.

His family sat near the front, with only two seats left, on the end.

She startled as Logan approached her from the left corner.

"You okay?"

She placed a hand over her heart. "I didn't see you standing there. I'm sorry it took me so long."

"You sure you're okay?"

"Yes, I'm looking forward to the program."

With an unconvinced gaze, Logan took her arm and led her down the stairs. When they reached their row, he moved to the side, allowing her to pass. Collapsing into the seat beside Mrs. Tant, she mentally surveyed her surroundings, her awareness of Logan's closeness elevating her already pounding heart.

Logan leaned closer, his concern far too intense, as if he could sense her weakness. He scrutinized her with unspoken questions swimming in his eyes.

Forcing a spirited smile, she nodded. She'd take anything Philip hurled her way, but tonight she would take comfort in Logan's nearness and cling to every moment.

1 8

After the presentation, the Tants' moved, along with everyone else, toward the tables set up for refreshments. Clutching her bag close to her side, Addison followed them, Logan right behind her.

Resisting the urge to stay even closer to Logan, she awkwardly took the only open seat, on the end of the table next to Ami.

It hadn't mattered. Logan grabbed an empty chair and positioned it on the end, right next to her. Addison straightened, eager to conceal her discomfort.

He reached beneath the table and took her hand. "Are you sure you're okay?"

She regarded Logan for a moment. His concern only deepened the magnetism drawing her to him. She chose her words cautiously, dodging the truth. "Yes, I'm so glad to be here with all of you."

Logan's tender smile resurfaced. The pressure of his hand connected to hers stretched through every ligament, causing even more turmoil inside her. A pleasant turmoil. One she missed when she wasn't in his presence. And it was when their hands connected that the warning signals flaring in her head weakened then faded completely that Philip was somewhere watching.

Addison glanced at Ami's plate. "You aren't eating much."

Zach leaned forward. "She's very picky and never eats anything mixed together and will only eat one thing at the time."

Ami frowned. "How do you know?"

The color in his cheeks deepened. "I've watched you eat a million times."

Addison laughed, her anxiety lessening until she glanced at Logan and found him leaning toward her. "Would you like some dessert?"

"Yeah, sure." Though she didn't think she'd be able to put another thing into her mouth. Not when his every word and deed pursued unexplored places in her heart.

After several minutes, he returned and set a piece of chocolate cake in front of her. "I wasn't sure what you liked, but this looked better than anything else," he said simply, as if he wasn't aware of his effect on her.

"Thank you."

Ami's sharp laugh cut through the moment. "If you know so much about me, why didn't you pick me out a dessert?"

Zach held his arms out. "I'm going, I'm going." He focused on Logan. "Women! They can be so bossy."

"Hey." Ami stood. "I am not."

Logan winked. And Addison's chest reacted.

After dinner, she followed Ami and Mrs. Tant to a larger room. Mr. Tant led Ami to the dance floor for the father-daughter dance and Addison reflected over the loss of her own father. Seeing Mr. Tant respond to Ami, witnessing their special bond—it was something Addison hadn't experienced in a long time.

"That's so sweet," she told Logan.

He said nothing, only regarded her with a crooked smile.

"What? Why are you looking at me that way?"

"The way you look at things. I see things differently when I'm with you."

For no reason, Addison laughed. "Would you like to hear my favorite memory with my daddy?" There was no need to wait for a verbal answer, it was clear in the delight that brightened his eyes. "He told me I had a special gift because I feel things so deeply. I could reach into the heart of anyone I dared and wrap them around my finger."

It was the crinkle of his smile that gave her the strength to go on. "It isn't true, but still my favorite memory." She never believed it to be a gift. Because she felt things so deeply, those hard things hurt even deeper. "I really don't know why I told you that."

"I believe it." His voice held warmth, his eyes even more affection. He slipped his fingers between hers and held them up. "Because I'm in very real danger of all these fingers." He pressed his lips to her hand. If he didn't stop, she would fall hard and never return. "Would you like to dance?"

Her stomach fluttered, the feel of his skin against hers once again electrifying every nerve ending. "Okay." Addison had dreamed of this moment for days.

Logan pulled her closer, riveting her attention with his gentle touch, as if she were something delicate, something to cherish. "I know I've already said this, but you look absolutely beautiful, Addison."

They swayed gently back and forth, closer than she dared imagine in all her fantasies of this moment.

The rhythm of the song, *Wonderful Tonight* by Eric Clapton was measured, the words echoing her feelings. When the music ended, she thought he would lead her to the table, but he didn't. Instead, he pulled back and looked into her eyes. "One more?"

She stared into his tender brown eyes, captivated. A new song had only started when Logan suddenly shifted.

"Mind if I cut in?"

Addison stumbled back. Nathan. She exhaled, taking several relieved deep breaths. Logan was staring at her, waiting for her reaction. She didn't want to hurt Nathan's feelings, but she didn't want to leave Logan. What if Logan didn't ask for another dance?

"Okay, but only this once," Logan said, winking at her before slowly releasing her waist.

She had no time to compose her thoughts, still aware of Logan's hands attached to her, before Nathan spun her around. "What's wrong?" he asked.

Her breath quickened. "What?"

"Don't lie and tell me everything's fine, because it won't work. You were so happy before. What happened? Did Logan say something?"

Turning from his scrutinizing gaze, she spotted Ami across the floor dancing with Zach. "Nothing's wrong."

"Addison." With an abrupt halt, he stopped dancing. "I know something's bothering you. There was something different in your eyes when you came into the auditorium and you've been acting funny ever since."

Funny? Had anyone else noticed how entranced she'd been while in Logan's arms?

Couples danced all around them, but Nathan remained still. He was embarrassing her. "Are you going to dance with me or not?"

He resumed motion as she stared into the space behind him, trying to gain control of her emotions. Logan had made her forget. Nathan was reminding her. Could she be honest with him? Why did he even care? "Your brother didn't do anything. He's been really ... nice." With a quick glance, she zeroed in on Logan sitting at a table in the corner, then her gaze skipped across the room and settled on Philip, who was glaring at her.

Suddenly the room blurred as uneasiness pricked her flesh.

"Okay, so what happened, then?"

Blinking the dizziness into submission, she tightened her grip on Nathan's arm. "Philip."

Nathan leaned back, his eyes wide. "Who's Philip?"

"Nobody important." Her voice broke as she glanced in his direction. Philip was still watching.

Logan stood by a table across the room, watching his brother talk easily with Addison. Resentment wove through his core, growing with each breath. He turned away. His brother could have any girl he wanted. Why did he have to invade on the one girl, the only girl Logan wanted?

"You're Logan, right? I've seen you around campus." The girl had appeared out of nowhere and was now leaning against his table. "Mind if I join you?"

"I guess not. No one else is sitting here."

She flipped her blond hair and reached across the table. "I'm Somer, and my sister's officially a débutante."

Logan shook her hand but looked across the dance floor. "Nice to meet you." His mind seethed. Addison and his brother moved in slow motion to a fast beat song. He hated this.

The blonde was trying to talk to him. Why wasn't he listening?

"I love this song. You want to dance?"

Logan looked into her dark green eyes. "Sure, why not?"

The song's lyrics went perfectly with this stupid decision. What was he doing? He glanced around the room, anywhere but the girl's face. He moved mechanically, regret filling him. The song lingered lasting longer than he remembered.

"I can tell you're not really into this."

"Sorry. I'm here with someone else." He hadn't meant to announce that. No matter how badly he wanted it, it wasn't the whole truth. Addison rode with him, but they weren't together.

"That's okay. I'm the one who should apologize. My date has been ignoring me all night, watching this other girl. I was trying to make him jealous."

Funny, he was attempting the same thing. The exact opposite of how Addison should be treated. He hadn't given her a fair chance to respond to his interest. Of course, he still wasn't sure he had a chance and still hadn't asked her out officially. But there was nothing stopping him. Except Nathan.

He wanted to return to Addison, but first he had to handle the situation in front of him. "I'm not trying to get my head busted."

"Don't worry. He's paying no mind to me," she added, looking toward the entrance.

His gaze followed hers and that's when Logan spotted him. "You're here with Philip?"

"You know him?"

"We play ball together."

Logan already knew what he'd find but looked in the direction that held Philip's attention anyway. Addison and Nathan were leaving the dance floor.

"Oh?" She turned back to face Logan. "Don't tell him what I said. Not that it would matter."

"Don't worry."

"Sorry for using you. You're a real sweetie. If things don't work out with your girlfriend, look me up."

Speechless, he watched the girl walk away.

1 9

L ogan was dancing with someone else. Refusing to look at Logan or in the direction she'd last seen Philip, she sat at a corner table and watched Ami dancing with Zach. Zach liked Ami. She could tell.

"I was hoping for another dance."

Blood raced through her veins hearing the familiar voice. Her gaze met Logan standing only a yard away.

Her heart pounded as Logan moved closer and didn't stop until they were only inches apart. "You at least owe me the one we didn't get to finish."

The song blaring through the speakers was fast paced. She held her breath for a full three seconds. "I would love to," she said softly, grateful for the diversion, "but I don't dance very well."

"Sorry, Miss Morgan, but that won't work." With his strong palm tucked securely in the middle of her back, he led her back to the floor. He pulled her along, his hand in hers, as they moved to the beat of the music.

Addison had no choice but to go along. She ignored the twinge in her gut that Philip was here still watching and probably waiting for the perfect opportunity to approach.

An older hip-hop song, *Stereo Hearts* by Gym Class Heroes with Adam Levine, sounded through the speakers and, with a rush of adrenaline, her body reacted naturally to the rhythm.

Logan laughed out loud, triggering a nervous laugh from her. "And you said you couldn't dance."

He twirled her around and she landed on his foot.

She pulled her gaze from his chest and focused on his face. "I'm so sorry."

Taking her by the shoulders and pulling her completely against him, he whispered close to her ear, "You can step on my feet anytime."

Tall and poised, the man mirrored strength. She closed her eyes, willing her anxiety to vanish. When she opened them, a single look at him reminded her she was living in the moment she'd been waiting for all day—to be in Logan's arms.

Her joy faltered when she met Logan's gaze. "What?"

"You just ... You're so beautiful when you smile that way."

She responded by resting her head against his chest for the span of a few heartbeats. He made her feel safe, made her feel important, made her want to soak in his strength and never let go.

He pulled her closer than before, his breath brushing against her face. "If it's okay with you, I don't want to share you with anyone else tonight."

Speechless, she allowed him to sway back and forth to the rhythm, holding her close. The scent of his cologne, the nearness of him roused comfort within her with each note.

They danced to three more songs before he led her from the floor. She let out a calm breath, still soaking in the warmth of Logan's arms.

———

Logan lowered his gaze to where Addison's hands twisted together as they left the dance floor. With caution, he seized one of them, letting their intertwined fingers hover in the space between them. "What time do you have to be home?"

"No specific time."

"Can we hang out a little longer?"

"Here?"

The hesitance in her question lured his gaze to hers. "No, somewhere else ... anywhere else."

"Oh," she said with a tense laugh. "I would like that."

It wasn't her words that convinced him. It was how her hand relaxed within his, like it had always belonged there.

After saying goodbye to his family, they walked out into the cool evening air.

He opened her door, helping her to climb inside his truck, and allowed his fingers to linger on the silky material of her dress.

Before starting the truck, he paused, adoring the tiny lines that crinkled across her forehead. "That was fun."

She shifted suddenly. "It was. I'm so glad Ami invited me." Her tone indicated a mix of doubt and expectation.

"Did you want to stop by your house and change?"

"No, I'm fine."

"Good." He kept his tone even. "But just so you know, I'm having a really hard time keeping my eyes off you."

The sound of her laughter drifting through his truck brought an unexpected rush. He could get used to that.

"Ami looked so beautiful, so happy tonight. What do you think of Zach?"

Her question caught him off guard. "He's a cool kid."

"He likes Ami. The way he looks at her. I mean, it's sweet," she mumbled, tucking her hands beneath her thighs.

Logan pulled the truck to a stop at the light and turned to look at her. "They've been friends forever. I guess it would be okay if they started dating." A moment of silent passion sparked between them at the mention of dating and Logan's breath caught in his throat. Did she feel it too?

They both faced the road as he drove the short distance toward the pier.

When he had parked, Addison cleared her throat. "Ami said Zach was going away to college this fall. And that she planned to take a few classes at the community college."

"I'm not sure what Zach is planning, but I'm relieved Ami will be home a couple more years."

"You're worried about her?"

"Can't help it."

"I agree with you. Even though I went straight to college from high school, if I had another option, I would've done the same thing." She glanced at him. "It's definitely cheaper."

"And will give her a chance to mature a little before jumping out there with all those who aren't."

Slipping his jacket off, he draped it around her bare shoulders. "It's cool tonight."

"Thank you." Her voice was gentle, soft like the flutter of butterfly wings.

He opened the passenger door and took her hand to help her down.

They walked across the wooden walkway that led to the ocean. A briny scent sifted through the air. They brushed against each other as they walked down the steps and a sudden urge to grab her hand assaulted him, but he resisted. This time. They were alone and it would be impossible to suppress his urge to kiss her. With a quick reach, she slipped her heels off and held them with two fingers. He led her onto the stretch of sand and then near the edge of the water. Her dress swished back and forth with each step, the black sequins sparkling in the moonlight.

As he rolled his pant legs up, Addison lifted her left leg and rubbed the skin above her foot.

"Did you hurt your ankle?"

"Yes, I—" Her voice caught, and her throat dipped with a hard swallow. "I'm so clumsy," she continued with a nervous laugh.

Logan studied her expression. Something wasn't right. The last words he'd use to describe Addison Morgan was clumsy. Each step, each movement she'd made since the first time he saw her was graceful. When she added nothing else to her story, he touched her elbow. "We don't have to walk."

"No, it's okay."

Without thinking, he took her hand. "Come on." He led her to a large rock set within a patch of wild grass.

"Logan, it's really okay."

"It's me. I danced all my energy out trying to keep up with you."

Full-blown feminine laughter exploded from her slim frame as she took a seat on the boulder and he fought his desire to sit closer.

"You're not a very good liar."

"Just let me see."

She scooted farther onto the rock, finding her balance. "See what?"

"Your leg." He tugged her foot toward him and searched for swelling. "Does that hurt?"

"It's just a little tender."

"It feels good to me." He glanced at her with a teasing gleam. "But maybe you should prop it up for the rest of the night."

Resting her foot across his leg, she smirked. "Starting now?"

"Absolutely." His gaze was sweeping across her bare legs as he wrapped both hands around them. "I'm more than happy to be your support."

She laughed and swatted at him as she retreated and positioned her feet beneath her. "I was kidding."

I wasn't. She was right though. The whole episode, all five seconds of it, did strange things to his pulse. Made him want to be closer to her. If he didn't look away, he would make a fool out of himself.

Gaze on the water, Addison sat silently for several heartbeats before lifting her lashes to him. "I love it here."

"Me too." His gaze shifted to her bare feet. "Do you walk down to the ocean a lot?"

"Not as much as I would like. I love walking on the beach, finding shells, watching children play, but my favorite is watching the sunset."

Listening to her talk, the passion in her voice when she spoke sent a thrill through him. He loved listening to the way she pronounced each word, her southern accent deeper than most.

Addison looked beyond where the waves were crashing before them. "I do try to sit on the back porch every night."

"Really? Every night?"

"I never get tired of it. Every sunrise, every sunset, every crashing wave. It's seeing proof of God's existence, even on life's darkest days."

20

When Logan dropped Addison off an hour later, she stepped inside and closed the door behind her. "Did that really just happen?"

"What did you say, honey?"

"Nothing, Aunt Brenda, I was talking to myself. What are you still doing up?"

"Couldn't sleep. Did you have a nice time with Ami?"

"It was great."

"That's wonderful. Can you come in here for a minute? I wanted to talk to you about something."

Addison sat on the couch.

Aunt Brenda studied her. "I'm thinking about spending some time on the West Coast."

Addison's stomach dropped. "What?"

"It wouldn't be until after graduation. I would love for you to come with me. We could do all kinds of exploring."

Addison didn't want to leave. Not now. Not after tonight.

Aunt Brenda tilted her head. "There are several properties that have caught my interest." She leaned against the sofa. "I've never been able to sit still for long. You know that."

Her heart broke for Aunt Brenda. Her aunt had sacrificed so much to give her and her sister a better life. Somewhere safe to stay. But Casey's death had been hard on them both. The reminders in this house, everywhere. But the reality of Aunt Brenda leaving her here alone disturbed her. "Are you selling the house?"

"Oh, no. I could never give up this place." Aunt Brenda stared into space for a long moment before speaking again. "I know you probably don't want to leave right now. But will you be okay, staying here by yourself?"

Addison breathed a sigh of relief. "Yes, I'll be fine."

"You have this new job you're trying to get. And I'm sure you'll be spending your last summer with your friends. Philip. I can't believe you're almost a college graduate."

Addison stared at the table, fighting her tortuous thoughts. She needed to explain about Philip.

"Is everything okay with you, darling? You've been acting so different lately."

She wanted to tell her about how she'd fallen in love with Ami's brother. About how Philip showed up at the débuette dance tonight and had hurt her, again. But it wasn't the right time. The last thing Aunt Brenda needed was to worry about her while she was away this summer.

Aunt Brenda's grin filled her whole face. "You know, you could invite one of your girlfriends to spend the summer with you." She leaned back. "Actually, the more I think about it, the more I like the idea of you having someone here with you."

Addison smiled against the tightening in her chest. "That's a great idea. I'll ask Taylor."

"That would make me feel much better."

"So, where exactly are you going?"

"I'll be traveling through California, but some of the properties are in Washington."

"Really? Wow, what a great experience for you! You have more guts than I do. I don't know that I could travel across the country by myself."

"Sure, you could. You never know what you'll do."

Addison shrugged her shoulders. "How long will you be gone?"

"No more than a few months." Aunt Brenda took a sip of her hot tea. "Have you talked to your mom lately?"

"I invited her to graduation, but I don't know if she'll come."

Aunt Brenda shook her head. "Of course, she'll be there for your graduation."

"I guess. I should visit more, but I feel like I'm in her way." She never wanted to return home.

"That's their loss and my gain." She wrapped both arms around Addison. "I have so enjoyed having you here with me."

"Me too."

Once alone in her room, magical moments of her night with Logan whirred through her memory. Addison glanced in the mirror, realizing suddenly that she still wore Logan's suit jacket. She pulled her arms tight around her waist, inhaling the scent of Logan's cologne. Another realization hit her at the same time. Aunt Brenda hadn't said a word about it.

Addison changed into her pajamas and climbed onto the bed tucking her feet beneath the blanket as *One Night with the King* played the opening credits.

Addison had watched the movie more times than she could count, but it would never get old. Sporadic thoughts of Logan filled her mind as the love story between a king and a Jewish girl named Esther was made queen unfolded. It was after one before the movie ended.

Addison lay back, still clinging to Logan's jacket. She wanted to stay wrapped in its warmth, but she didn't want to wrinkle it. Unable to part with it, she placed it carefully on the extra pillow.

Addison's cell phone beeped, and she froze. The ring tone meant she had a text message. The thudding of her heart roared in her ears. Philip saw her with Logan. She hadn't thought about that once since Logan dropped her off. Had Philip stayed the whole time? Though she'd managed to detach from her anxiety over the encounter with Philip, it lingered just below the surface. She waited one full minute before she grabbed her phone. An unknown number appeared attached to a message.

I know it's late and you're probably sleeping but I couldn't wait another minute to tell you. I had a really good time tonight. And this is Logan, by the way.

Within an instant, she was sitting straight up. Her stomach quivered in response as she read the message two more times.

Should she reply? Should she wait? The questions filled her as she held her fingers above the keypad of her phone. There was no point trying to regulate her pulse, it had been skittering all over the place the entire evening.

Me too. She erased it and started over. *I did too.*

Ugh. How could it be so hard to reply to a text message?

I had a good time too.

Heart in her throat, Addison's fingers sped across the keypad.

It was a perfect night. I hope to see you again tomorrow and the next day.

If only. She quickly erased her silly ramblings, before she made the mistake of hitting send. She would die of embarrassment.

I did too. I have your jacket. Forgot I was wearing it.

She pressed send and held the phone against her chest, anticipating his response. She should've offered to take it to him tomorrow.

Then her phone beeped again.

I didn't forget. I'll get it next time I see you. Hopefully that will be soon. Goodnight, beautiful.

Collapsing against the pillow, she nestled into Logan's jacket, no longer caring about wrinkles.

She read his message twenty more times before placing her phone on the table. A smile filled her face as every gentle touch, every endearing word, every single memory of being in his arms left her staring at the ceiling in wonder.

21

The following Thursday morning, Addison headed to campus for one final meeting with her professor, the tenderness of her twisted ankle from her confrontation with Philip was now only a fading memory.

"Congratulations on a successful year. I have been given nothing but good reports and look forward to seeing you at graduation."

"Thank you so much for everything." She grabbed her purse and headed for the door. With only a half day left in the classroom, she'd be free to relax until the commencement services Friday afternoon. Walking through the double doors, Taylor met her on the walkway.

"Hey, how'd it go?"

"Great. Now I just have to find a job." Addison scanned the surrounding area.

"What about your student teaching school?"

"They still have no openings this fall."

"Oh no. I'm sorry. Don't worry, you'll find something."

"It's fine." Addison sauntered forward, her head shifting from left to right.

"Are you looking for somebody?"

Taylor knew her better than anyone. "You don't miss anything. I need to talk to you about something."

"Please tell me it isn't about Philip."

Addison ignored the shudder rattling her at the mention of Philip's name. "No, of course not. Do you think your mom would let you stay with me this summer? My aunt's visiting the West Coast for a while. And she's leaving Sunday."

At Taylor's outright laughter, Addison joined her. "Are you kidding me? Yes, I would love to."

"Shouldn't you ask first?"

"She'll say yes."

Addison stared as a few students started drifting from the building across the yard. "We'll talk more later, but right now I've got to go. I still have half a day left."

"Wait! How was Saturday night?"

"One of the best nights of my life."

"What happened?" Taylor stopped in her tracks. "I want to hear everything."

"I'll tell you everything later. I really have to go."

"Addison?"

Addison's eyes widened at the sound of Logan's voice calling her name. "It's him," Addison whispered. She turned away from Taylor's thrilled smile and faced him.

Taylor whispered near her ear, "I'll catch up with you later."

Addison smiled, a shiver pitching her forward. "Okay, call me."

Logan came to a halt only inches from her. "This is my lucky day. I never expected to see you here."

"I had a meeting." Addison's smile widened, and biting her lower lip, she looked away from his steady gaze. The other night, she'd detected warmth, maybe even adoration in his eyes. But now, his expression was indecipherable. It left her feeling vulnerable, unsteady.

"I found this in my truck," he said, handing her the bracelet she had worn Saturday night.

"Oh, I didn't realize it had fallen off."

He chuckled. "I seem to keep ending up with your things. I wasn't sure if I'd see you before Friday, but just in case, I brought it with me."

Desperate for something to do, she wriggled the bracelet onto her wrist. It was impossible to fasten with her hands trembling. She would never get it latched.

He reached for the bracelet. "Here, allow me."

Taking the silver strand into the palm of his hand, Logan dropped it across her wrist, his fingers brushing against her skin, creating a wave of sensations.

"You know it's really too bad." He still held to her arm, though he'd already snapped the lock into place.

She glanced at him, her brows crinkled. "What?"

"That I didn't see you on campus until our last semester of college." Her legs wobbled at the intense look in his eyes. "We've been in college together four years, and now we're graduating."

"Maybe you just didn't notice me." On impulse, she looked away, unable to contain her deepening smile. "I probably walked by you every day."

"I would've noticed. Believe me."

A skeptical laugh wrenched her chest. Maybe it camouflaged her flaming cheeks.

"Where are you headed now?"

"To my kindergarten class. Half a day left, and I'm finished."

"Care if I walk with you to the parking lot?"

"I would like that," she admitted, even though it would be torture. His nearness made her blood race and her breathing irregular. "Your jacket's in my car."

"Oh, okay."

"I wasn't sure if it was rented and you needed to return it today."

"No—"

"There's my car. Let me get your jacket." Her stride lengthened as she neared her car. She took her time with the door, needing a moment to catch her breath from all those untamed emotions swirling in her chest.

"Do you mind keeping it? So, I'm not toting it around?"

She turned, lifting unsteady eyes to him. "No, of course not. I wasn't sure if you needed it."

"Not planning to attend a dance anytime soon." The abrupt twist of his lips into a relaxed smile hinted at his confidence. "Not unless you'll be there."

Heat flooded her cheeks. Her inability to control any of her emotions in his presence was daunting.

"You ready for graduation?"

She took a vital deep breath. "So ready."

"You finished your exams?"

"Here on campus, yes. But I still have the state teachers' exam." Their conversation made standing this close easier. "What about you?"

"Only one. French."

For no reason at all, she laughed. "You took French?"

"There were no available spots in Spanish." His smile hitched into a full grin. "*Comment allez-vous?*"

From one breath to the next, she wanted him more. "*J'vais tres bein.*"

"You're fluent?"

She moistened her lips. "*Non.*" Clearing her throat, she hoped her voice sounded as unaffected as his. "No."

"The words are like exotic poetry tumbling from your lips." His gaze once again fell to her mouth, and she swallowed hard. "What time do you have to be there?"

She exhaled, thankful for the sudden change in subject, and glanced at her watch. "Now."

"I'm holding you up."

She studied the ground beneath her feet and took a deep breath. "I wasn't sure how long my meeting would last. It's fine. The kids are having a fun day outside."

He reached behind her and opened her door. "Allow me, Mademoiselle." He waited until she was settled inside before stretching an arm across her hood. "I hope to see you again very soon."

His gaze lowered to her lips and fire blazed through her veins.

148

22

The frame gave a low squeak as she sprawled across the mattress and tucked in the last corner of the sheet, still warm from the dryer. Addison positioned the last throw pillow and turned to find Aunt Brenda standing in the doorway.

"Philip's here."

"Philip?" Addison groaned. What was he doing here? Her attempt to ignore him at graduation this morning had been successful. And from her brief observation of Philip's attention centered on the blonde, Addison was convinced he had moved on. The short distance to the living room wasn't enough time to think of something civilized to say. For Aunt Brenda's sake.

No matter, she didn't intend to give Philip even the slightest ounce of hope. Without looking in his direction, she hurried past him and headed straight for the front door.

"Addison, wait."

Whirling around to face him as soon as she exited the house, she ignored his tear-streaked face. She wouldn't give in to him. "What do you want?" She walked toward him, seeing more clearly how his eyes were swollen. "What's wrong with you?"

"I miss you. I'm so messed up." He tousled the loose strands of hair dangling around his face. "I need to quit drinking, but I can't. I need us."

Us? There is no us. But the unspoken words hidden in his tears softened her heart. Every grieving emotion from her own past materialized, nearly taking her breath. Memories of Philip by her side during years of neglect from her parents, every tear she'd shed, and even the darkest moments before she'd finally moved out choked out the resentment from only moments before. How could she turn her back on him completely?

"Just stop. Don't do it anymore."

"I tried, but I'm hurting so bad. I feel like I've lost you. I don't know what to do."

"I'm sorry, Philip, I'll always be here for you as a friend, but I don't know what else I can do."

"You don't have to do anything. I just need to know we're okay. I never meant to hurt you. I'm sorry. I know I've done some things, but you are the one who has my heart. I love you."

Her stomach tensed. This was getting out of control fast.

There had to be a gentle way to explain that she didn't feel that way for him and never would again. "Philip—"

"I don't deserve you. Or another chance, but I can't do this without you."

Aunt Brenda stepped outside onto the porch. "Philip, I'm going to need you to keep an eye on Addison for me. I'll be gone this summer. I've decided to head to the West Coast for a while."

"Aunt Brenda!" She had to stop her. She hadn't explained about Philip and knew instantly that had been a grave mistake.

Addison didn't miss the change in Philip's expression. It scared her the way the light in his eyes brightened then darkened so suddenly. She had to set this straight. Now.

"Taylor's staying with me. There's no need to worry about it, or to check on me."

"I'll feel better having Philip check on you occasionally. You'll be seeing each other anyway, so it'll be natural for him to come by."

"Of course, I will. I'll be more than happy to check in on her."

Addison stepped between him and Aunt Brenda. "No, Philip, you shouldn't, we—" It wasn't okay for him to just come by. Not anymore. Addison cringed. They continued to talk as if she wasn't there.

Philip finally left but so did Aunt Brenda. She couldn't let Philip believe that she was giving in to him. Or that anything had changed. And she needed to tell her aunt about their break-up.

She couldn't believe Aunt Brenda had told him she would be alone.

A few minutes later, after her aunt and Philip had both left, Addison stepped outside onto the back porch, still fuming over Philip's audacity to pretend nothing had changed.

Leaning against the railing, Addison looked across the yard just as a sea gull landed in the grassy area at the edge of her aunt's property. The bird walked toward something—or was it someone? Dark hair fluttered in the wind just barely above the tall grass. Inhaling a shaky breath, she grabbed the railing.

She'd almost missed seeing Logan sitting there. Only a few days had passed since she'd spent time alone with Logan, but it felt like weeks. With the graduation commencement services this morning and her obligation to spend time with Aunt Brenda before her trip, there hadn't been time to be alone with him.

What was he doing here? She tried to restrain the hope welling within her. If it wasn't him, her disappointment would be crushing.

Taking several deep breaths, she walked across the porch and took the narrow path leading to the ocean.

Logan stood when she took a few steps across the wooden planks leading to the stairs. "I should've called first." His assured pose, his steady gaze left her breathless and she had to focus before she tumbled down the stairs. "I would've knocked, but Philip—"

"I didn't see your truck." Addison slipped off her shoes. "Where did you park?"

"Across the street." Logan lifted his hand to indicate the direction, then stepped forward, distress deepening the already dark brown of his eyes. "I didn't want to intrude. If you want me to leave—"

"No." How was she supposed to explain Philip's presence? Eluding the question, she stepped closer. "I'm glad you came."

151

Exposing a quirked brow, he didn't press but took her hand as she reached the last step.

With an exhale, she absorbed snippets of the young man standing before her. Hardened muscles beneath soft flesh. Heavy breaths, deep and even. "Thank you," she whispered.

Up to now, her day had treaded along on rocky terrain. She endured the unexpected visit from Philip. Aunt Brenda blurted about her move, and Philip jumped at the opportunity to check in on her.

But now, the day was slowly correcting onto even ground. Logan Tant walked by her side toward the water. The wind skimmed the tips of the swells and a trace of moisture drizzled over her bare arms. They stood facing the lapping waves crashing against the shore, the cool water rushing over their bare feet. Neither of them spoke.

The sun slowly dropped and reddish orange slashed across the water.

"Can I—" He rubbed the back of his neck, his expression thoughtful. "Can I ask a personal question?"

Oh no. "Okay."

The last rays of sunlight warmed her face from their glow while she stared ahead motionless, waiting.

"Are you and Philip still involved?"

She stiffened as the sudden desire to spill her heart engulfed her. With a quick shift, she met his gaze. He watched her, uncertainty filling his expression. "No!" she exclaimed, shaking her head all at the same time.

His eyes crinkled with a smile, but he didn't say anything for a long time.

"How would you feel about me calling you?"

A nervous, shy smile filled her lips. "I would like that."

She should explain about Philip, but it was complicated. Besides, it wasn't Logan's responsibility. And it might send him running in the opposite direction. Even Aunt Brenda knew nothing about how Philip treated her, and she was leaving tomorrow. The timing hadn't been right to talk to her. Aunt Brenda might change her mind about letting her stay here. And the last thing she wanted was to return to her mom's house.

There would be a better time to explain that they had broken up.

When Aunt Brenda returned.

Making her decision to keep her problems with Philip to herself, she veered toward safer conversation. "My aunt's leaving tomorrow." Her throat felt dry, parched like she hadn't had a drink in days.

"Where's she going?"

"California."

His eyes widened. "Really? But you're not going?"

"No."

"How long will she be gone?"

"Possibly the whole summer."

Logan studied her for an extended, unblinking moment. Did he grasp from her discomfort that there was more to the story? That she longed for his touch, his love, his protection? "You'll be staying here alone?"

"No." Addison didn't miss the concern edging his voice. "My best friend Taylor's spending the summer with me."

"Good." Logan's glint of relief was instant. "Did you need to get back inside since she's leaving tomorrow?"

"No." She inhaled the warm summer air. "She's not here anyway."

After walking a few more minutes, they turned back toward the house, and the closer they came, the more she dreaded it. She didn't want their time together to end.

"What time is she leaving?"

Addison slowed and slid her feet into her flip-flops. "Before lunch."

"So, Taylor's staying tomorrow night?" He fumbled with getting his feet into his shoes.

"Yes."

"Is it okay if I stop by and check on you?"

"Check on me?" She shifted closer and affectionately leaned into him. "When?"

He responded by taking her hand and pulling her fingers to his lips. "As often as you'll allow me." The heat of his breath smoldered through her fingers with the hushed words. After a gentle press of his lips against her skin, he let their hands drop but didn't release her fingers.

"You don't have to do that."

Hesitation deepened the tiny lines surrounding his eyes as his gaze lingered. "It's as much for me as it is for you."

"Is that so?"

"Absolutely." He was confident as usual, his tone captivating, while she tried not to trip over her feet as they ascended the stairs. He secured his grip on her hand and awarded her with a smile that was both charming and genuine.

When she opened her mouth to respond, he interjected, "I won't be able to help worrying about you. One of the perks of my job."

Her desire to be near him deepened. When he motioned for her to step up onto the porch, she looked away. How long had she been staring up at him? He had caught her, but she was too elated to care.

He led her to the porch swing. "Make sure you keep the doors locked."

"I will." She could easily get used to all this attention. "Where do you patrol?"

"This area and south of here."

"Really?" Taking the seat closest to the water, she forced her shoulders to loosen. "So, my neighborhood? My house?"

He nodded. "Is in my district."

"That makes me feel better already."

"For now, anyway. We move around the city. But call me anytime you need anything. Even if I'm not working."

"I will." And she meant it.

They sat side by side on the swing while Logan lazily pushed his foot against the wood slats creating an unhurried motion. She couldn't see his face clearly, but his eyes twinkled in the moonlight.

"What's your favorite thing about your job?"

"Helping people." The hum of cicadas rang through the silence. "What about you?"

"The same. Loving the kids. Seeing them learn new things. Maybe once I get a full-time position, you can visit my class, be my show-and-tell." She tugged at a lock of her hair while Logan's eyes moved over her face slow and steady.

"Your show-and-tell, huh?"

It was impossible to hide her delighted smile.

She glanced lazily at her watch. They'd been out here for a while, yet it seemed like only minutes.

Logan brought the swing to a halt and she lifted her gaze, already dreading his departure. "I better go," he said. "It's getting late."

They stood and, before she knew what was happening, he pulled her against him, and she nestled into his chest as if it was where she'd always belonged. She drew in a deep breath, savoring the fragrance of his cologne.

The rumble of crunching rocks reverberated from the driveway. *Aunt Brenda.* Addison had barely detached from his embrace when it hit her. She'd made a mistake.

"Sounds like someone drove up."

Her pulse kicked up with a jolt. Aunt Brenda couldn't see her with Logan. There had been no time to explain. She wouldn't understand.

He lengthened the space between them. "Is everything all right?"

"Yes. Yes, of course." *She cannot see us together. Not yet.* "It's my aunt. I should go in and help her."

"Do you need me to stay and help?"

"No, I just meant she'll need me for some last-minute stuff." Her body stiffened as her aunt's car door slammed. "But thank you."

"Okay, I'll see you later."

"Okay." Hands trembling by her sides, she watched him until he disappeared beyond her view.

Then raced inside.

23

The next morning, Aunt Brenda climbed into her car, excitement filling her eyes. "I'll be calling you very often. Have a great summer and I'll miss you so much, honey."

"Me too and don't worry, I'll be fine. Enjoy your time and take lots of pictures." Addison stood on the curb waving as Aunt Brenda drove away, but then Philip wrapped his hands around Addison's waist.

"Wow, I can't believe she's leaving you with the whole house to yourself."

"She needed to get away for a while, Philip."

"Yeah, but still, the house is yours." His hands roamed lower down her back, still holding her tight.

"Stop it. You shouldn't be here, and my neighbors might be watching."

"Let's go in then, so we can be alone." He traced her neck with his lips, and chills sliced through her skin.

"What're you doing?" In one fluid motion, she yanked from his grip. She had already risked too much by ignoring his intentions this long.

"We're going in."

"No, we're not. You're leaving. I have to work this afternoon and need to get ready."

"You have plenty of time before you have to be there. I thought we would celebrate."

"Celebrate what, Philip? There's nothing to celebrate. What's wrong with you?" Addison asked, trimming her volume so the neighbors wouldn't hear.

"What's wrong with you? You're no fun anymore. You're always so serious."

"Why don't you find someone else to have fun with? There's nothing stopping you anymore, remember?" She hated how wobbly her voice sounded.

He laughed and grabbed her again, sending icy slithers down her arm. "I don't want someone else." His eyes grazed over her and she cringed. "You've made me wait long enough." His voice was sharp. "But now we have more than enough privacy."

"Philip, stop." Using all her strength, she pushed him away. "I said stop. You need to go, now."

Within seconds, Taylor pulled into the driveway and parked. She jumped out quickly and grabbed her suitcase.

"Perfect timing, Taylor." Addison said as she helped Taylor with her bags. Without looking back, Addison hurried up the porch steps after Taylor and closed the door behind them.

After securing the lock, she stole across the room to the nearest window and peered through the crack along the curtain to make sure he was leaving. Philip staggered to his car, still looking toward the house. He punched the hood of his car and, after one last look over his shoulder, climbed in.

Addison breathed a sigh of relief. The curtain slipped from her trembling fingers and she leaned against the wall for support.

"What was he doing here?"

"Pretending to care that Aunt Brenda's leaving."

"What?" Taylor plopped down on the couch.

"Nothing. What matters is he's gone."

. . .

The restaurant was already busy at five o'clock. Addison fell into the routine quickly, all thoughts on keeping her guests happy. She tamped down her hope that Logan would show up here tonight with each hour that passed.

On the drive home, Taylor talked on her phone the entire time and Addison's mind transported to Logan's visit last night. Was he working tonight? If he rode by, would he stop?

All evening, she glanced at her phone set on silent, hoping Logan had sent something. At 12:45, she noticed she had one text message. She swiped the screen, her pulse racing.

I just wanted to say hi. I hope you had a good night. How long would he wait to see her again? What if he changed his mind? Especially after the way she rushed him away Saturday night.

She started typing, not sure how to respond. *Just got home from work. I hope you had a good night too.*

Addison stepped into the shower, the hot water stinging her skin. She stood motionless, too tired to move, too exhausted to think.

A fresh wave of disappointment roused her thoughts when she climbed under her cold sheets.

Logan didn't ask to see her tomorrow.

"Why don't you invite Addison to our cookout this weekend?" Matt asked.

"What?"

"Y'all are talking, right?" Matt punched him in the arm.

"Sort of."

"Ask her to come. Shelley won't leave me alone. Besides, we need to break her in."

"No. We are *not* breaking her in."

"I'm kidding, man." He chuckled innocently, then shrugged. "I wouldn't do that to you."

"I don't know."

"Bring her. I'll behave. I promise."

Logan hated himself for not stopping by her place last night, but he had already taken his dinner break and couldn't come up with a good reason to stop. Not at one o'clock in the morning. Not when Taylor's car was parked beside Addison's in the driveway and they seemed to be secure inside her home. He didn't want to be too presumptuous or push things too fast. After all, she had dated Philip a long time and didn't want to be her rebound. And he still wasn't sure where he stood. Especially after the way she rushed him off the other night when her aunt came home.

Still, he worried about her most of the night and had almost asked Nathan to go by and check on her today, but he'd stopped himself. He wouldn't make the same mistake twice.

But now, tonight, there was only one car parked in her driveway and the living room light was still burning. It was late, but he couldn't wait another day to see her.

He typed the first few letters of her name into his phone and pressed call before changing his mind.

She answered on the second ring. "Hello."

"Addison, hey, it's Logan."

"Hey." Relief filled the simple word.

"I know it's late, but I'm on my dinner break." He hesitated as he pondered whether to invite himself, now, at this hour. "Would it be okay if I stopped by for a few minutes?"

Silence filled the line between them.

"I mean, if you think it's inappropriate for me to be there with your aunt not home, I understand completely."

"No, I just wasn't expecting ... Yes, I would love for you to stop by."

Logan took several deep breaths. "I'm pulling in."

24

Addison's heart seized before skipping away with her breath. Logan was here now. Already in her pajamas, she was lying on the couch watching a tearjerker of all things. Her eyes were probably puffed out to her ears. With a paper towel, she wiped at the smeared mascara under her eyes. It only made it worse.

Starting over with a fresh towel, she managed to wipe it off and took an extra minute to brush her teeth.

She glanced through the window to make sure it was him before opening the door. He stood on the porch facing the yard, the dim light flickering off his badge. At the sight of his tall form dressed out to protect her city, the anxiety that had bound her for several hours shriveled to the size of a pea.

She blew out a breath, then opened the door. "Hi."

"Hey." He made no motion to enter the house. "Do you want to sit out here?"

The idea seemed wonderful, with her swollen eyes. "Okay, but let's go to the back." They'd have more privacy. No one would see them back there. She couldn't have her nosy neighbors talking, especially with his patrol car parked on the curb.

They walked through the kitchen, but she didn't switch on the light.

"Would you like something to drink? I have sweet tea, orange juice, and lemonade."

Logan looked around the kitchen as she watched him carefully. She had never seen him in uniform. He was something to behold. And it was hard to look away.

Thank goodness he wasn't paying attention.

"Sweet tea would be great."

With a slight tremble, she grabbed two glasses from the cabinet. "How long is your break?"

"Thirty minutes."

"Did you already eat?"

"Not hungry."

After filling both glasses with sweetened iced tea, she followed Logan through the screened back door.

Logan took a seat on the swing and she moved into the space beside him, careful not to brush against his gear when she sat.

It had been several days since they'd sat in this very spot, and after he punched through a few break-the-ice questions, he reached for her pinky with his. His touch kicked up her pulse a notch. She plunged her free hand beneath her leg, wrestling against tingling sensations stirring commotion through her veins.

"Did your aunt get to her destination? Or is she still traveling?"

"She made it about half-way today before stopping at a motel for the night." The evening air was warm and briny. She pulled a breath deep into her lungs.

"How are you doing here without her?"

She stared at his darkened form before answering. "It's different and I miss her, but I'm okay." She loved sitting here, talking to him. It was everything she longed for in a relationship, longed for in a man. A longing she'd never thought would come true. And still wasn't sure was real.

"Your friend's still staying with you this summer?"

"Yes."

"You don't like staying alone, do you?" There was no ridicule, no agenda, only concern. And it deepened her affection.

161

"No, not really. I feel safer with Taylor here."

He didn't speak for several seconds as he pushed the swing back and forth with his boot. "My apartment's only a mile from here, so even when I'm off duty, if you ever need anything, call me." It was impossible to read his expression, but his tone expressed sincerity and her voice rejected a response. "Is everything okay? You look like you've been crying."

Addison laughed. "I was hoping you wouldn't notice."

He stiffened. "Is something wrong?"

"No, I was watching a good movie."

"So, good movies make you cry?" He regarded her with a warm smile. "I'll have to remember that and only watch bad movies with you."

"Ha, ha, ha. Very funny," she told him, her gaze caressing his darkened form.

"How's the teaching job search going?"

She lifted a hand to brush loose strands of hair away from her face. "I have a couple of interviews lined up."

"For schools here in Wilmington?"

"One is, yes. But the other school is in Jacksonville." She steeled herself for his reaction—a bad habit—one she intended to break.

"Jacksonville?" His jaw twitched. "That's a good hour drive."

"I know. But there aren't many positions available." Too aware of his thigh pressing against hers, she stretched out her legs. "What about you? Are you still planning to become a detective?"

"As soon as a position becomes available, I'll be the first in line."

Peace bordered the perimeter of her heart, struggling to gain entry, wrestling against the pain of her past.

With a deep breath, she warded off the internal battle stealing her short, precious time with Logan. "What time do you get off?"

"Seven in the morning."

She imagined him working those long nights, those dark brown eyes tormented as he patrolled the streets of Wilmington. She grimaced, visualizing the danger he faced shift after shift. "Do you like working this shift?"

"I'm getting used to it. Working different shifts during college was a challenge, but now that I'm on this shift permanently, it's easier." He pivoted slightly. "Are you working tomorrow night?"

Having trouble concentrating, she peered into the darkened sky, into something ordinary. "Me? Tomorrow, no."

He released her pinky and gently maneuvered his fingers between hers. The thrill of his touch flowed through every nerve ending as he continued to push the swing lazily with his boot. Waves just beyond the hill crashed through the silence.

"There's a cookout tomorrow night at a friend's house. Would you go with me?"

"I would love to." The electric current that flowed between them intensified with each second his fingers lingered with hers.

"I want you to meet my friends."

Her mind raced ahead with anticipation and she smiled. "I would love to meet your friends."

"We usually build a bonfire and sit around and talk for hours."

Addison gazed down the trail leading to the ocean. "Sounds fun."

He leaned against her gently. "So, I can pick you up around five?"

"That'll be great," she whispered, a jolt hammering through her chest.

"All right." A slight shift in his tone seized her attention. "Well, that was easier than I thought it would be."

"What's that?"

"Asking you out?"

Instinct might have warned her that the question was coming, but nothing prepared her for the stirring of emotions that stole her breath.

2 5

Looking through the kitchen window, Addison's gaze zeroed in on Logan's truck pulling into her drive. He was five minutes early, but she was ready—had been for over an hour. He climbed from the truck and she met him at the door. Senses suddenly sharper in his presence, she absorbed the blue jeans and white polo he wore with heightened appreciation.

"Hi," he said when she fully opened the door. "You look beautiful."

Her cheeks warmed and her lips curved into an exhilarated smile. "Thank you."

Moments later, they were driving through town, sitting in a comfortable silence.

Reaching a stop light, Logan turned his head quickly, before she could look away, and she instinctively swallowed the tremors that emerged in her throat.

He reached for the stereo; his eyes still fixed on hers. "What kind of music do you listen to?"

His expression made her pause before she took several slow, deep breaths. "A mixture, but I love certain songs more than a specific style." The disobedient squeak in her voice screamed in her ears.

"What about the music at Ami's débuette dance?" A deep throaty laugh fell from his lips and he leaned toward her. "You seemed into that." His low voice was hypnotic, forcing the memory of his arms around her to surface.

For a second she said nothing, willing her mouth to be more cooperative. "I enjoyed dancing."

"Me too."

She had enjoyed every moment she spent with him. It had ended way too soon.

"Have you been to the aquarium lately?"

She willed the awkwardness away and focused on the road, trying to manipulate her inner consciousness. It was getting out of control. Fast. "Years ago."

"I was trying to think of something fun to do for our second date."

"Our second date, huh?" The thought, the simple idea of being with him here like this, was more than she dared dream for. "You may not want a second date, you know like what's her name at the restaurant?"

Logan laughed out loud. "Surely you don't think—it was her decision." He faced her again. "I guess it didn't help that she was jealous of the waitress."

Addison's neck flamed.

"I had trouble keeping my eyes off her," Logan teased, scrunching his cheeks.

A flutter bounced across her chest. "So, she was jealous, huh? Her first drink was diet."

"I know."

"How?"

"I took a sip when she was complaining."

She stared at him. "Did you ever talk to her again?"

"No, she was pretty mad when she left. I feel bad now using her like that."

"What do you mean?" She kept her voice composed, not wanting him to know her heart. Not yet.

"I was trying to forget about this girl, but it didn't work."

Her throat closed. What girl? Was it the same one she had overheard him and Nathan talking about?

"Oh." Addison didn't need any more information. It would only cast a shadow on their first date. Logan said nothing more about it. But if he still had feelings for the girl, why was he talking to her this way? And where was she now? Disappointment wove a wedge through her middle. She didn't like this and decided to get it over with. "So, this girl, she's an old girlfriend?"

Logan stared ahead at the road for several seconds before turning to look at her. "No, it was you."

"Me?" She was too afraid to hope, so she teased him instead. "You want to forget about me?"

"I did … before … I tried. But I gave up. Nothing worked."

Addison allowed his words to filter through her mind, her soul. She had to be dreaming.

"I really did try. You're way out of my league."

She felt Logan's gaze on her. "Yeah right, I'm definitely not out of your league."

"You don't see yourself very clearly, do you?"

Speechless, Addison stared straight ahead, trying not to let his compliments embarrass her. She didn't know how to respond and changed the subject. "How's Ami?"

"Good. She's very excited about our date today."

He was relentless. She giggled. "Really?"

"Yeah, she tried talking me into letting her come."

Addison glanced at Logan, fascinated by his words, by the change in the way he was speaking to her. His warm gaze made her weak.

He didn't wait for her to answer. "My friends are ... very loud."

"Loud?"

"And a little pushy." He released a playful grin that probably melted the hearts of countless others, including hers. "Don't be surprised at anything they say."

He continued to tease her as he drove down the main strip heading toward Carolina Beach. The drive seemed faster than she'd ever remembered. It seemed like moments later he was parking his truck.

As they walked toward the house, Addison smiled remembering

the expressions he made while teasing her. While she was staring ahead, the feel of Logan taking her hand startled her.

"Do you mind?" he asked, slipping his fingers between hers.

She nodded, chewing her bottom lip.

They walked hand in hand toward the backyard where there were two guys standing near the grill.

"Hey guys, this is Addison."

The one standing closest to her reached for her free hand. "I'm Matt. It's so nice to finally meet you. I've heard all about you."

"It's about time you brought her, man." The other guy punched Logan before wrapping an arm around her. "The girls are inside. They've been waiting for you to get here."

After Logan introduced her to Matt's wife and Tommy's wife, the ladies shooed the men out of the kitchen.

Addison fumbled through the list of things to say and not to say, but nothing materialized.

"I'm Shelley." Matt's wife stared at her with crinkled brows. "You look nervous."

"Am I that obvious?" Her response was nothing more than an awkward whisper.

"You have no reason to be. Me and Matt have known Logan our whole lives. And we've never seen him this happy."

Addison's heart flittered wildly. "Really?"

"Matt said you were all he talked about."

"She's right." Tommy's wife wrapped an arm around her. "Welcome to the family, Addison."

The family? On those comforting words, she lifted a genuine smile.

After a few minutes of finishing the preparations for dinner, they joined the guys outside.

"The chops are about done. Can you grab the cabbage?" Logan asked Matt as he headed her way. "Hey, the girls didn't scare you away, did they?"

It was the exact opposite. Only she couldn't tell him that. "They were great. I like your friends," she replied with a warm smile.

Under his breath he sputtered, "Now I just have to keep a leash on the guys. They're determined to embarrass me."

After dinner, his group of friends sat around the fire talking among each other, their laughter growing in volume. Their intention to tease Logan by sharing embarrassing stories made the time move at a faster rate. And she was content sitting back and taking it all in.

After hours of sitting around the bonfire, eating and talking, Logan led her to his truck and drove her home. Taking her hand, he helped her down and closed the door.

"What did you think of my friends?"

"They were great."

Since it was already after one in the morning, she was surprised when he joined her on the back porch.

"Thanks for inviting me."

He leaned back, pushing the swing into motion with his boot. "How long have you worked at the Olive Garden?"

"Four years."

"You must like it?"

"Most of the time. There are certain customers that can make things difficult though."

"Like those loud guys harassing you, promising to come back when your shift ended." He pursed his lips and exhaled hard.

Chills smothered the length of both arms. "You heard what they were saying?"

"You have no idea how hard it was to stay in my seat and not pound them."

Startled, she glanced at the wooden slats, freeing herself from his piercing gaze. "That was the same night you came back to wait for me."

He reached across and took her hand. "I never left." A slow smile played across his lips. "I wanted to protect you ... I felt responsible for you. Then, on top of that, my date, blind date insulted you more than once."

Speechless, she stared at him. He never left, but stayed the entire night waiting for her shift to end?

His profile blurred as drowsiness billowed, thrusting her into reality. With Logan, time felt distorted, unending, each moment magical.

"I better go. It's late. And you're getting sleepy."

Addison had been anticipating it all day, but it wasn't until he led her to the front door, and they stood facing each other that it happened. Hidden by the shadows they stood in silence, while in the distance, waves crashed against the seashore. Logan placed his finger against her cheek compelling her to look at him.

"I had a really good time with you today."

"Me too." Her voice quivered with emotion.

His gaze fell to her lips, and her awareness intensified.

Logan leaned forward, gently pressing his lips against hers, his breath warm against her skin. With her lips parted, she inhaled the taste of him. She trembled with a mix of pleasure and disbelief. He pulled away, his eyes locked with hers.

A mischievous grin spread across his lips. He paused, still watching her, then seconds later captured her in another moment of passion. Spellbound, Addison braced herself against the yearning flooding her soul.

He smiled at her wistfully. "Can we do this again soon?"

She nodded, her throat tightening with expectancy. "Yes."

"I'm leaving first thing in the morning for Indiana."

Addison gave the door frame a good portion of her weight, praying her disappointment wasn't too obvious.

"I'm riding with Matt. He has to take a load there for his dad. So, I'll be gone for a few days." He paused like he wasn't sure what to say. "Can I call you when I get back?"

"I would like that."

"Okay, then. Go get some sleep." He finished with a tender look into her eyes and a gentle touch to her cheek before he descended the stairs, leaving her with a warmth she may never get used to.

26

Taylor plopped down on the couch next to Addison Friday afternoon. "Tell me everything."

Details of her first date with Logan trickled through their conversation over the next few minutes. The date had been flawless, right down to the very last moment. "Taylor, I've never felt this way."

"He kissed you." Taylor fell back on the couch, her arms flailing toward the ceiling. "Finally."

"This is serious."

Taylor shot straight up, a mischievous smile curving the corners of her mouth. "He did, didn't he?"

"Yes! It's like being launched into a fantasy, and I never want to leave."

Taylor's smile broadened. "I'm so happy for you. You deserve this more than anybody I know."

Stretching her arms and legs, Addison grinned at her friend. "What would I do without you?"

"You would be lost without me, so don't even try."

Addison grabbed her phone off the table where it had rested all morning. Turning it over, she stared at the screen. "What in the world?"

"What's wrong?"

"I have thirty-five missed calls."

"Wow, when did you become so popular?"

"Ha, ha." Her clipped, edgy laugh dimmed as she swiped the screen and saw Philip's name. It was only a few less than yesterday. Uneasiness settled in her stomach. "It was Philip."

"What do you mean it was Philip?"

Addison glanced at it again, hoping she'd see other callers, different names, a different number, Logan's number. She didn't. "He called thirty-five times."

Taylor stared at her, horror stricken. "Talk about an obsession."

Addison stared at the phone, her hand trembling. What did she ever see in him? "Should I call him back?"

"Are you crazy?"

"He won't stop until I talk to him."

"Do not call him back. You owe him nothing. Besides, that's the last thing you need right now. Enjoy your happiness. You know he'll ruin it."

Whatever his purpose was for doing this, it frightened her. "Taylor, I can't just keep ignoring him. What if he shows up here?"

"If he does, don't answer the door. Eventually he'll get the hint that you want nothing to do with him. He doesn't even deserve your friendship."

Releasing a swift breath, she turned toward Taylor. "Do you think it would do any good to take out a restraining order?"

"A restraining order is the best idea I've heard from you yet." Taylor frowned. "Did he do something to you?"

"I just don't want him to think he can come here whenever he wants. Because he can't. I don't want to see him. Ever again."

"I'm so proud of you."

"No one can know about this. Logan being a cop and everything, he may think I'm being overdramatic. Or it may scare him off."

"My lips are sealed. Now, enough about Philip, when are you seeing Logan again?"

"He's been out of town a few days. But he did say he wanted to get together soon." Remembering, she smiled. "I hope he calls when he gets back in town, but I shouldn't be too anxious."

"Yes, you should. It's okay to be anxious. You wasted a lot of years on you-know-who. You can really start living now."

"I don't know if I can go through with it." She stared at her phone.

"With what?"

"The restraining order." Addison fell back against the couch. "I will feel so guilty."

"You have no reason to. It's his fault. That is definitely considered stalking."

Addison looked at her friend, her very best friend, and wanted to squeeze her. Taylor was right. She'd done nothing wrong. She was only trying to move on with her life. There couldn't be anything wrong with that. And since Philip wouldn't listen, maybe this would make him take her seriously.

But most of all, she was worried. Really worried. What if he came and lost his temper when no one was there to stop him? She told herself this over and over, trying to convince herself, but still it wasn't easy. Even when she walked through the police station doors an hour later, she was still trying to talk herself out of it.

"Addison?"

Throat constricting, she turned.

"What are you doing here?" When Matt moved toward her, tugging his hat into place, she berated herself. Wasn't Matt supposed to be in Indiana with Logan?

"Well, I uh ... I was ... " she stuttered. No matter how she searched, she couldn't find a sensible explanation. And it didn't matter that reading people was part of his job description and he would definitely be able to read her. She couldn't tell him the truth.

"You're here to see Logan?"

Or hopefully he would think that. A sigh left her throat before she could stop it. "I was in the neighborhood."

"He isn't scheduled to work tonight." Matt fished for something in his pocket, then pulled out his phone. "You haven't talked to him?"

"Not today."

"Huh," Matt murmured more to himself, but then tilted his head slightly as if assessing the situation. "Is something wrong?"

"No, I was on my way to work and just thought ... but it's okay." *What have I done?* "Okay, well, thanks. I better go." After giving him a brief hug, she moved toward the door. "See you later."

"I'll tell him you came by."

Swallowing the lump in her throat, she turned but still moved backward, closer to the door. "Uh, no ... please don't. I'll tell him when I talk to him." If he called her. She hadn't talked to him since he left for Indiana. It was ridiculous to worry because he didn't call her when he came back. And was off today. No, she would not go there. "Bye."

Six hours later, after a long night of waiting on twenty couples and families combined, Addison was following Taylor to her car when his familiar voice called her name. "Addison."

She slowed and looked back. "Logan? What're you doing here?"

"I came to follow you home, but I could drive you."

"That's so sweet," Taylor said, not even trying to disguise her excitement. "See you at home."

"Okay, bye."

Shifting her focus, she turned to face Logan, amazed that he was standing here waiting for her. "How was Indiana?"

"Good. We came back sooner than expected. I'm glad to be back."

She forced a smile as a jolt of insecurity surged through her. "I'm glad you had a good trip."

"I know it's late, but I couldn't wait until tomorrow to see you again." Logan took a step closer, his eyes sparkling like diamonds against the moonlight.

Her cheeks burned as Logan took her hand and helped her into the truck. A warm glow expanded through her body when he closed the door.

"Are you too tired to grab a drink with me?"

Her stomach lurched in response to his question. "I don't drink." She winced, suddenly aware of how harsh that had sounded.

"Me either. I meant a Coke. Like a soft drink. I'm sorry. I guess it did sound like that."

Swallowing a measure of remorse, she fixed her gaze on him, thankful for his presence. She'd missed him more than she'd realized. "I would love to."

"Okay, how about Baker's Sandwich Shop?"

"I love Mr. Baker."

"He's a nice guy. It's hard to believe he never married. It's always been just him and his dog."

"Posie," they both said in unison with a laugh.

"I used to stop there when I visited Aunt Brenda every summer." Addison had always secretly wished he was her grandfather, something she never had. "When did you get back in town?"

"Last night. I had a hundred things to do today or I would've called you earlier."

At least he didn't lie about it. The lasting effects of her toxic relationship with Philip tugged and pressed. But Logan had nothing to do with any of that and he didn't deserve her insecure thoughts at his expense. So instead she said, "I'm glad you're back."

Her victory was rewarded with a long tender glance, and he reached for her fingers and tucked them securely within his. "Me too. I missed you."

There was a moment of awkward silence, but the smile that graced his lips remained sincere. "What have you been up to?"

"Working mostly."

After Logan parked, they walked inside to the scent of fresh cinnamon rolls. Logan led her to a corner booth.

"I should probably let Taylor know I'm not coming straight home."

"Okay, I'll be right back. Got to wash my hands. I stopped for gas earlier."

Addison grabbed her phone, watching Logan walk away. She skipped over Philip's name in the visible notifications, fighting the warning signals knotting in her stomach that she'd not taken out the restraining order earlier today. And how she hadn't mentioned seeing Matt.

Logan brought me to a sandwich shop to grab a drink, so I'll be home later.

Taylor's response caused a lighthearted laugh. She slipped her phone into her purse just as Logan returned. Logan ... a considerate, kindhearted gentleman. The type of man she didn't believe existed. Until now. And she never wanted to let him go.

They talked for what seemed like only minutes, but when she glanced at her phone it was two hours later. "Do you know what time it is?"

Logan looked at his watch. "I'm so sorry. I didn't mean to keep you out this late."

"I could've sat here all night."

"Me too. I can't believe it's after two."

Addison yawned, stifling a chuckle. "It doesn't seem that late."

"It doesn't, but I know you're tired. Your aunt would not appreciate me keeping you out this late."

The drive to her house was too short. But even after they arrived at her house, he didn't leave immediately. They sat in his truck still talking, still in each other's presence. It was as if he wanted to stay near her as badly as she didn't want to see him go.

With another glance at the clock on the dashboard, she couldn't put it off any longer. "I really should go. Thank you for bringing me home."

His gaze flicked to her lips and her body trembled in response. He jumped out of the truck, walked around to her side, and lifted her into his arms. In slow motion, he gently lowered her until her feet were steady on the ground, but he left no space between them. Their arms enfolded, they clung to each other with a dangerous longing.

Every movement, every sound of the night stilled when Logan pulled her closer and muttered heated words against her neck. "I have never—" Lifting his hand gently, he brushed the back of his fingers against her cheek his gaze following silently. And she could sense the sheer, inescapable desire raging through his fingertips.

Suddenly the air wasn't entering her lungs fast enough as her heart vibrated in her throat.

"I've wanted you from that first day. It drove me mad not knowing who you were, not knowing your name."

A reckless thrill sealed her lips shut.

"And then that day you were there ... standing in my living room." His hands traveled down the length of her arms, and his fingers rested on the small of her waist. "I can't get you out my head."

"I know how you feel." Her voice was husky, breathy. She longed for him to close the distance between them as she relived the feel of his mouth on hers.

Smoldering sensations raced through her veins when his lips brushed against her cheek, tracing the line of her jaw, her lips. Something inside her awakened as her lips parted and she gave into her passion as a quiet whimper escaped. When he eagerly bound her mouth in a ravenous kiss, her ache transformed from a delightful thrill to a deep craving. The sound of his struggling breath ignited those sparks into a blazing fire.

His face was in her hair, his mouth at the base of her neck. Pressing herself even closer, her inner voice exerted itself. But she ignored the warnings. She closed her eyes for a moment. She wanted him, wanted him to want her.

She crushed her mouth to his again, the taste of him intoxicating.

With a jolt, he broke their connection and pulled back. "I have to go."

Stunned, she watched as he hurried to get inside his truck.

"Goodnight, Addison."

She backed away unaware of her surroundings, only the tingling sensation lingering on her lips.

Addison stood at the bottom of the stairs waiting until his truck disappeared down the street. Turning, she took the first step up the stairs and glanced over her shoulder for one last glimpse when someone grabbed her.

She screamed, her piercing voice lost on the breeze between the trees.

27

"Philip? What're you doing?"

"I was going to ask you the same question." His voice was strained.

A disturbing grip of fear crept into her airway, robbing her breath. She gasped for air as she prayed Taylor would hear them. But it had been over two hours since she'd texted her. Taylor would be dead asleep by now. As if reading her mind, Philip grabbed her arm, pulling her toward the back of the house.

"Let go of me," she cried out, as loud as she could.

He ignored her and kept walking, his stride too fast, causing her to trip over her feet. She stumbled and landed hard on the wooden planks beneath her. Through watery eyes, she searched the area behind her, but there was no one there to save her. A flood of tears overflowed onto her cheeks, splashing onto her lips.

Tugging her with a tightened grip, Philip didn't stop until he reached the sand dunes just beyond the stairway leading to the ocean. "What were you doing with Tant?"

Every poor decision she'd made regarding Philip taunted her.

"Answer me," he demanded.

"Nothing." She closed her eyes and tilted her head slightly, anticipating her punishment. "He just drove me home from work."

He snatched her in one fluid motion, and she was suddenly face-to-face with him. "And you thought that was a good idea?"

"It was nothing." The lie was vital, yet the truth bled through her veins. He knew. His fingers dug into her skin and the pain doubled with her fear dimmed her vision. "You're hurting me."

"Hurting you?" With a sharp blow, he slapped her against the head and knocked her feet out from under her. Strips of bright light flashed before her eyes.

She cried out as pain seared through her head.

"You were all over him." His grip tightened as he yanked her back to her feet. "You think you can ignore me and pretend I no longer exist?" His voice had a sarcastic edge. He forced his lips hard against hers.

She bit his lip, and he pushed her backward. "Ouch!" Philip shouted. "You—"

"Philip, please, it's not what you think." Through blurred eyes, she begged him, though Philip knew perfectly well what was happening after witnessing her with Logan only moments ago.

"You liar!" With a dark glance, Philip slapped her again, the sting immediate and sharp like needles poking through her scalp.

He knew just where to hit her—where there'd be no proof. Philip wouldn't stop until he beat the truth from her. She couldn't take much more. His breath reeked of alcohol and something else.

"Please, Philip, I'm sorry." She pulled back, but he yanked her hard to the ground.

He lowered onto his knees pinning her arms to the ground. "You're not going anywhere." His voice was low, the menace behind his words slicing chills across her skin. "I'm giving you exactly what you were begging Tant to do."

"Please, Philip. Please, you're hurting me."

"You will not make a fool of me," he sneered through gritted teeth as he ripped her shirt from her chest.

On Saturday morning, the sun radiated through Logan's blinds, waking him. His first thought before opening his eyes was Addison, centered on that last moment. The pivotal second when he made the decision to leave her standing there. He had to. Things had almost gone too far. He wanted her more than he'd ever wanted anything.

After a five-mile run, he took his time preparing for the day. After keeping her out so late he didn't want to call her too early, so he waited.

Two hours later, he could wait no longer. He paced back and forth when the call went straight to voice mail. After trying again for an hour and sending several text messages, he got worried and drove toward her house. He was overreacting, but he couldn't help it. He had to see her. What if it had upset her him leaving so suddenly with no explanation after his reckless behavior?

His ring tone echoed as he pulled to a stoplight. Peeking at the name across the screen, he exhaled. It wasn't Addison, it was Nathan. He dropped the phone onto the seat, disappointed.

Moments later, he pulled his truck into Addison's empty parking space. Disappointment washed over him. Taylor was standing by her car and waved at him, but she wasn't smiling. He parked his car and, after climbing out, he walked toward her. Taylor would know where Addison had gone. She must have had to work this morning. Guilt washed over him. He shouldn't have kept her out so late.

"What are you doing here so early?"

"I was hoping to see Addison. Her phone went straight to voice-mail. Did she have to work this morning?"

"No, but she was already gone when I got up. There was a note saying she had to go home. I thought maybe she told you." Taylor laughed. "I actually thought she was taking you home to meet her mama."

"No, she didn't say anything last night." She had never spoke much of her family.

Taylor's brow furrowed. "Did something happen last night?"

179

"What do you mean?"

"I don't know, early this morning I could've sworn I heard her crying. I thought I was dreaming. But then it stopped."

A rush of panic seized Logan. "Why would she be crying?" he said more to himself.

"I don't know. Like I said, maybe I was dreaming."

Logan's phone vibrated and he pulled it from his pocket, hoping it was her. Nathan's name appeared across the screen. Pressing mute, he slipped it back into his pocket.

"Have you talked to her this morning?" he asked, Taylor.

"No, I didn't think about calling. I just assumed she missed her mama and wanted to visit. I know she's scheduled to work tonight, so I guess she'll be back this afternoon."

Logan braced himself for the next question. He didn't want to seem possessive, but he really wanted to see her. "What time does she have to be at work?"

"Four-thirty. If I talk to her before then, I'll tell her to call you." Taylor said, running down the stairs. "I better go, I'm running late for an appointment."

Taylor left and Logan returned to his truck.

He dialed her number one more time after climbing into the truck. The voicemail instructions burned his eardrums. Just as he closed the phone, it vibrated. Again.

Logan decided to listen to the message Nathan left, instead of calling him back. "Call me as soon as you get this message."

Not right now, Nathan.

He typed another message to Addison before turning the truck around. He erased it. What was the use? Her phone was either dead or she had it powered off.

Throwing the phone in the seat, irrational thoughts crossed his mind, and with tightened lips, he exhaled hard.

He left with only a feeble plan to be at the Olive Garden by four-fifteen.

28

Addison arrived at her mama's house in Raleigh on Saturday morning, not really remembering anything about the drive. She only knew as she walked toward the house, she had nowhere else to go. Her leg muscles tightened as she climbed the few steps onto the porch just as Mama walked out the front door. A swirl of cigarette smoke hovering in the air between them.

"Addison, what on earth are you doing here?" Mama's voice should have been soothing to her soul; instead the sound caused her lungs to constrict, making breathing difficult.

Addison's tears threatened to escape, but she kept her chin up, her sunglasses on. "I haven't been by in so long."

"And we both know that's for the best. You never know what kind of mood your daddy will be in." She grunted. "I was getting ready to leave."

"Could we go somewhere? I need to talk to you."

"I don't have time right now. I was supposed to be there ten minutes ago."

Addison stared ahead, ignoring the way her stomach lurched in response to Mama's cold words. "But it's important."

"And what I'm doing ain't important? You can't just drop in when-

181

ever you want to. Now, go on. Next time call me first. Hurry before I wake your daddy from his nap with all this arguing."

Instantly regret swept through her. Mama's gaze kept shifting between Addison and the bedroom door. "I'm sorry, baby girl. You should've called first."

Addison hurried to her car leaving behind the trail of smoke burning her nose. With one last glance at her mama, she blinked back tears. There was no regret in her mama's eyes, only unease.

"Call me first the next time."

With more verbal lashings from her mama than she could count, Addison had developed a thick skin over the years. It was necessary in order to survive in a world where hugs and kisses were non-existent. But right now, her skin felt paper thin and her legs wobbly as she climbed in her car.

Why had she come here? Four years might have passed since she'd left this place, but Addison remembered every detail of the landscape, every detail of what drove her away. She sped down the long stretch of road, her mind whirling in pain, dark memories surfacing.

It was several years before Daddy died that Mama had another baby.

When Addison first saw the baby, she was excited. She was a big sister, but something in their little world changed from that day on. Mama was suddenly nervous all the time, smoking even more cigarettes back to back. And Daddy acted different. There was something sad about his eyes, a sadness that never went away.

It wasn't until years after Daddy died that Addison's long-forgotten memories unveiled what had happened.

There were always different men visiting with Mama when Daddy was off at work. But one of those men had dark red hair, and so did her baby sister.

When that same red-headed man appeared at their front door with a bouquet of flowers after Casey arrived, Mama had shooed him off and told him to never return.

Addison never said anything to her mama, but instead carried the dark secret deep inside. It wasn't a sickness that had killed her daddy. Mama had killed him.

Daddy had died of a broken heart.

There was nowhere to go. Driving home to Wilmington and facing Taylor or Logan was the last thing she needed. Taylor would see right through her, and Addison would tell her everything.

Logan would comfort her. He had already in the short period of time she'd spent with him, softened her skin, made her believe that happily ever afters could be real.

But they weren't.

And the only way to avoid that kind of love he'd introduced to her heart, was to keep her distance.

She needed time to think, even though, thinking was the one thing she couldn't escape no matter how she tried. So, she pulled into the Triangle Town Center parking lot.

While walking along the mall, she studied the displays in the store windows, trying to free her mind from the violent images.

People of all ages passed, some sitting on the mall benches, others shopping. Small children played in the kid zone area, while others were led by their mamas. With no warning, a flood of tears tumbled out in a desperate race. She cared nothing about what people thought, her sorrow swelling with each moment. She walked faster, but with each step, her sobs deepened.

No one here knew her anyway. In a city this big, it was unusual to run into anyone she recognized. Then she spotted a lady, she recognized from the church she attended as a child, walking on the opposite side. Turning quickly, she slammed into someone behind her.

Nathan grabbed her arms. "I thought that was you. Why are you wearing sunglasses inside the building?"

Stunned to see his familiar face, she instinctively fell into Nathan as he wrapped his arms around her.

"Is something wrong?" he asked.

She composed herself and looked up into his worried eyes. "I have to get out of here," she told him, her voice hoarse.

A heaving sound escaped her lips as she hurried toward the exit.

Nathan grabbed her hand pulling her to a stop. "Addison, what is it? Has something happened?"

He was so familiar, so like Logan, she didn't want to let go. She shook her head over and over at the clamor of her shattered life, breaking into a million pieces. Pieces that would never find their way back together. "I need to get out of here." Turning, she wiped the errant tears from her chin, straightening her posture.

"Okay. I'll walk with you." When they reached Nathan's truck, she removed her sunglasses and Nathan gasped. Harsh sobs swept through her body, the unforgiving ache in her chest, rocking her back and forth.

"You're coming with me."

As Nathan drove away from the mall, she stared across the parking lot, wishing to wake from a horrid nightmare. But when they reached his apartment, she knew she would never wake from this terrible dream. Everything she had experienced was real and even now her body ached from where she had wrestled with all her might last night.

Unable to share any details, Addison could only nod as Nathan asked endless questions. Until he figured out what had happened right after Logan dropped her off. How she had lost the battle—how Philip had won.

29

L ater that night, Addison pulled into her driveway and climbed from her car, relieved, yet unsettled. As hard as she'd tried to convince herself to call Logan, to explain what happened, she knew she couldn't.

Logan could never know.

Taylor wasn't here and for the first time she was glad she'd have the house to herself for a while. She sprawled across her bed, the many tears she'd cried claiming her once again. A hazy film dimmed her vision and minutes later, sleep prevailed.

The sound of the doorbell roused her, and she stood clumsily to walk toward the door. "Logan, you're here."

"Oh, Addison, I missed you. Why didn't you call me? I have been worried sick about you."

"I'm sorry. I just didn't know what to do. I didn't think you'd understand."

"Nathan told me everything. It's okay, don't blame him. He was only trying to help."

"But now you know we can never be together."

He leaned in and brushed his lips across her cheek, her mouth, her neck. "Addison, we can never be apart. I'll never leave your side. Nothing else matters. It will only be you and me for eternity ... eternity ... eternity ..."

She could feel his lips, could taste his breath. Darkness invaded the room, as he wrapped his arms around her waist pulling her down beside him, ripping her shirt. The floor felt hard, the sand sticking to her skin.

"No, don't. Please stop. You're hurting me, please."

She opened her heavy eyelids, fighting her way to consciousness, and then she saw his face. Philip.

She shot up, dark shadows covering the room as a shrill scream escaped her lips.

Monday afternoon, Logan stared into space as he sat on Matt's couch across from him. "I still haven't heard from her."

"Hey, don't let it bother you. If something was wrong, she would've told you, right? And if she doesn't want whatever is going on with y'all ... it's better to find out now, before you get too serious."

It was too late for that. But maybe that was it. He had pushed her too far the other night. Let things get way out of hand. And then left her standing there like she had done something wrong—like it was her fault.

"It doesn't make sense though. I thought she was really into you."

"Me too." Logan leaned back.

"I mean, if she didn't want to see you anymore, why would she stop by the station?"

Matt's question jerked Logan forward. "The station? Addison came to the station? When?"

"The other day."

This new revelation helped Logan stuff unpleasant thoughts of this being his fault to a lower level. "Which day?"

"The Friday after we came back from Indiana. It was weird though."

"What do you mean? What did she say?"

"She said she hadn't heard from you. Which was weird for her to come by if she didn't even know you were back."

Those unpleasant thoughts were creeping back to the surface. Why hadn't he called her? It was a foolish assumption to wait a whole day before contacting her. What if that combined with his reckless display of emotions the other night scared her off?

"She was acting different."

"Like how?"

"I don't know exactly. She just acted nervous. Like she was really surprised to see me there. Which was weird 'cause she knows we work together," he added for clarification. "Did she not tell you?"

"No, she didn't." Clearly, he had missed something. Nothing Matt said was making any sense. "What was she doing there?"

"You think something's wrong?"

"I don't know. She won't return my calls, and she didn't show up for work last night. Why didn't she say anything about stopping by the station?"

"I'm sure she'll have a good explanation. It's only been two days. And if it doesn't work out with her, there are other girls out there."

Wrong. There is only one girl for me.

As Logan drove away from Matt's house, the last night, the last week he'd spent with her replayed through his brain until he thought he'd scream.

Addison reached for her phone in the dark room, reeling inside. The dream was so real, so vivid, she could still feel Philip's fingers lingering on her. She wanted Logan. She needed to see him.

187

Unlocking the phone, she searched for his name, eager to hear his voice. She read the two messages he'd sent earlier.

Hey, I was just thinking of you. Logan

Hey, I was getting worried. I hope everything's okay. Call me. Logan

Gripping the direct passageway to Logan in her palm, she turned the power off and leaned against the bed frame.

I can't call him.

She couldn't bear it if Logan called again. She wouldn't be able to stop herself from answering this time.

Tuesday morning brought a mixture of relief and regret. Addison was glad to be released from the relentless nightmares haunting her sleep, though now she was faced with reality. Forcing herself from the bed, she walked into the kitchen still wearing her pajamas.

Taylor stood against the counter pouring a cup of coffee. "Hey, it's about time. I've been worried sick about you. How was your visit with your mom?"

"She was busy."

"What? But I thought your note said … " Taylor gasped when she glanced at her. "What's wrong?"

"It's a long story. I really don't feel up to talking about it right now. Is there any more coffee?"

Taylor poured another cup. "Did something happen with Logan? He's been trying to reach you. He said he hadn't heard from you. I tried calling you too."

"Yeah, I know."

"So, you talked to him?"

She forced a fake smile, her tears threatening to escape. "No."

"Did something happen between you two? He seemed really anxious to talk to you."

The thought of him ripped through her heart. She studied the countertops as she moved in slow motion.

"He has come by here every day."

Addison snatched her coffee, spilling some on the counter. "He came here?" She tried to keep the eagerness from her voice, but it was unsuccessful.

"Why are you so surprised?"

Addison stared across the room at her best friend. She should tell her the truth. She sat down at the kitchen table across from Taylor. "I'm not surprised. I just can't see him anymore."

Taylor grabbed her arms. "What? What're you talking about? You're in love with that boy. What happened?"

There was a soft tapping at the front door. Addison froze. "I'm not here."

"But your car's out there? I can't keep putting him off. He knows you're here."

Addison scrambled out of her chair and rushed to her room. "I can't see him, Taylor. I'm not here, no matter who it is."

Once safely hidden in her bedroom, Addison peeked through the window. It was Logan. Taking a moment to catch her breath, she slid down against the door frame, sobs wracking her body.

Logan paced back and forth on Addison's front porch, his determination to see her unsettling him. He needed answers. Was she with Philip right now? No, he didn't believe that. He wouldn't. Not until he spoke with her. But why hadn't she responded to his messages, his calls?

Taking several slow deep breaths, he knocked on the door. Taylor opened the door, stepping onto the front step before he had a chance to knock again.

"She's not here."

Logan glanced at her car before peering around Taylor through the living room. She pulled the door closed. "Her car's here. I have to see her, Taylor."

"What happened?" A note of contempt rang through her voice.

His eyes darted around her. He looked through the window. "What do you mean?"

"The other night? Why is she so upset?" Taylor glared at him. "Her eyes are almost swollen shut."

"What?" His stomach tensed, his pulse spiking. "She's here?" He reached for the door. "I need to see her."

"No, she doesn't want to see you."

"I don't understand."

"Me either. All I know is she's stayed locked up in her room since Saturday night. I thought she was sick. But that wasn't it. Something's wrong and it all points to you."

His pulse quickened. "Has she been with Philip any this weekend?"

Her nose crinkled, but he didn't miss the flash of uncertainty. "Philip?" Taylor rolled her eyes and started to close the door.

"Wait, please, Taylor? I have to see her."

"She doesn't want to see you." Taylor slammed the door. Logan stared at the door, dumbfounded.

Addison woke still curled in a ball, lying on the floor in front of her door. Her body ached as she pulled herself into a sitting position. She stood, dizziness sweeping through her. After taking a few moments to gather her strength, she moved toward the bed and turned on her lamp.

She stumbled through the darkened house, toward the kitchen, her throat burning with thirst. A note attached to the refrigerator caught her attention.

Had to go to work, we'll talk later if you're awake when I get home. If not, definitely tomorrow. Call me if you need anything!! Taylor

Queasiness rippled through her chest as she recalled Taylor's conversation with Logan. She couldn't bear to let him believe this had anything to do with him. But what did it matter? She needed to let Logan go.

Addison looked through the window, her reflection staring back at her. There was a part of her that would've given into Logan that night. The same night everything had been stolen from her. If Philip hadn't witnessed that moment she lost herself with Logan, something she had never allowed with Philip, maybe none of this would've happened.

Logan deserved better than her—better than this.

Feeling like she was suffocating, Addison stepped outside the back door to get some fresh air. The sun had already descended from the sky and the moon was hidden behind thick, dark clouds. Memories of her night dancing with Logan then standing by the seaside, his hand in hers, brought on a fresh wave of tears. The beauty of that night was forever ruined. Too afraid to walk any closer, she sat on the edge of her porch and buried her face in her hands, her tears flowing freely from all she'd lost.

She screamed when warm hands grasped her bare shoulders.

Logan stumbled back in shock at the shrill cry that escaped Addison's lips. Her arms flailed wildly at him and he grabbed them in an attempt to calm her.

"No, please, no," she repeated over and over, her voice rasping in terror.

"Addison, it's okay, it's just me."

"Logan?"

The instant change in her expression alarmed him. The dark sky hid her face, but her tears sparkled against the light from the kitchen window.

"What are you doing here? You scared me to death." A wave of relief leaked into her voice.

"I'm sorry. I came by earlier, but Taylor wouldn't let me see you."

Her brow furrowed as she scooted over.

He took the space next to her, but she stood, walking toward the door.

"What's wrong?" He drew a breath through his constricted throat. "I've been trying to call."

"I ... I had to go out of town."

"I know. Taylor told me you were visiting your mom." He stood and walked toward her.

She stumbled back, putting distance between them.

"Did something happen?"

Her eyes softened, filling with fresh tears. "I ..." Her voice broke and she cleared her throat. "I've just got a lot going on right now."

He took a step closer with slow deliberation. "Did I do something?" He came to a stop, leaving only inches between them.

"No."

He took her hand, the soft feel of her skin tormenting him. Her eyes fell to their hands intertwined and a rush of sobs erupted from her. Pulling her against his chest, he held her tight. With each moment that passed, the more vigorously she held to him. She trembled against him and his mind raced. Something had happened, but what?

"I'm so sorry." Slowly, she pulled away from him, wiping at her eyes.

"Addison, please tell me what's going on."

She took a step back and straightened, but she said nothing.

Desperation to end her pain gripped him. "Will you walk with me?"

"I can't." She glanced toward the ocean beyond the yard, her expression torn. "It would be better if you just left. I'm so sorry."

Her words took a moment to register. His knees buckled and he grabbed the rail to support his weight. "What?"

She kept her gaze averted, the pain in her eyes evident.

"Look at me."

She lifted her chin to meet his gaze and he cupped her face in his hands. "Addison, please? Tell me what's going on."

"You are such a nice guy. I have enjoyed spending time with you, but I only want to be friends."

She gazed at him, the violet blue revealing a spark of affection. He couldn't look away as the depth of her stare drew him to her, and his body shifted closer.

He couldn't believe it—he wouldn't.

Leaning forward, his eyes fell to her parted mouth. His lips pressed against hers, and he savored the taste of her mouth. She responded to his kiss, with a desperation he hadn't felt before. It couldn't be over. He held her, and in that embrace, he felt everything they had meant to each other, the unspoken love leaving his body aching with defeat.

He wasn't sure how long they stood there. Those three words were on the tip of his tongue, but before he could speak, she escaped his embrace and stepped through the back door.

"Bye, Logan. I'm sorry," she whispered, her eyes spilling over with fresh tears as she closed the door behind her.

In shock, he stared at the door, willing her to open it. To come back to him—to explain what had happened. A few minutes passed before he took the few steps to his truck parked across the street. His hands trembling, he dropped his keys and it produced a chinking sound against the concrete driveway. He glanced back at her house. The curtain was pulled away from the window and a soft light glimmered, beckoning him to return. But then seconds later, the curtain fell back into place.

Oh, Addison, what happened? Logan climbed into his truck, his hope crushed.

Two weeks later, Addison stared at the ocean from the safety of her back porch. The beauty that had once led her to the body of water now stretched in front of her like a looming, shadowy landscape that only produced frightening memories.

As ridiculous as it was, Addison hoped Logan would show up again, demand that he would never let her go, never let anyone hurt her ever again, and love her for all eternity. But she got exactly what she'd asked for even though that last kiss had changed everything, and she wanted to take it all back.

But it was too late.

She no longer had any faith that he would return. Not now. Not after weeks had already crept by without hearing a word from him.

"Addison?"

A frightened wail squeaked from her throat. Logan's sister rounded the corner of her house. "Ami, what are you doing here?"

Ami stepped onto the porch. "I came to see you. I thought about calling first, but I was scared you would tell me not to come."

Seeing Ami was like a breath of fresh air. On impulse Addison rushed to her, wrapping her arms around her. "Are you crazy? I would never tell you not to come. It's so good to see you."

"How are you?"

"I'm good." Addison forced a smile. "I've missed you so much. Do you want to come in?"

"Of course, I do."

They spent the next hour talking around everything that had anything to do with Logan. At least Ami wasn't upset with her. If Nathan had told Logan, she would know by now, unless Logan blamed her.

She shook the disturbing thought free. Nathan promised to never tell anyone. And she'd only told Taylor a few details. Enough to settle her curiosity.

On Ami's departure, Addison observed too late that she had promised Ami that she would stop by her house soon. She missed Ami's family.

She missed Logan.

Logan drove through the neighborhood for the twentieth time, making sure there was no one lurking around.

"You've covered every inch of this area. And driven by her house enough already. She's sleeping. Take another route," Matt said, typing something into the computer, "before you get pulled from this zone."

Logan stared straight ahead. "I can't. I have to make sure she's all right."

"Why don't you take tomorrow off and do something for yourself for a change?"

Logan turned the car around so that he would have to drive by her house once more before heading to the coffee shop down the street. "There's nothing to do."

"Logan, I'm your best friend, but also your coworker. It's not okay to stalk her like this. Take some time off," Matt said, stepping from the vehicle. "It's been over a month."

Restlessness moved within him, growing in capacity, mounting his frustration, stretching his doubt. He snatched the keys from the ignition and stormed from the cruiser to the restaurant.

When did his concern for Addison become stalking? Why did everything have to remind him of Addison? Everything was going so perfectly.

He refused to believe she only thought of him as a friend.

The chemistry flowing between them wasn't one-sided. Her reaction, the emotion, was more real than anything he'd ever felt. And made his decision to leave her standing there even more unbearable.

After regulating his breathing from the sharp memory of those last moments, and his internal lecture beating him down for the hundredth time, his attention jerked back to reality.

That couldn't be the only reason. It had to be Philip. She wasn't over him. And he knew deep down that was his reason for driving by her house every night. He had to know if Philip was hanging around her house. Spending time with her. Taking his place.

When his shift ended at the break of dawn, he drove toward his apartment but had no desire to see anyone. He worked every available hour, took extra shifts, a part-time position at a local high school for summer school. From sundown to sunup, then noon through the evening he worked, then slept, then worked.

But now it was Saturday morning, and there was no school today. His roommates would be home.

Slamming his fists against the steering wheel, he pulled to a stop at the intersection. He turned the truck and headed to his mom's. At least there, in his old bedroom, he could have some privacy.

Ami met him at the door. "What are you doing here?"

"Am I not allowed to come here either?"

She took a step back, her brows crinkled. "What's wrong with you?"

He pushed past her. "Nothing. I just want to be alone."

"Why, so you can sulk? Why don't you just call her already?"

He turned and glared at his sister, but seeing tears in her eyes, he bit his tongue. He grabbed Ami and pulled her into a hug. "I'm sorry. I'm just a little touchy."

She sobbed against him, and he took a deep, pained breath.

"Please call her. This isn't right. You're so angry." She hicupped. "And she doesn't sound like herself anymore. She looks so sad. I don't understand. What happened?"

He braced himself. "Ami, I can't talk about this. I'm sorry. I just came here to be alone. I worked all night and need some sleep. I'll see you later, okay?" He jogged up the stairs, leaving her standing in the hall.

"Well, I think you're both stupid."

Her words replayed in his mind over and over for the entire afternoon, until he believed it himself. Why hadn't he called her? Why hadn't he tried to find out the real reason she no longer wanted to see him?

Addison frowned at the bright puffy clouds scattered across the blue sky like patches of white cotton candy. Rain and dark brooding clouds would suit her mood much better.

"Hey." Taylor sat on the swing next to her. "Are you working tonight?"

"No, this is my only day off this week."

"Good, you need a day off. You need to get out of this house."

"I'm supposed to go to Ami's today."

Taylor's gaze rose, along with her curious smile. "Ami Tant?"

"I should call her and cancel. What if I run into Logan?"

"So, what if you do? I wish you would run into him. That's what

197

you want, to be with him." Her voice was exceptionally compassionate. "Talk to him. He deserves at least that."

Addison stiffened in anticipation. It had been over a month since she'd spoken to Logan. "Don't look at me like that."

"I don't know what happened between you two, but I know you're in love with him. I've never seen you this way over anyone. You might as well admit it. I *am* your best friend."

Addison laughed, a quick throaty sound. Her first laugh in over a month. "The night Philip was waiting for me when I came home—"

Taylor leaned back against her chair, her eyebrows furrowed.

"He was waiting outside, around the corner. He saw me kissing Logan." Addison studied the wood planks beneath her feet. She stared at the cracks so hard, they started moving. Clearing her vision, she glanced beyond the yard where the water shimmered in the sunlight. Her resolve to tell her the whole truth collapsed with each second.

"So, it's none of his business. You did nothing wrong. Go to Ami's, and I hope Logan shows up."

Addison aimed her gaze at Taylor. The truth of that night was better left in the past. It would only strip away at hardened scabs and expose fresh wounds to more pain. Staying silent and pretending it had never happened would help her heal faster.

A single thought circulated in slow motion like the clouds shifting across the sky, all sensible doubt dissolving.

What if Logan was there?

31

The sun had already dipped beyond the trees when Addison finally found the nerve to drive to the Tants'. It had been so long since she'd been there. With her stomach in knots, she parked at the curb just like she had that first time.

A light breeze whipped her hair around her shoulders as she climbed from the car. And in that breeze, she could almost smell Logan's grill burning charcoal from the back yard. But it wasn't. Logan wasn't here. And a sharp sting of disappointment spiraled through her chest.

Nathan met her at the door. "Addison." He stepped outside and, after closing the door, pulled her into a warm embrace.

Seeing him brought back a rush of dark memories. She clung to him for only a moment before pulling away. "I wasn't expecting to see you here."

"Just visiting for a few hours before I head back home to Raleigh." His worried gaze zeroed in on her. "How are you?"

"I'm okay." She paused, not wanting to ask the next question, but it was unavoidable. "You didn't—"

He stopped her before she could finish and took her hand. "No, of course not. Did you press charges?" At the mention of the crime, Nathan's face softened.

Addison blinked into the darkening sky. "I don't live in the same kind of world as you."

"What's that supposed to mean?"

"Your family. My family. It's as if they're from different planets. My mama is too self-absorbed to care about anything that happens to me." *And my stepdaddy's too drunk.* Her past was a piece of her she kept buried. But she had just given away a snippet to a man who was like a brother. A brother that came from a family she wanted to call her own.

Nathan considered her with a baffled expression. "I don't believe that. Surely your mom would—"

"My aunt ... she's done so much for me ... I could never ask her to return from her trip. Besides, it doesn't matter."

"Of course, it matters."

"He probably doesn't remember." She emphasized the phrase to affirm the truth for herself. "It's better to just forget."

"We will support you."

"I can't, Nathan." The countless hours she'd contemplated a charge against Philip had left her on edge and always with the same conclusion. "I really appreciate you being there for me. I don't know what I would've done if you hadn't found me." To steady herself, she placed a hand against the railing. "Please just let it go."

"What about Logan?"

"What about him?"

"I've never seen him this way. You distancing yourself has almost killed him. Talk to him."

The engine of a truck roared, and she glanced absentmindedly. Logan's Silverado pulled into the driveway. The sight of him sucked the air from her lungs. "I don't know if I can do this."

"Don't let that monster steal all your joy. Give Logan a chance."

In the wake of Nathan's words, silence fell between them as she considered his advice.

"I'll wait here and talk to him."

"Good," Nathan said as he stepped past her and entered the house as the sound of the truck's engine faded.

Addison tried to imagine a life where nothing had happened, and they could pick up where they had left off. But she had glimpsed a world where darkness could slash through your hopes and dreams and leave you shattered and broken.

———

Logan's heart raced seeing Addison standing on his parents' front porch. Immediately he was transported to a time when his days of anticipation of being with her weren't laced with an uncomfortable longing and sorrow.

He stayed in the truck, every fiber of his being silently indulging in her presence. When Nathan walked inside, Addison didn't. She stood there, waiting for him.

Logan climbed from the truck, confused and physically aching at the sight of her. She had lost weight and looked weak, as if she could tumble over at the slightest flutter of wind.

"Logan, I—"

All logic abandoned him, and he surrendered to his first instinct. He went to her and, without restraint, wrapped her inside his arms. He was admitting to himself, to her, that he couldn't live without her. That it didn't matter if something was still going on between her and Philip.

"I'm sorry," she cried, her voice crushed, broken.

He clung tighter, unable to let go. "I've missed you so much."

Pulling her only a few inches away, he tilted his head to get a better look at her. Her apprehension ruffled his insides. In her silence, he studied her closer. She swayed, her stance shaky, as if she would shatter into a thousand pieces. "Are you okay?"

Tears trickled down her cheeks. "I just—"

There was more, but she stopped. He had been so worried. Had been unable to get a full night's sleep for weeks. Whatever had happened had devastated her.

Maybe it had something to do with her parents. Everything had been fine that night before she went to see her mother. A longing, wistful smile had filled her face as he drove away. He had replayed that image a thousand times over the last few weeks. The words to his question hung on the tip of his tongue, but he didn't want to impose, to push her further away.

There was something in her gaze, a storm brewing behind those eyes. Their undeniable connection nearly brought him to his knees.

Suddenly, she said, "Does this mean we can still be friends?"

Friends? The muscle in his jaw tightened. "Of course." He rubbed the back of his neck, his thoughts on all the reasons he couldn't let her go. The temptation to demand an explanation faded. The main thing was her presence. Nothing else mattered, he tried telling himself, sharing the small area of space with her. "Did I do something?"

"No, Logan, you have been so good to me. If only I ... I don't deserve—"

It made no sense. What did her parents have to do with their relationship? He knew hardly anything about them. Why hadn't he asked more questions?

It had to be Philip. Or maybe it was all him. But her response didn't match her body language that was clearly screaming *I need you.* "Do you want to come in?"

"Yes, Ami's expecting me."

Ami. She was here to see his sister, not him. But she was here. And that was all that mattered.

He glanced at his twin brother as they entered the house, his brother's darkened gaze full of questions.

Addison ran up the stairs to Ami's room, leaving him standing there, his hands clasped behind his back, his heart breaking for her.

"How did it go?"

Logan forced a smile. "She still just wants to be friends."

"Oh, man."

"I don't understand."

"Maybe she just needs time."

"For what?" Logan registered the way Nathan excused her actions as if he knew more than he was saying. And something twisted in his gut. "How would you know anything about this?"

"I'm just trying to help."

Logan grabbed a Coke from the refrigerator and twisted off the top. "She just wants to be friends and that's that." It was likely that would never be enough for his heart. He took a long drink of the beverage. "Being friends is better than nothing right?"

Logan cringed at the words and nothing about them made sense. But he had no choice. The last few weeks had been torture. Remaining friends would be better than not seeing her at all.

When Ami brought her downstairs for a few minutes, Logan kept his distance. Every time Addison caught his gaze, her cheeks flamed a deep pink, her shy smile filled with regret. Her eyes were warm and intimate, and his stomach fluttered with each glance.

Ami dragged her back upstairs after a few minutes, and he shoved aside wasted thoughts. She was here now, and she was safe.

Eventually she'd give in and talk to him. And he would do the only thing he could. He would wait.

Logan followed Nathan to his truck. "Just give her some time. She'll come around."

Logan narrowed his eyes. "What makes you say that?"

"I see the way she looks at you. What can I say? I know women better than you." Nathan punched him in the arm. "Trust me, Logan. Be patient with her, just like you were today. I was actually proud of you."

"I hope you're right."

"I've never seen you act this way. Not even over Carrie."

Logan flinched. It was still hard hearing her name. "Carrie was different. I spent most of my time worrying what she was doing and who she was doing it with."

Nathan frowned. "I never meant to hurt you, Logan. I was tired of seeing her hurt you."

Logan's stomach tensed. "Were you together that night?"

"No, I would never do that to you. I despised her. I only wanted you to catch her, so you'd know the truth—so that you could move on. I'm sorry it ended the way it did. It wasn't your fault, Logan."

Painful memories emerged and he brushed them away as Nathan pulled him into a quick hug. "You're my brother. I love you, man."

He glanced up at Ami's bedroom window and caught a glimpse of Addison standing there staring down at him.

He wanted to rush upstairs, to steal her away, to hold her in his arms, but he couldn't. He entered the house and with each step asked himself—how would this ever be enough?

"What do you think of this one?"

Addison moved away from the window, glad for the distraction. "I like that."

Ami wore white pants with a black sleeveless top that hung lower in the back, flowing as she twirled in front of the mirror. She looked delicate in the lamplight, her blond hair teased for volume and bundled into a messy pile on top of her head.

Addison sat on the white lacy comforter covering Ami's bed thankful for their friendship.

The only reminder of the accident was a tiny pink scar on Ami's forehead. A scar that wasn't even noticeable unless you were looking for it. "What time is Zach picking you up?"

Ami applied a thin layer of clear lip gloss, the shine matching the sparkle in her light gray eye shadow. "I'm not going with Zach."

"Really?"

"I mean, he's going. A group of our friends are all going." She lowered her gaze. "There's a new guy."

"A new guy?"

For a wonderful few minutes, they talked about something ordinary, while Ami fussed over her makeup, reapplying powder and mascara. In those minutes, Addison escaped the constant turbulence of her thoughts.

"Yeah, he's really cute. I met him at a homeschooling event. I think he likes me." Ami walked across the room with a confident swing of her hips, a confidence that Addison was sure stemmed from a secure, tight-knit family.

"What about Zach? I thought you liked him."

Ami sulked, her lips puckered. "I do, but what does it matter? He treats me like a little sister."

Addison nodded in understanding. "Don't worry. Sometimes it takes longer for guys to catch on."

"Tell me about it. I can't wait on that boy forever."

Ami sprayed a mist of perfume and the floral fragrance lingered in the air, mixing with the clean, delicate scent of the Tants' home. The same scent that clung to Logan.

"Where are you going?"

"Carolina Beach Amusement Park." Ami sat on the bed next to her, the bounce of her landing bringing them so close they were touching. "Will you come with us?"

"Me?" Addison swallowed the knot forming in her throat as Ami rested her head on Addison's shoulder. "I don't want to intrude on your group thing."

"Are you kidding me? I want you there. I've missed you so much."

Addison knew exactly how she felt. She'd missed her too. She'd missed all of them. "I guess I can."

"Oh, thank you, Addison. Do you think it would work if I acted like I like Maverick a little? You know, to make Zach jealous?"

Addison ran her fingers over the lacy material of the bed spread. "Jealousy is the last thing you want in a boy you're dating. It might seem flattering at first, but it has nothing to do with the way he feels about you as a person. Jealousy leads a person to do things he wouldn't normally do ... sometimes really terrible things."

"I've never thought about it that way. Besides, I wouldn't want to use Maverick. He's really a nice guy, and I do like him." Ami's cheeks scrunched with her smile. "Oh, by the way, Logan's coming too."

Addison's pulse raced in an uneven rhythm and she stood. "Ami, I don't think—"

"It won't be like that. You'll be with me."

"But you don't understand."

"Yes, I do. You're in love with him, even though you can't be with him for some reason. You don't have to explain. It's none of my business. But please come with me, Addison."

"Does he know you were planning to ask me?"

There was something thrilling about being near him again. After not seeing him for weeks, she'd almost forgotten the stirring effect he had on her.

"No, but he won't care. Besides, he's boring and never rides anything. Do you like the rides?"

"Only a few."

"I want Maverick to ask me to ride but what if he tries to hold my hand?" Ami shuddered and Addison laughed. "I mean, I like Maverick, but I still like Zach. I think. I'm so confused."

"Just enjoy spending time with your friends. You're a smart girl. Things will work out as they should."

A few minutes later, Addison stood next to Logan's truck. She felt like a schoolgirl, butterflies raging war within her. She'd stayed away from Logan the entire afternoon, but now she was standing next to him and every nerve ending in her body stood on edge.

She inhaled his fresh, clean scent mixed with the familiar woodsy, spicy notes of his cologne. A quiver of awareness flowed through her. There wasn't a waking moment she hadn't thought of him. Longed to call him. Longed to be in his arms. She stared as Logan walked around the truck after helping her in, his gentle touch still lingering on her skin.

Logan paid for parking at the amusement park and listened to the girls chatter beside him. He had a hard time concentrating on the drive here with Addison sitting right next to him and was glad to finally arrive at the park.

Logan allowed Addison to walk ahead of him with Ami as they met up with a group of kids. They headed through the entrance gate, then Maverick slowed and walked next to him.

"Ami likes to come here, doesn't she?"

Logan glanced at the boy. His face was so red. "Yeah, she comes all the time."

"Do you like the rides?"

"No." *If Addison wants to ride with me, I'd reconsider.* Ami would keep Addison to herself though. It would be better that way. He wasn't sure how long he'd be able to handle being near her without giving in to his need to be closer.

As if reading his thoughts, Addison turned and looked at him. He'd thought of her all afternoon. He had to make this friendship thing work. If he only avoided eye contact with her, he'd survive.

Then everything changed.

Maverick walked toward Logan's sister. "Ami, will you ride something with me?"

Ami glanced over her shoulder at Addison. "Do you want to come with us."

"I'm okay, Ami. You go ahead."

Ami pulled her to the side and whispered against her hair. Addison shook her head. He scolded himself and turned immediately to remove his temptation to study her every move.

Moments later, when the voices subsided, he looked over his shoulder. Addison stood against the fence, her arms folded against her chest, her expression distraught. He ached for her.

He moved into the space next to her and stared into the evening sky, praying that he would say the right thing.

"Ami told me you were going to be teaching at the academy in Jacksonville this fall."

Addison glanced at him, her gaze charged, the connection between them electrifying. "Yes, they called me last week."

"Were you able to get a kindergarten class?" he asked, keeping their conversation safe. He had to gain control of his emotions before he pulled her against him.

"Yes."

Logan blew a lungful of air from his chest. "I'm so happy for you."

"Thank you, Logan." Addison's smile increased as she stared starry-eyed into the flashing carnival lights. She was fighting their attraction too.

Logan lost his train of thought, watching her relax, watching her lips curve into a charming smile, but then suddenly she straightened, and her posture tensed.

33

Addison deliberated a moment too long. "Logan, I need to go to the truck."

"Is something wrong?"

Her delay was going to cost her.

"Addison, Logan, it's so good to see you." Philip's disgustingly fake voice sickened her.

Addison stared at the blonde hanging to Philip's sleeve avoiding Philip's eyes.

With a brief tilt of her head, she met Philip's gaze and that's all it took. Addison spun around, unable to stand there another moment. Philip had violated her in the worst way yet stood here facing her as if nothing had happened.

Dizziness swept through her, nausea rolled in her stomach, and she grabbed the fence rail to steady herself.

In search of an escape, she scoped the surroundings to no avail. The fried dough smoking from the trailer directly in front of them bled through the air and she took a step away.

"Addison." Philip called her name and she froze. With each step that brought him closer, her pulse quickened. "I need to talk to you."

Anger consumed her every breath. He had caused her unimaginable torture, but he didn't remember or didn't care.

She glanced at Logan in desperation. "Will you walk with me?"

Philip grabbed her arm. "I said I need to talk to you." Addison tried to snatch away from him, but he yanked her toward him. "Let go of me." The next seconds were a blur as Logan's hand breezed past her making contact with Philip's mouth.

"She said"—Logan's tone deepened—"let go." Philip stumbled backward, landing against the fence.

"Are you crazy?" the blonde yelled.

Commanding her heart palpitations to cease, Addison moved forward without looking back.

Moments later, Maverick and Ami stepped around the opposite side of a carnival ride startling Addison's heart into another round.

Ami took her arm. "Hey, we're going to play some games. You want to come?"

Addison met Logan's gaze and drew in a deep breath. Forcing a smile, she straightened. "No, you guys go ahead. We'll catch up with you later."

Ami's smile widened. "Okay, see you in a little bit."

Addison glanced down and, seeing blood, she grabbed Logan's hand and yanked it toward her. "You're bleeding!"

"You're shaking."

She ignored his perception. "Do you have napkins in your truck?"

"Addison, it's okay."

"No, it's not. Come on," she said, pulling him forward.

"It's nothing."

"We need to make sure." Addison pulled at the locked handle. "Where're the keys? I need some light."

He leaned against the truck, ignoring her question. "Are you okay?"

"Yes, of course. I'm fine. You're the one that's hurt."

He leaned in closer, still staring at her, unwilling to give in. "Why won't you be honest with me?"

"Please, Logan. I'm worried about your hand."

"I'm worried about you," he said as he unlocked the truck.

"Don't be." Addison opened the passenger door and unlatched the glove compartment. She grabbed a wad of napkins and poured some of the liquid from her water bottle onto the crumpled pile. "I'm so sorry. This is all my fault." She dabbed at the small cut on his index finger under the interior light of his truck.

He gently touched her shoulder, drawing her gaze to his. "It's not your fault."

Tenderness welled inside her as he smiled down on her. His fingers were still attached to her shoulder, his touch quickly distorting all sensible thought. How she had missed him! If she wasn't careful, she would most certainly give in to his charm and never look back. She continued pressing the napkin to his cut, tearing her gaze from his. "I shouldn't be here."

"Where should you be?"

A broken laugh, blended with a guttural sob, escaped her lips. "What do you mean?" she whispered tearfully as she looked at him.

"If you shouldn't be here with me, where should you be?"

Her hands stilled as his hand lowered down the length of her arm. His lips quirked slightly as if eager to claim hers, the touch of his fingers still lightly grasping her bare arm. He gave her no time to respond. "Would it make you feel better to go back and find Philip?"

Her brow furrowed. "No." But immediately understanding dawned on her. "You don't think ..." She paused, unsure how to finish.

Addison glanced across the parking lot just as Philip's truck pulled out of the gate.

"It's none of my business, but I understand you being upset seeing him with someone else."

"No, that wasn't it."

Logan didn't say anything, and she regretted her words immediately. How could she explain it to him? She couldn't. Not without telling him the whole story.

"Really, it isn't what you think," she said, still dabbing his knuckles with the napkins. His breath tickled her cheek and her mind went blank.

"Do you want me to take you back to your car?" His voice was low and bleak, and his nearness had an undeniable effect on her. Caution filtered her affection. She was only millimeters from crossing an invisible line she had drawn.

She didn't want to go home, to be lonely, despairing in her own thoughts. This is what she wanted. To be here with Logan, where she felt safe.

Mistaking her silence for an affirmative, he said, "I understand, Addison. It's okay. You don't have to stay. I'll find Ami and let her know that I'll come back after I drop you off."

He hesitated, waiting for her to respond, and she cleared her throat, driving away the tears clouding her vision. "I don't want to worry Ami." She immersed her attention in the warmth of his hand as she folded hers within his. "I would really like to stay here with you."

"Are you sure?" His quietly spoken words brought her closer.

She smiled. There was something freeing about being near Logan. The tender way he regarded her as if she was the most important thing in his world. "I've never been more sure of anything."

"What do you want to do?"

"I want to ride something." An electric current pulled them toward each other. His intense stare mesmerized her, just as his eyes fell to her lips. "With you."

They stood in line for the pirate ship and Logan told himself to quit worrying about Philip, but to enjoy this moment with Addison. Demanding the truth from her was out of the question. But something was wrong. And it had everything to do with Philip. It was in the uptight way she'd held to his hand, the way she constantly looked over her shoulder, the way she never left his side.

Logan had to tread carefully where she was concerned. This may be his last chance to spend time with her like this.

Addison's eyes held a mixture of fear and confusion. "Do you like this ride?"

He stood taller, staring at the big machine swinging back and forth in midair. "I've never ridden it."

"You were telling Maverick you don't like to ride." She turned to face him, her gaze wandering somewhere behind him. "This probably isn't the best one to start with."

He had to remain neutral, her stronghold for the moment. "I want to. It looks … fun."

She chewed on her lower lip, studying the passengers screaming as they floated by. This ride was nothing to her but a deliberate diversion, but to him it would be much more than that.

"It is, but it takes your stomach. Like really bad."

"What does that mean to you?"

She blinked. "What?"

"What does it feel like to have your stomach taken?"

"Wait! You don't know how that feels?"

Weary of the pretense that they could only be friends, he leaned in closer. "I don't know what it feels like to you."

"It's like a rush of a thousand butterflies sweeping through your body all at once, taking your breath." Her hands were animated as she described the sensation and her voice was too warm, drawing him in like a magnet. If she didn't stop talking, he would kiss her.

He held her gaze, wanting to reach out to her, but kept his hands stuffed in his pockets. "Then I do know how that feels." *Because that's exactly the way I feel when I look into your eyes.*

"Okay, good." She studied his face. The tiny lines on her forehead crumpled and she looked away.

His lungs expanded as he examined her movements. She squeezed her eyes shut and seemed to be holding her breath. Fear mixed with excitement shaded her face. He fixed a tight smile on his lips; confident he would kiss her if he allowed them to relax. The gate opened and they walked to the top of the ship and he took the seat next to her. They had plenty of room to spread out, but she slid closer to him.

"I'm scared," he said.

"You are?" Her voice jumped an octave.

He wrapped his arm around the back of the seat. "Aren't you?"

"A little. Do you want to get off?" She grabbed the rail, her fingers just millimeters from his other hand.

"Not on your life."

Feminine laughter came crashing from her and his heart lifted.

As the ride started, she leaned closer to him and he welcomed the pleasant feel of her body against his. He allowed his arm to fall onto her shoulder and she snuggled deeper into him. The ride was exhilarating, but it was nothing compared to the way she made him feel.

Minutes later they stepped from the platform onto the safe grassy earth beneath them.

He held out his hand to help her down and she took it.

"How did you like it?" she asked.

"It was amazing."

She laughed. "You didn't even flinch. I did all the screaming."

"Believe me, Addison. I felt your rush of butterflies." He was having way too much fun watching her blush.

They walked side by side, careful not to touch each other but close enough that the electricity flowing between them sparked thrilling moments throughout the rest of the night.

34

On Monday morning, Addison arrived at the elementary school and climbed from her car as Principal Andrews, her new boss, walked toward her.

"Miss Morgan, good morning. I hope you're doing well."

"Yes, ma'am," she said. "I hope you are."

After her second interview with Mrs. Andrews a week earlier, Addison could hardly wait to get started.

"It won't be long now. Enjoy your time preparing your room for your students."

"Yes, ma'am, I will."

Mrs. Andrews walked toward her car and climbed in. "See you tomorrow if not before."

Addison knew without looking back that Mrs. Andrews still wore a huge grin. She was always smiling, the kind that could brighten any dull room.

Addison had applied to several different schools but had prayed she'd get this position. It was a longer drive, but it would be worth it to work for a principal like Mrs. Andrews.

Addison unloaded the first few boxes from her car then walked to her new classroom. Mrs. Andrews had shown her the room yesterday, but today it looked bigger.

A soft knock on the door startled her. "Hi, you're Addison Morgan, right? I'm Charlotte Avery. I heard you come in."

Addison walked across the room to meet the pregnant, pretty blonde halfway and offered her hand. "It's so nice to meet you."

"You too. We'll be teaching partners this year, until I go on maternity leave. That just means we'll do our lesson plans together and work out a strategy that will boost our students learning capabilities. It sounds boring, but it can really be a lot of fun."

Nothing about it sounded boring. "I'm excited. This is my first year, so I'm ready to get started." *Ready to get my mind focused on something else.*

"Good, I was hoping we could start working on the first six weeks. It will take a few days to go through everything and gather the materials."

"That sounds good. Tell me when and I'll be there."

"Let's meet after lunch. For now, I'll leave you to go through all this stuff. Don't feel like you have to use everything and if you need anything, I'm right next door."

"Thanks." Addison smiled as Charlotte slipped from the room.

By the end of the week, Addison had a daily schedule planned out for the first six weeks and had transformed each corner of her classroom into different learning centers.

On Friday afternoon, Addison placed twenty-three name tags carefully on each desk. "Perfect."

She pulled her classroom door closed in anticipation of Tuesday morning. She then drove home to prepare for her last night at Olive Garden. Aunt Brenda had returned, Taylor had moved back home, and school was starting next week.

Sunlight streamed through the kitchen window as Aunt Brenda stood at the sink washing dishes as Addison headed for the front door. "I was hoping to talk to you."

Addison moved in the space beside Aunt Brenda. "Okay. I have a few minutes."

Aunt Brenda rinsed her hands and dried them on a tattered towel. "What happened with you and Philip?"

Addison hugged herself against her sudden chill. "We're not seeing each other anymore."

"That's what I thought. He hasn't been coming around. Did something happen?"

She tightened the strings of her apron, warding off painful memories. "He's unfaithful and hateful when he drinks."

The hard lines of Aunt Brenda's face softened with tenderness. "Oh, honey, I feel bad leaving you all alone while this was happening. I can see how hard it's been on you. You're better off without him."

Tears burned her throat. What Aunt Brenda witnessed lately had more to do with Logan than that slime ball who didn't deserve space in her head.

"I'm glad you were able to go to California. I'm okay, really. I've got to go, but I'll be home early. We can talk when I get home. I'm not closing tonight."

"That's good. You look so tired. Are you feeling okay, honey?"

"I'm fine, really." She kissed her on the cheek. "I'll see you tonight."

Addison was relieved to have her aunt home. She had missed her bigger-than-life laugh. Her finger-licking good butter sauce that paired with just about any seafood dish. Her big hugs and undeniable love.

The first part of the summer had been magical, until that devastating night. And then there was that trip to the amusement park. One more enchanted night, filled with thrilling rides, more than one innocent, yet stimulating touch, and a cautious goodbye. She hadn't seen Logan since that night. And though her heart ached to see him again, she knew it was best.

Once clocked in and ready for her shift, she served customers with her usual devotion, as if they were personal guests in her home.

She stepped from the kitchen just as the hostess walked away from her booth, revealing Ami and Logan sitting across from each other.

Anticipation fluttered in her chest. She walked toward them, but they hadn't noticed her yet.

Ami looked her way first. Logan's eyes stayed glued to the menu. "Hey, Addison."

She kept her eyes locked with Ami's, unable to contain her smile. "Hey." She didn't look at Logan again until she asked for their drink orders and regretted it immediately.

"I'll take a Coke," he told her, his eyes burning through her with such depth that warmth spread through her and she was unable to regain her composure as she walked away. Entering the kitchen, she gathered the wandering hope skipping around her heart and set out to prepare their drinks.

While placing the two beverages on the tray, a wave of dizziness slid across her vision. All sounds were sucked into a vacuum and black dots scattered the world around her. "Can you drop this off for me? I need to—" She muttered to whoever was standing next to her.

"What table? Addison?"

The girl's voice was muddled, in a tunnel of haziness. Addison couldn't stop. Not now. She hurried around the corner, desperate to find somewhere to sit as a sea of darkness engulfed her.

Logan looked up and saw Addison come through the kitchen door. She leaned against the wall for one split second, before she sank to the floor.

He scrambled from his seat in such a hurry, silverware went flying across the table. He hurried across the dining room, dodging other tables, chairs, customers and kneeled in front of her, his stomach twisting in knots. Slowly her eyes fluttered open and she blinked as she focused on him.

"Addison?"

Addison gaped at him for several seconds before her gaze flitted across the dining room. "Oh no." She frowned as she tried to sit up but stopped midway.

"Does anything hurt?"

"No."

In his eagerness to help her, he lifted her into his arms.

Lids partially closed, she snuggled into the nook of his neck as if that was where she belonged. Then she whispered against the soft flesh of his neck, "I'm so sorry."

"Do you have a break room?" Logan asked one of the guys who hovered around them.

"Follow me."

Logan carried her to the break room and set her down on a bench. Several others, including Ami, followed them into the small room.

Bending in front of her, Logan took her hand. "How do you feel?"

"Still a little woozy." She pressed her free hand to her forehead. "I passed out in front of everybody," she whispered. "This is so embarrassing."

"It was graceful. You just scared the daylights out of me."

She relaxed against the wall and let go of his hand. "I'm so sorry."

The manager stepped toward them and Logan scooted to the side, making room for him. "How're you feeling?"

"I'm okay. I'm so sorry."

It was so like her to worry about everyone else before herself.

"The other girls will take your tables. You go on home and feel better, okay, sweetheart?"

Logan flinched at the endearment. He was young, not much older than they were.

"Yes, sir. Thank you."

"Do I need to get someone to take you home?"

"I can take her."

The manager looked to Addison for her approval and she nodded. "Thank you so much." He held out his hand and grasped Logan's in a firm grip.

"Logan Tant. We're friends," he told the man to settle his curiosity.

"Logan, I'll feel better knowing she's in good hands."

Everyone dispersed, except for Ami. She was still crying.

Ami sat beside her when Logan backed away. Addison hugged her. "I'm so sorry. I didn't mean to scare you."

In the short span of time after she had fallen to the floor, she apologized four different times, though none of them were necessary. As if she didn't believe she was worth any trouble.

To him, she was worth everything.

Addison followed Logan to his truck and, though she still felt light-headed, her stomach fluttered for more than that reason alone.

Logan didn't talk much as he drove her home. Mortified that she'd fainted in front of all those people, she was absorbed in her own thoughts.

They reached her house and he climbed from the truck too. "It's okay, Logan. I can make it now," she said.

Logan's gaze roamed over her with a slow assessment, ascertaining her condition. "I need to make sure you're settled."

He finished his inspection with a tender brush of her forehead, and she helplessly leaned into his touch. "Thank you for being there. For bringing me home."

Ami pulled in beside them and climbed from Addison's car, joining them in the yard.

The whole episode had shaken Ami, so her brother opened the passenger door for her. "Why don't you wait in the truck? I'll be right back."

"I hope you feel better, Addison. I'll call you tomorrow."

Addison reached for Ami and pulled her into a hug. "Thank you, Ami. Don't worry. I'm fine. I'm so glad you came to see me. And I'm sorry for messing up your dinner."

Logan wrapped his arm around Addison's waist and led her to the front door.

"My Aunt Brenda's back home."

"Good, I wouldn't want to leave you alone right now."

Her nerves on edge, she nearly tripped over the first step. He took her hand.

"You better be more careful if you don't want me carrying you."

A small laugh escaped her lips as she opened the front door.

Aunt Brenda was already there waiting. "I thought I heard two vehicles. What are you doing home so early?"

Logan kept his grip on Addison but offered his other hand to Aunt Brenda. "Hi, I'm Logan. Addison passed out at the restaurant, so I drove her home."

Aunt Brenda wailed, "Addison?"

"It's okay. Really, I'm fine."

Aunt Brenda's gaze danced back and forth between her and Logan. She released his hand and smiled. "Well, don't just stand there, come on in." Her eyes were swimming with questions. "How can I ever thank you?"

"I'm glad I was there."

"Where did you find this nice young man?"

Heat warmed Addison's cheeks. "Logan is Ami's brother."

"Ami Tant?" She looked at Logan as if seeing him for the first time.

"Yes, ma'am."

"Well, it's so nice to meet you. I didn't know Ami had a brother."

Addison could almost imagine the disappointment flowing through Logan and settling in the crevices around his eyes. "Actually, she has two. Logan has a twin brother."

"How nice!"

She stared ahead as Logan led her into the living room.

"I'm so glad you were there too." Aunt Brenda paused. "Addison, are you sure you're all right?"

"Yes, I'm fine," Addison told her, twirling her apron string around her finger.

"You're working too hard. Why don't you sit down, honey?"

Addison obeyed, the weightlessness of the moment catching up to her. Logan took a seat next to her leaving only inches between them.

"I'm okay, really." Addison cast a glance at Aunt Brenda, hoping to persuade her aunt to veer the conversation toward something else. But it didn't work.

"The night of the accident, she ..."

"Aunt Brenda, please, I don't ..."

Logan sat back, his fingers gracing her lower back. "No, please, tell me. What about the accident?"

Addison's hand rested in the small crevice of space between them, nestled against Logan's thigh, her senses shamelessly engrossed with his presence, his nearness.

"The same thing happened. Her blacking out caused the accident."

Aunt Brenda's words registered through her brain a second too late. She peeked at Logan, his concern evident by his expression. Her chest rose and fell on a longing sigh.

"Addison was so worried about your sister. She tells me she is doing very well now."

A guilty blush heated Addison's cheeks.

"Yes, she's doing great." Logan reached for Addison's hand and that simple act gave her heart a thrill. "I'm so thankful it wasn't any worse for either of them."

"Me too."

After a gentle squeeze, Logan released Addison's hand. "Ami's waiting outside. I should probably go."

Aunt Brenda stood.

Logan stood too and reached for her aunt's hand. "It's so very nice to finally meet you, Ms. Morgan. I hope to see you again."

"Yes, I hope so too, Logan. I'll be back right back, young lady. You stay put." Aunt Brenda winked at Addison as she rounded the corner leaving them alone.

Addison stood and moved into the space next to Logan. He captured her pinky in his as he had done so many times before. Breathing deeply, she allowed him to pull her closer.

"Call me if you need anything," he told her.

She shuddered at the remembrance of that night Philip showed up and how she should've called him but didn't. And how that decision affected everything good in her life. "I will. I promise."

Though there was a flicker of skepticism in his gaze, he gently pressed his lips to her forehead. "I'll check on you tomorrow."

Her throat closed, so she nodded. He squeezed her hand, his gaze never wavering as he groped to find the doorknob. "I'll see you later."

He walked through the front door and it wasn't until Aunt Brenda returned, and after seeing him out, that she noticed her aunt's expression.

"Oh, my goodness. He is really something. I like him."

So, do I.

"Was it the same feeling as when you blacked out driving?"

"I'm not sure, but I don't think so. I was fixing drinks when my ears closed. Everything around me became dark shadows. I asked whoever was standing next to me to take the drinks, so I could sit down, but as soon as I turned the corner ... I didn't make it."

"Do you still feel dizzy?"

"No, I'm just tired."

Aunt Brenda took the chair across from her. "Take it easy for a couple of days. If you start feeling that way again, we're going to the hospital."

Addison nodded.

Aunt Brenda rested her elbow on one of her legs. "Logan was there when this happened?"

"He and Ami came in for dinner."

Aunt Brenda leaned back in the recliner. "How well do you know him?"

"We hung out some over the summer."

Aunt Brenda stared off into space for a long moment, then she suddenly seemed to recall what she wanted to say. "When did you and Philip decide to go your separate ways?"

Her stomach tensed. "I saw him with someone else the night of my accident."

Aunt Brenda leaned forward. "That same night? Oh, honey, why didn't you tell me?"

"I told him we were finished several times before you left, but he wouldn't listen to me. He kept denying everything. He's been drinking more than usual."

They sat in silence, tormenting thoughts invading her.

"I'm so disappointed in him."

Jagged emotions ripped through her and Addison stood. "If it's okay with you, I think I'll lay down. I'm not feeling so great. I'll see you in the morning."

Tears burned the backs of her eyelids as she settled under her covers. She wanted to tell Aunt Brenda the whole truth, but no one else would be able to make it right. No one else could take the pain away.

It would be easier to forget if she kept the dark secret to herself.

35

Addison found Aunt Brenda in the kitchen cooking breakfast on Saturday morning. The crisp scent of bacon and freshly ground coffee turned her stomach with an angry swell.

"I hope you're hungry. I went overboard."

Addison's phone chimed with a text notification. She turned and swiped at the screen giving herself a moment to swallow the heave growing in her chest.

Good morning, beautiful. I hope you're feeling better.

The words displayed on the screen eased the bitter taste in her mouth.

"Invite him for breakfast."

Addison pulled her fingers away from the screen. "What?"

Aunt Brenda gave her a sideways glance. "It's Logan isn't it?"

"How did you know?"

"The obvious smile on your face." Aunt Brenda winked. "Invite him. We have plenty."

Her stomach fluttered at the thought of being near him again.

Would you like to come for breakfast?

Yes! I would love to. Should I come now?

Yes!

I'm on the way.

"He's coming." She blew out a deep breath. "I shouldn't have done that."

Aunt Brenda stopped and turned to face her. "If you two are going to be seeing each other, I'd like to get to know this young man better."

"We aren't seeing each other."

"Oh, well, either way, it's obvious he cares a great deal about you."

Heat rushed to her face. "Why do you say that?"

"I'm fifty-eight, but I'm not blind. I saw the way he looked at you. That boy is smitten. And if I'm not mistaken, you looked just as love struck."

Addison couldn't hide her smile. Did he really look at her like that? "He's coming now and I'm not ready," she said, already heading to her bedroom to change.

The thought of only being friends twisted a jagged edge straight through to her soul.

Logan tried to control the emotions building inside him, knowing he had to take it easy. Addison had said she wanted to remain only friends, but the warmth radiating through her voice told a different story.

He reached her front door and kicked around a pebble until Ms. Morgan answered the door. "Come in, Logan. I'm so glad you'll be joining us for breakfast. Addison will be out in just a moment. Have a seat and I'll fix you something to drink. Would you like orange juice or coffee?"

Logan smiled at Ms. Morgan, relaxing immediately. "Orange juice will be great."

Moments later, Addison entered the kitchen. He caught a trace of her clean, fresh scent as she took the seat next to him. "Hey."

He bit his lip to hide his smile. "How're you feeling?"

"Much better."

She smiled tentatively and he couldn't look away. "Are you working today?"

Addison laughed. "Last night was my last night."

He leaned back in his seat and faced her. "So, you decided to go out with a bang?"

Her dimples deepened. "Very funny."

"Do you have plans today?"

"No," Addison said, a touch of genuine delight blending with the curiosity in her simple answer.

"Do you feel like coming over and hanging out with Ami a while?"

Addison glanced at her aunt. She nodded. "I would love to. I'll call her to find out what time to come?"

"I was planning to drive you, if that's okay."

"You don't have to do that. It will be out of—"

Before she could finish, Logan took her arm. "Actually, I'm going that way."

"But still you'd have to bring me back and I don't want to put you through any trouble."

She wasn't going to make this easy. He looked at Ms. Morgan. "Do you mind if I drive her?"

"Not at all, Logan. In fact, that will make me feel more comfortable after her fainting spell last night."

Addison rolled her eyes dramatically, but a weak smile escaped, and he relaxed.

After breakfast he led her to his truck, ecstatic to have her next to him again. He waited until he started the truck before asking the question that had bugged him all morning. "Are you sure you're feeling better?"

"Yes." She lifted her chin to meet his gaze and his pulse raced.

Unable to speak, he stared at her, an intense thrill claiming his awareness.

"I promise, Logan. I'm fine."

He turned facing the steering wheel, facing away from the girl who'd stolen his heart. He could see in her expression that she knew how he felt too. "Good." He looked straight ahead, afraid if he looked at her a moment more, he'd blow his commitment to just being friends.

"I feel bad for upsetting Ami." She shifted in her seat. "Does she know I'm coming?"

"No. I wasn't sure if you'd be able to go."

"That was sweet for you to do that for her."

I'm doing it for both of us, he wanted to tell her.

"Thank you for bringing me, Logan." Addison walked through the front door after Logan. She suspected Ami was upstairs, so she climbed the few steps toward her room.

She knocked but pushed the already open door. "Hello, can I come in?"

Ami sat at her desk but turned at the sound of her voice. "Addison, what are you doing here?"

"Your brother brought me."

Ami stood, coming toward her, and smiled. "You're feeling better?"

"Yes, I'm fine. And there's no need for you to worry about me." Addison met her in the middle of the room. "What are you doing? I don't want to interrupt."

"Working on my senior project."

Addison sat on the bed across from Ami. "You don't get a break for summer?"

"Yes, just getting a head start on it."

"Smart girl." Addison fiddled with a button on her top. "What's your topic?"

Ami stood and crossed the room holding a poster board toward her. "Adoption in America."

"That sounds interesting."

"I'm showing the entire process from beginning to end. That's what I'm trying to do, anyway."

"What do you have so far?"

"This is my opening sentence. 'Adoption is a wonderful opportunity for parents who aren't physically able to raise their own child, and for married women who aren't able to conceive.'"

"Great start."

"I don't know." Ami plopped down on the bed next to her. "Maybe you could help me. You could be my mentor."

"Me?"

"Yes, I'm supposed to find one and you would be perfect. You've graduated from college, you're a teacher. What could be better than that?"

"I don't really know anything about adoption though."

"That doesn't matter. I'll just let you read my notes and you can give me suggestions on how to make my paper better. If you want to."

"I would be honored." Before Addison could say more, Ami captured her in an enthusiastic embrace.

They spent the next two hours researching information for her paper. There were so many options. Different rules applied for different agencies and Ami worked to pull the information together in an informative yet appealing way. Some adoptions could take years to complete an adoption, where others were finalized within a couple of months.

Ami stretched her arms over her head. "I'm getting hungry. Let's go find out what Mom's fixing for lunch."

A nervous rush assaulted Addison as they descended the stairs. She'd been helping Ami all morning and hadn't seen Logan since they'd arrived. Was he still here? Would she see him now?

Ami bounced into the kitchen, crossing the room toward her mother. "What's for lunch?"

"I'm putting together some BLTs for you girls and Logan."

Addison turned and came face-to-face with the object of her affliction.

"You girls having fun?" His cheeks lifted with his smile, and then his gaze fell to her lips.

"She's helping me with my project. Addison's agreed to be my mentor."

His smile bound them to each other, in a subtle, yet overpowering way. No one existed in that brief instant, but the two of them.

Addison walked toward the table, and the smell of bacon grease sifted through the air and into her nose. Bile rose in the back of her throat and she covered her mouth.

Logan had moved next to her and placed his hand on her shoulder. "What's wrong?"

"Nothing. I ... I left something in Ami's room. I'll be right back."

The queasiness intensified and she ran upstairs to Ami's bathroom, closing the door behind her, making it just in time.

Ami had followed her, and her panicked voice echoed through the sheetrock wall separating them. "Addison?"

She couldn't answer. She couldn't breathe. The burning sensation was suffocating, and she grasped the toilet, praying for relief. Her body rejected every ounce of breakfast she'd eaten, within the next three seconds.

Desperate to get Ami's attention, she kicked at the door with her foot. But Ami didn't hear her attempt. What if she had already run back downstairs to get help? She wanted no one to know about this.

After wiping her mouth and rinsing the ends of her hair in the sink, she returned to the bedroom. But she was too late. Ami was already gone. Sitting on the bed and still suffering from the effects of the nausea, she searched for an excuse as she held to her stomach.

"Addison?" At the sound of Logan's voice, she stood too quickly. The room slid across her vision and she slowly sat back down. Logan crossed the room and sat next to her, his hand reaching for hers. "What's wrong?"

Within a second, Ami was next to her on the bed. "Are you okay?"

"I'm not feeling well." Her throat burned, the foreign acid sizzling against the back of her tongue. She coughed, the effort scratching her throat. "I'm so sorry. I should probably go."

Ami shifted onto her knees beside her.

"Of course." Logan grasped her arm, helping her to her feet, and led her down the stairs and out the front door. All the time never speaking, never even looking at her. Until they were outside.

"Do you feel any better?"

When he did speak and their eyes met, something happened. Could he read the desperation in her eyes? He looked worried. Really worried.

"Not really. I don't know what's wrong with me."

"Do you think it's a virus or something?"

"It has to be. I felt sick earlier, but then it went away."

He reached across and grazed his strong fingers against her cheek. Warmth bloomed launching a frisson of excitement at his tender touch. "You feel warm."

"I hope it's not contagious." She needed this to be a simple virus but knew it wasn't.

"Don't worry about that. You just get some rest, drink plenty of fluids, and call me in the morning."

She had no means to protect herself against his charm. Addison was convinced she would never feel this way about another man, ever again. "I wish. I still have a few things to do for school."

"Today?"

"School starts next week."

Addison leaned back against the seat and relaxed as Logan started the truck and pulled onto the highway.

"Do you need help?"

"No, it's just a few last-minute details. I'm so excited but so worried about having my own class. Everything has to be perfect."

"I'm sure you'll be great. And I already know your children will love you."

"Thank you, Logan."

When they arrived at her house, he parked in the driveway and turned to face her. His gaze held hers, unwilling to break its hold.

A battle raged within her to give in, to allow him to embrace her. But reality slammed its way to the core of her heart, its razor-sharp edge ripping through her consciousness. A reality she'd been trying to ignore for days. She was late. And she was never late.

Turning her face from him, she slipped her clammy hands from beneath her legs. "I better go."

"Okay," he said, staring at her, his expression too intense. "Don't forget to call me if you need anything."

She wouldn't make the mistake of looking at him again. His eyes confused her, making her believe that everything could be as it was before.

It wasn't real, it was a delusion.

"Thank you for everything, Logan. Tell Ami I'll call her later."

Addison hurried into the house and through the living room, unable to get to the bedroom fast enough. Reaching under her bed, she grabbed the hidden box that would give her the results that could change the rest of her life.

After following the directions, she paced the bathroom, squeezing her upper arms. *Please be negative. Please, God, I'm begging you.*

Gasping for breath in uneven rhythms and with sweaty palms, she lifted the strip from the counter.

3 6

T he bathroom felt too warm, too small. The cinnamon spice scent swirling from the wax melt churned her stomach. Keeping her eyes shut tight, Addison twisted around, grasping the counter as she slowly sank to the floor.

Positive. How can this be happening? What am I going to do?

Her first instinct was to run to Aunt Brenda. She'd know what to do. But what would she tell her? Philip took advantage of her? He raped her? She wasn't even sure herself what to call it. How could it be rape, when she'd dated him for so many years? She screamed no at him, over and over, but he wouldn't listen. Still somehow, she should have been able to stop him. She should've been stronger.

Memories of that night came rushing back and a wave of nausea caused tiny beads of sweat to gather across her forehead. Because of her weakness, she was pregnant.

Pulling herself up, she took the box, the results, and pushed them into the bottom of the trash, burying the proof.

She couldn't think about this right now, there was too much to do.

The first day of school came and went at an accelerated pace. It hadn't been a perfect day but instead had been filled with a few tears and a minor bathroom accident. Still, she enjoyed getting to know her students, discovering the many different personalities, and getting a small grasp on what to expect in the days to follow.

By the end of the first week, Addison had her class settled into a smoother routine and was able to call each child by name effortlessly. The last few heartbroken tears of being separated from mommas had finally dwindled. Addison had also managed to keep her hands and mind busy until she could no longer hold her eyes open every night.

But now the weekend had arrived, and she couldn't put off verifying the results any longer.

Addison walked into the downtown women's clinic first thing Saturday morning. Over-the-counter tests were sometimes wrong, weren't they? Plus, she hadn't taken it at the recommended time, first thing in the morning. But she already knew that a false result wouldn't be the case.

Walking up to the building, her insides churned as if she were contemplating a morbid crime.

"Hi, welcome to our clinic. May I help you?"

"Yes, I um ... I need a pregnancy test."

"Of course." The girl behind the desk handed her a clipboard with a form. "Fill this out for me. It shouldn't take too long."

After filling out the one-page form and returning it to the front desk, Addison grabbed a brochure from the rack. The first thing that caught her attention was the no surgery abortion option. She didn't have time to finish reading before someone called her name.

A numbing sensation encased Addison as she went through the motions of collecting and giving the nurse her sample for the test.

While she waited, she scanned the brochure almost heaving at the words, the large numbers she was seeing.

This clinic alone had provided abortion care to over 100,000 patients over the last 20 years. The statistic made her physically ill. She held her breath, not even realizing that she did so until the nurse approached her.

"It's positive."

The outcome didn't come as a shock, it was the result she'd been expecting. And that small fact alone gave her the strength to ask a question.

"Can you give me more information about the pill?"

Logan hadn't seen Addison all week determined to keep some distance as he worked out the best way to remain friends. Between working his regular hours and still taking on part-time hours, there was little time for anything else. Even though he longed to stop by on his lunch breaks, he didn't. It was always too late, and he didn't want to be responsible for keeping her up late her first week of school. Especially with her fainting spell and then getting that virus.

By Saturday morning, he could wait no longer. After spending two extra hours at the station for paperwork for a shots fired call, he left the station by 10:00 and drove straight to her house. Her car wasn't parked in its usual spot in her driveway. Ignoring his disappointment, he pulled out his phone to text her, but then Addison pulled in behind him and parked to the side of his truck. He squinted against the morning sunlight as he climbed from the truck.

"Hey, I just got off work. I just wanted to stop by to see you for a minute." As soon as the words left his mouth, he regretted them. He left no room ... no excuse to spend time with her later today.

It wasn't until he walked closer, that he saw dried tear streaks across her face. He pretended not to notice, but he ached for her. Her lips curved, but the smile she tried forcing, didn't reach her eyes. He had never seen her so disheartened.

Not wanting to waste time and disregarding his better judgment, he gently took her hand, slipping her keys into his pocket, and led her down the narrow path leading to the beach. She never spoke but stared straight ahead. The moment they hit the wooden bridge, she stiffened. He turned to find her staring at a spot near where they stood, surrounded by overgrown grass.

Ignoring his impulse to ask her what was wrong, he led her down the stairs, caressing her hand with tender strokes. It no longer mattered that he'd promised he wouldn't do this; he couldn't stop now. His actions came as natural as his next breath. Here with Addison was where he belonged, where he knew he wanted to spend the rest of his life.

Her tension seemed to disappear, and she walked closer to him, their bodies brushing against each other with each step. They walked slower, almost mechanically, as if they were the only couple in the world at this very moment.

An ember of awareness burned within him, intensifying when he glanced at her. She watched him, her eyes awestruck, her mouth enticing. Her lips parted and he thought she would speak, but instead she licked them slowly, her eyes softening. An invigorating force stopped him from moving another step and he pulled her closer until their lips melded into each other.

"I love you, Addison." He breathed the words against her mouth.

A flicker of yearning danced across her eyes and within a fraction of a second, part laugh, part cry escaped her lips as she collapsed against him. "I love you."

She squeezed her eyes shut and expectancy filled him.

Addison held her breath, afraid if she exhaled, Logan would disappear. He led her back to the house and sat next to her on the wooden swing. Flowers surrounded the base of the porch, the bright yellows and pinks bursting with a sweet fragrance making everything brighter. Logan leaned against her, pushing her playfully. Her gaze fell to her hand still tucked inside his.

"I like this," he said, his words soothing her like a lullaby taking away all her fears, lulling her into a fantasy where happily-ever-afters were real.

He wrapped his other arm around her shoulder, and she leaned into him, drinking in the magnificence of this moment.

When he lifted his head and rested his gaze on her lips, she slowly leaned in, fusing the space between them until nothing separated them. His mouth was warm, tasting of mint and sweat. Secure in his grip, she relaxed savoring the passion swirling through every ounce of her. His declaration rang in her ears, the sweet melody playing over and over again through the deepest trenches of her soul. She wanted to hold onto him forever, to never let go. She couldn't imagine spending the rest of her life without him by her side.

How would she ever survive letting him go?

The nurse had given her the answer this morning to her most feared question. She was going to have Philip's baby.

How could she be sitting here next to Logan as if nothing had changed? But she only wanted this one last moment with him. One last chance to pretend she was free to love him for the rest of her life.

The nurse at the abortion clinic gave her several options this morning, and her thoughts were on nothing else the entire drive home.

Sitting here with Logan gave her a new perspective on everything. If she had an abortion, no one would ever have to find out and she and Logan could be together. It didn't change the fact that abortion was wrong. She'd grown up believing that. But now that she was in this situation, the lines blurred. After all, it was against her will. Philip had forced her.

Had God sent Logan this morning to keep her from saying anything to Aunt Brenda? He had come just in time. She'd planned to tell Aunt Brenda as soon as she arrived home. But God wouldn't want her to get an abortion. That went against everything she'd been taught.

A faithful neighbor who'd seen two young girls who needed the Lord had taken her and her sister to church every time the doors were open. And it had made a huge difference in her life. Addison couldn't imagine a life without those countless lessons of Jesus, lessons that had become more than just stories, lessons of a Father who loved her, a Father she leaned on when she had nothing else.

Logan squeezed her fingers softly between his, breaking her thoughts, and a shudder of anticipation flowed through her.

She leaned back, hope filling her heart. Hope that must have shown on her face, because Logan smiled. That soft, tender, smile of his that never failed to melt her from the inside out.

If only hope could erase all her doubt and fears.

She licked her dry lips and kept her smile even in an effort to redirect the unwanted thoughts. She had to make a decision; it just wouldn't be today.

37

Two weeks later on Friday afternoon, Addison stood in her classroom facing her children standing in a crooked line, waiting patiently for the last bell. She touched each one as they walked past, giving them best wishes for the weekend. Her children. All twenty-three of them were precious in their own special way.

Her baby, the one she carried right now, would be special too. One day, he or she would be starting kindergarten just like these little ones. How could she consider destroying the baby's life? But this child she carried wasn't conceived out of love—but from something repulsive, horrid.

Philip had hurt her.

No matter how many times she tried to convince herself he couldn't have done something like that. He had. And she carried the proof of that horrific night inside her.

She followed her class to the buses and helped each bus rider to their line and then led the car riders to the parking lot.

A beautiful, dark-haired, brown-eyed girl, with two perfectly braided strands hanging down her back, was the last to be picked up.

The girl's mother, when she reached them, lowered as she leaned toward the opened passenger window. "Hey there, baby girl," she told her child as Addison held the back door open for her. "Sorry I'm late. I got stuck at the train again."

Addison wanted to say, *you aren't late*. Because she wasn't. Her daughter was just the last child of her class to be picked up. All her parents always arrived early. But being the last one would make a parent feel late, she imagined. Though she had a hard time with that too. It was something her parents would never have worried about.

Reeled back in time, Addison remembered a time when her and Casey stepped off the school bus on a Monday afternoon, but no one was home to let them in. Four hours later, sweat clinging to their skin as the sun lowered beyond the trees, their mouths parched from thirst, their family's small rusty car pulled into the drive. Mama and and her step-daddy both exited the car laughing. And the only thing given to her and her sister was another one of Mama's flawed excuses.

Addison returned to her classroom, her thoughts fading from her own memories to the mother's words. The tiniest of things sparked the reality of her current situation to the forefront of her mind. The child she carried. The idea of a child growing inside her made her blood spike and her breathing irregular. It took every bit of strength Addison had to not ask questions about Charlotte's pregnancy.

After wiping down all the tables with a bottle of cleaner to kill all the germs that tiny fingers could carry, she straightened the tables in each row. She placed the already copied papers on the edge of each cleaned desk for Monday morning. Each box she carefully placed inside the appropriate cubby, then grabbed her tote and walked across the parking lot to her car. Alone.

She thought of Logan and physically ached to see him. Each moment spent with him was evidence that they were meant to be together. But not like this. Not pregnant with Philip's baby. She had to make a decision about carrying the baby and putting it up for adoption, or the only other alternative. The choice that would allow her to keep Logan but would end the baby's life.

And she was running out of time.

Pulling her car onto the highway, she drove in the opposite direction of home. And before she knew what was happening, she merged onto I-40 heading west.

As she came closer to the area where she'd grown up, the signs started looking familiar. The same buildings that had been there her whole life stood in the same places, with cars still crowding the parking lot at this hour. Traffic had already thickened with the nearing of the close of another workday. She should feel something like peace, returning to a place she called home, but she felt nothing but emptiness.

She climbed the stairway to the apartment and pressed the doorbell. An out-of-body feeling plagued her. She shouldn't be here.

"Addison, what are you doing here?"

Looking into Nathan's worried eyes, the tears she'd fought all the way here now freely streamed from her eyes. The reality she'd avoided the last two weeks had caught up to her and her knees buckled against the weight of the truth. "I'm so sorry, I shouldn't have come. I just don't know what else to do."

Nathan took her hand and led her inside. "What's going on?"

Hysterical sobs choked through and she struggled to catch a full breath. "I didn't know who else to talk to."

"It's okay. Why don't you just start at the beginning?"

"It's Logan." His name fell from her lips in a rasping sound, like her heart had been ripped in two.

"Is everything okay? I haven't talked to him in a couple of weeks."

"I'm all wrong for him." Fresh tears spilled onto her cheeks.

Nathan's gaze sharpened. "Is this because of Philip? You should tell Logan what happened. It wasn't your fault."

Addison didn't believe that for one minute. It *was* her fault. She should've been honest with Philip from the beginning. None of this would've happened if only she'd been honest.

"I'm pregnant."

His confident expression twisted into a fierce straight line and he drew in several, slow deep breaths. He fell back against the couch, bringing his bawled fist to his mouth. "That slime." His gaze flicked to hers for an instant, his assurance traded for helplessness.

She walked across the room. "I don't know what to do."

"Are you sure? I mean, you've already seen a doctor?"

"Yes, I'm sure."

"Have you told anybody else?"

"No, I planned to tell my aunt as soon as I came home from the clinic Saturday morning two weeks ago, but Logan was there." She stared through the window, studying the trees lining the parking lot. "I couldn't. I still don't know what to do. I'm running out of time. I need to make a choice." Saying the words out loud created a torrent of guilt and twisted the knot in her stomach even deeper, stealing her breath.

She faced Nathan, waiting for his response. His elbows were propped on his knees, his face hidden behind his hands, and he said nothing. He stayed that way for a long moment before he looked up at her. His lips parted, but no sound emerged from his mouth. He seemed to take on the regret as if it were his responsibility.

"This is not your problem, Nathan."

He shook his head and leaned back against the couch.

"If I give the baby up for adoption, everyone would find out. I would have to explain what Philip did to me."

He looked at her with such compassion, it stole her breath. "What Philip did to you was wrong. It was very wrong, Addison."

"Would God be okay with ... it, if it was ... against my will?" She still couldn't voice the word *rape* or *abortion*. Not out loud.

Nathan stood, pacing back and forth. "Did you talk to a nurse? I mean, did you tell her what happened?"

"I started to, but something stopped me. You're the only one I've told."

Determination swept across his expression. "And if you have an abortion, no one would ever have to know?"

A small ounce of hope settled upon her. "No one but you ... and me."

"I'm the last person you should be getting advice from, Addison."

"I know I should've talked to my aunt or Taylor. But I didn't want them to know ... just in case. I didn't want anyone else to know."

"Okay, so let me ask you a question. If you go through with this—

abortion; do you really believe everything will be fine? That it will be like none of this ever happened?"

His words played over in her mind, the real meaning behind them piercing her soul. Slowly a bitter, stabbing pain webbed its way through her heart. Knowing that every single child in her classroom, in her school, in the world, would remind her that this child's chance at life had been stolen by her choice. "No, I don't believe that."

"You'll be starting a relationship with Logan built on lies."

"I don't want to hurt him. I don't want to lose him. I love him, Nathan."

He took a deep breath, still watching her, his eyes squinted as if considering his words. "Two close friends of mine dated all through high school. The circumstances were different, but she became pregnant, and because she was still in high school, she aborted the baby. Her boyfriend agreed it was the right thing to do. They were too young to have a baby and weren't ready to get married. That happened five years ago just before her seventeenth birthday."

Addison leaned forward, absorbing every word. "Wow, she was so young! How is she now? Are you still friends?"

"Yes, she comes over occasionally. They both do."

Her eyes widened. "So, they're still together?"

"No, they broke up weeks after the procedure. A procedure that is more horrifying than most people realize. She still struggles with the decision she made to destroy her child. She can't talk about it without crying. She has asked the same question a million times. Why didn't I just give her up for adoption?" The shift in his tone was unmistakable.

Nausea rolled in her stomach and she stood, fighting against it. She was only thinking of herself, selfishly thinking of how to keep from suffering any consequences, when this baby growing every minute inside her had done nothing wrong. It wasn't her fault. How could it be fair to punish, to murder her unborn baby? "You said *she*. But she couldn't have known." A little girl just out of her reach, repeating the word *Mommy* over and over had filled her dreams every night since she took the pregnancy test.

Nathan closed his eyes. "She knew."

She fell back against the cushion, her body heaving in response to his words. She knew. She saw. But how? She couldn't ask the forbidden question. Her mouth opened, but no sound escaped.

"I know this is hard to hear, but you should know everything. It's not simply taking care of it. It will never go away. This will always be a part of you … something you will carry with you for the rest of your life. I know your situation is different, but will you be able to live with your decision? That's what you need to decide. And really, Addison, this isn't about Logan. This is about you. Even if you were able to keep Logan, would it be enough?" Nathan sat in the space next to her. "My brother loves you, Addison. I know him better than anyone. I see the way he watches you, the way he acts around you. There's no doubt in my mind how he feels about you. Just think about telling him. I can't even imagine how you must feel—how scared you must be, but it will make you feel better. It will be okay."

Uncontrollable sobs broke through and she lay back down and curled into a ball, resting her head against the arm of the loveseat.

"I'm sorry," she told him, between sobs. "I don't mean to keep doing this to you. This isn't your problem."

She only had a few weeks left to make her decision, before it was too late. The counselor at the center had told her the earlier, the better. How the pill was the most popular choice but was only available up to ten weeks from conception. How it would be much like a period, only heavier. How ending her pregnancy would be easy, ending her baby's life would be too easy.

How had she even considered it as an option?

Logan hadn't known what to expect as he merged onto I-40 toward Raleigh after receiving a text from Nathan asking him to come over.

Things had been going great with Addison and he was anxious to talk to his brother.

Pulling into Nathan's apartment parking lot two hours later, he shut off his lights that already glared with dusk upon them.

He found a spot on the back side of the parking lot and took a deep breath.

He twisted one of his shirt buttons as he walked across the lot, glancing toward Nathan's door. Turning sideways to walk between Nathan's truck and a white Camry parked at an angle, he took a second look. The car looked like Addison's. He had never paid attention to white Camrys until he met her, he thought, climbing the stairs to Nathan's upper-level apartment.

It wasn't until he glanced again, after knocking on the door, that he noticed the wired figure hanging from the rearview mirror ... identical to the one that hung in Addison's car.

The soft knock roused Addison from her dream. She opened her eyes to find the room dark. She sat straight up, realizing after a few jumbled seconds that she'd fallen asleep on Nathan's couch.

Unable to clear her blurred vision, she glanced at the large clock hanging on the opposite wall. Eight-thirty. How long had she been sleeping? Soft voices filtered into the living room.

The door burst open and, startled, she turned. Logan stood in the doorway staring at her. She stood quickly, the sudden motion awkward. Had Nathan called him? Nathan followed behind him, his tanned cheeks a full shade lighter.

Logan stared at her with skepticism, his frown slowly deepening with sorrow. He spoke tensely, cautiously. "What are you doing here?"

Dread washed over her as her betrayal seemed to ooze from his pores, seeping into her skin like poison.

Addison crossed the room and reached out to him, a sudden longing to feel his touch directing her. He flinched, taking a step back. She glanced at Nathan, desperation bleeding through her veins.

That one look of betrayal changed everything.

Logan turned and hurried through the front door, not once looking back. Addison froze, waiting until she could no longer see him before she screamed out his name. "Logan—"

Nathan blew out a frustrated breath. "Stay here. Let me talk to him."

What would Nathan say? Would he tell Logan the truth? She fell into the loveseat, pulling her legs to her waist, and prayed like she never had before.

Her emotions unbalanced, she took a risk on hope, stood and rushed through the front door.

Logan jumped in his truck, anxious to get away. The agony crushing his chest raced against him. He should've known better than to trust her or his brother. How could he have let this happen again? How could he have been so blind?

Addison's guilty expression would forever be burned in his memory. She'd been caught and didn't even try to deny it. She just stood there, her face a mixture of shame and regret. But what did she regret? Hurting him, or getting caught?

Logan slammed the truck into reverse, ready to speed from the parking space as fast as he could. Music blared through the speakers, drowning out the voices desperate to make him crazy.

What was he thinking?

He couldn't afford to lose his temper. It might cost him his job. Plus, he couldn't just leave without answers.

Logan threw the gear in park and scrambled from the truck.

Nathan leaned against the rail. "Are you finished throwing your temper tantrum?"

Logan charged his brother, and within seconds he was pushing him against the building, until a shrill cry came from upstairs.

"Stop! Please don't fight," Addison screamed, her voice breaking with each word.

Logan stepped backward. He couldn't do this in front of Addison, no matter how badly she'd hurt him.

"Logan, please—"

What was she doing here? Why? Nothing made sense as he meandered away.

"Can you please come back upstairs? This is ridiculous, Logan. I really can't believe ..." Nathan shook his head in disgust. "You just need to calm down."

Nathan reached out to grab him, but Logan shook his arm away. It would be better to leave before he did something he'd regret. Still facing his brother, he felt Addison's presence and turned at the sound of her heavy breathing.

Agony twisted through him, hate seeping into every muscle of his body with each thought of catching them together. Blinded by fury, he turned to her.

He couldn't let this happen again. Not because of his brother. Not this time. Addison loved him. She wasn't Carrie. He needed to calm down and hear her out. "What are you doing here?"

She slumped against him, digging her fingers into his shirt, hanging onto him. Nathan turned and took a step leading to his apartment.

"I'll leave you two to talk. Don't do anything stupid, Logan."

Icy chills sliced through Logan's skin. He wanted to rip Nathan's arrogant head off his shoulders.

Addison pulled back, still clinging to him, watching his every move. Her eyes were red and swollen. He'd been too angry earlier to notice.

She took a step closer, fear lacing her expression. "Can we go somewhere?"

Weary from it all, he let his arms hang limp by his sides and he didn't budge, unwilling to give in to her.

Addison had never seen Logan so angry. Even when he'd thought she'd been drinking and driving that night, his eyes didn't hold this much hate. Now she was responsible once again for coming between Logan and his brother.

From one breath to the next, something in his demeanor transformed and Logan took her hand. "Let's go."

Addison surrendered to his touch, comforted by the connection, but her jaw was still shaking, her heart fluttering restlessly.

Logan led her along the sidewalk, the thick rasp of his breath an indication he was still upset. Very upset.

His shoulders slumped in defeat with each step. How would she ever survive this?

Thanking God for this time to think about what she wanted to say, she prayed for a solution, a miracle. But there was no other way. She had already caused too much strife for Ami's family. Being responsible for separating Ami's brothers was something she could never live with.

Logan envied Nathan. Her years of experience with Philip gave her more insight than she needed on how a man reacted when faced with the corruption of jealousy. She'd avoided the truth for months, not wanting to believe it, but she could no longer do that.

It was obvious and this was all her fault.

The hazy light of the moon filtered down on them from the darkened sky as they walked hand in hand toward the nearby park. Reaching the slide, Logan stopped walking, the same question flooding his mind. Nothing he came up with made any sense, nothing except his biggest fear. "Are you going to tell me why you're here?"

She kept a safe distance, backing away and keeping her gaze glued to the concrete beneath her feet.

"Logan, first of all ..." she started, her words a jerky whisper. "Your brother had nothing to do with this. I showed up at his apartment. He had no idea I was coming. I wasn't invited. Nathan did nothing wrong. It was all me."

Logan pressed against the steel ladder holding himself upright, defeat constricting his lungs. "You have feelings for him?"

"Not the way you're thinking. But yes, I love your whole family. Nathan's like a brother, but that's all." She touched Logan's arm, speaking softly yet determined. "You shouldn't fight. He's your brother. You're so blessed to have each other."

"We're not fighting, he just … I don't know. I let him get to me. I still don't understand what you're doing here."

She shook her head, her distress a silent shrill, foreboding winding a coil around his chest.

"There's something you should know." He fixed his gaze on her. A glimpse of hope flashed across her face. "I dated a girl in high school. Her name was Carrie." He had her attention. She waited expectantly. "We'd made plans to go out on a Friday night, so I drove to her house to pick her up. But on the way, I saw her and Nathan walking from one of the high school hangouts. At first, I thought nothing of it, not until I saw the way she looked at him, and then she stretched up and kissed him on the mouth." Addison gasped and he stopped. He wanted to explain, but he could tell she was hurting. Was this really what he should say right now?

She blinked and took a step closer. "What happened?"

Logan stared at her for a few seconds, willing her to understand. "Nathan noticed me first. His expression … I'll never forget how he looked at me. His face was full of regret." *Just like tonight*, though he kept that to himself. "When Carrie saw me, she pretended nothing had happened."

The memories of that night had a bittersweet feel. He knew the truth, and for the first time in years, he felt free from the pain it had caused him, yet he stood here tonight for a very similar reason.

"I'm so sorry, Logan. I know how that feels … how much it hurts. Is that why you broke up?"

With a thorough sweep of every feature of her face, Logan found hope in the affection spilling from her eyes. "We didn't break up. I killed her."

39

A heavy feeling settled in Addison's stomach. What did he mean? "You killed her?"

He stared at her without really seeing her. He seemed to have gone to another time, another place.

"We were in a car accident, that same night. I should've left. I shouldn't have let her climb in my car. I was so angry, I couldn't see straight." He paused, his gaze fixed on Addison, though something in his eyes was still distant. "She told me as I pulled onto the highway that she needed to talk to me. She said it would be better if we went our separate ways, because ..." He cleared his throat. "Because she was pregnant. The one thing she knew I couldn't live with ... her having another man's baby. I sped through the intersection and, out of nowhere, a drunk driver slammed into the passenger side. I never even saw the truck coming. She died later than night."

She wanted more than anything to comfort him, but she couldn't. There was nothing she could do.

He ran a hand over his face. "I believed Nathan was the baby's father for a long time. But I should've known better. I wasted so much time with him, with my family. I'm sorry, Addison. I didn't mean to react that way. It brought up so many terrible memories when I saw you together, but that's no excuse."

Understanding dawned on her and the reality of what she was about to do smothered her, making it hard to breathe. "Logan—"

"You have every right to be upset. I should never have treated you that way, either of you. Please forgive me."

She needed to get away from here. She would never be able to tell him the truth. Not now. Not after hearing the pain Carrie had caused him. He deserved better than this—better than her.

She wanted to wrap her arms around him and never let go. "Logan, I'm so sorry. I don't know what to say." Before her love for Logan Tant could alter her course, she kept her hands tucked inside her arms and shifted a half step back. "I'm moving. I've been thinking about it for a while. The hour drive both ways is too much."

There was a charged silence as he slowly inched backward, toward the curb. Moments later he moved closer, facing her, his eyes cloudy, blank. "What? When?" His voice was low, muddled.

She fought the tears that threatened to escape, and she looked away. "I don't know. As soon as possible."

The lines of their relationship had blurred over the last two weeks, and she knew she had to break it off with him, once and for all. Because she had no choice but to carry Philip's baby.

She pleaded with her eyes for him to understand. "You deserve better than me."

He pulled her against him. "How can you say that? You're everything to me. Please don't push me away. I'm sorry, I shouldn't jump to conclusions. I have a terrible habit of doing that."

"Logan, you've done nothing wrong. But nothing has changed. I shouldn't have—"

He pulled away and took several steps back. "What are you saying?" His confusion blended with hopelessness.

"I'm sorry. I can't see you anymore." She turned and hurried to her car, unable to look at his pleading gaze a moment longer.

She drove away and watched in the rear-view mirror as his posture crumpled in defeat.

The two-hour drive of replaying her conversation, of how she never should've given him false hope. The sight of him in agony, of finding her with his brother, broke her heart.

When she reached the house, deep sobs stole all her strength. *God, I don't know if I can do this? Please help me. I want to do the right thing. I want to do what you would want me to do.* Her stomach ached in her mourning. *I love him, Jesus. Please heal my broken heart.*

Pulling herself together, Addison walked through the front door and into the kitchen as Aunt Brenda stepped from the sink to face her. Addison collapsed in her aunt's arms.

Aunt Brenda detached slightly from the embrace and pulled back to look at her. "What's wrong, honey? Why are you crying?"

Slumping into a chair, Addison supported her elbows on the kitchen table, propping her chin in her hands. "I'm pregnant."

Aunt Brenda's mouth dropped open and her hands flew to her chest.

"It's Philip's."

Her aunt fell into the chair across from her, her eyes stricken. "How far along are you?"

Addison blinked, lifting her tear obstructed gaze to her aunt. "Two months, maybe ten weeks." They lapsed into silence for a few troubled moments. "There's something else you should know."

Her aunt's startled eyes stole over her with a worried sweep.

"Philip did it against my will."

Aunt Brenda stood, pushing her chair back all in one motion. "What?" The muscles around her aunt's jaw tightened. "What do you mean, he did this against your will?"

"Philip was waiting for me that night when I got home from work. Logan had brought me home and—" Addison's lower lip trembled as the memories of those moments came rushing back. "Philip saw us ... together. He was so angry. It all happened so fast and then he was gone."

"Where was Taylor?"

"Asleep. We rode to work together that night. When Logan showed up to drive me home, Taylor left. It was two in the morning before I got home." How could she have been so stupid? "I fought him as hard as I could. I just wasn't strong enough."

"Oh, honey, why didn't you tell me?"

Addison covered her mouth, stifling the sobs escaping, and shook her head. "I couldn't. I didn't know how."

Aunt Brenda dropped into the seat again slumping back, her head tilted toward the ceiling. Addison watched in silence as her aunt battled with her emotions. A tinge of guilt pervaded her at keeping this secret from her aunt for over two months.

"I should've been stronger. I should've been able to stop him."

Aunt Brenda leaned forward and slammed her fist on the table. "Don't you dare blame yourself!" Tears filled her aunt's eyes. "You are a precious, wonderful, beautiful person. I've never known anyone more giving, more caring. How dare that boy do this to you! Does he know you're pregnant?"

A hiccup escaped from deep inside. "No. And I don't want him to find out … I haven't seen him. He didn't know what he was doing. He was drunk. He probably doesn't remember."

Aunt Brenda took several, slow deep breaths and released them. "That's no excuse."

"Philip can't know. So, I can't press charges against him."

Aunt Brenda raised her brows. "But—"

"I'm going to have the baby," Addison said, her words softening. "I went to an abortion clinic two weeks ago to confirm the pregnancy." She inhaled a shaky breath. "I'm not going to lie, I thought about ending the pregnancy." Addison rubbed her stomach as the verse she'd learned as a girl lingered in her mind. *For you created my inmost being, you knit me together in my mother's womb.* The same verse the lady from the Pregnancy Resource Center mobile unit quoted after their short conversation as Addison was leaving the abortion clinic. The lady had given Addison other options, had given her hope. "I can't, Aunt Brenda. I just can't. It isn't the baby's fault. And God has given me peace."

"Don't you worry." Aunt Brenda declared as she bent to plant a kiss Addison's cheek. "We'll figure this thing out together."

Her aunt's acceptance soothed the jagged edges around her heart.

Logan spent the next few weeks in a daze. He poured himself into work, unable to focus on anything else. Nathan had called him every day, but he'd refused all his calls. Deep down, something told him it had nothing to do with Nathan, but he wasn't mentally prepared for the truth. So, he'd avoided any opportunity of finding out what really happened—why Addison had been at his apartment.

At the end of Logan's shift, Matt walked with him to the parking lot. "I'm worried about you."

"Don't be."

Matt stood by his car, his arms crossed over his chest. "Come by tonight. We're grilling out. And you know Shelley. There will be plenty."

"I can't."

"You can't or you won't." Matt had asked him to come over every weekend for weeks, so had his mom, but he always found an excuse. "You can't keep avoiding everyone."

Logan snatched his keys from his pocket and unlocked the door. He didn't feel like seeing all his friends or his family. They would have too many questions about Addison that he had no answers for.

"I promised my mom I would have dinner with them tonight." The admission left a sour taste on his tongue. He couldn't keep putting it off. "Maybe another time."

"Okay, bud. Give your mom a hug for me."

An hour later, Logan sat across from his family at dinner, intent on the food in front of him. No one spoke of Addison as he'd been expecting. He reached into the depths of his soul, salvaging any normalcy he could find.

"This is good, Mom."

"Thank you, Logan. I'm so glad you could join us for dinner tonight." Her motherly tone echoed through the dining room.

He glanced at Ami sitting across from him, her face downcast. She hadn't spoken to him all night. She glanced up just before he could look away.

Her glare bore a hole through his soul. "What did you do to her this time?"

"Ami." Mom's sharp tone held a warning.

Ami didn't heed it. "She's my friend." Ami's voice broke as sobs wracked her body. "Why did you have to ruin everything?"

Logan leaned back, his anger rising with each second. "You can still be her friend. I didn't do anything," he yelled across the table at his sister. "It was her choice. Not mine."

Dad slammed his fist on the table. "That's enough, you two."

Logan stood. "I'm sorry, Mom." The deep ache just below the surface threatened to engulf him. "I have to go."

Ami came running out the front door. He glanced back just as tears spilled onto her cheeks. "Call her, Logan. Make it right. She needs us." She took a quivering breath and walked toward him in longer strides. "Please, you can make it right." Her voice jumped an octave and she begged him again and again.

"I can't. It's over between us and that's the way it's going to stay."

He hurried to his truck, desperate for an escape. The metal rock screamed from his radio as he started his truck and he slammed all memories of the violet-eyed girl from his mind. She would never hurt him again.

40

Addison arrived at her classroom, a few weeks later surprised to find Charlotte Avery sitting in her desk.

"Hey. Did I forget to do something?" Addison scrambled through her memory trying to locate anything she may have forgotten from her to-do list.

"No, I just wanted to talk." Charlotte's normally bright eyes were now troubled.

Addison set her bag on the other side of the desk and busied herself with passing out the morning papers. "About what?"

"I'm worried about you. The first few weeks of school you were so happy, but something changed. You look so sad, and it's breaking my heart."

"It's a long story."

"I'm a good listener."

She couldn't talk about this. Even thinking of Logan and all she'd lost caused her eyes to burn with unshed tears.

"I have a lot going on, but it's nothing I can't handle."

"We don't know each other very well, seeing how we've only been working together for a while. But I know you're pregnant."

Addison spun around from the middle of the classroom and faced her. "What?"

"Aren't you?"

Addison glanced at her midsection. "How did you know?"

"I'm a woman. And look at me." Charlotte ran both hands over her protruding belly. "We girls can sense these things."

Addison took a first-row seat. "It's complicated. And I'm really tired. The hour drive every morning and afternoon is wearing me out. What I really need is to move here to Jacksonville."

"My parents have rental property and there's a small house available. It's only a mile down the road."

"Are you serious?" Addison's mind raced ahead. That's exactly what she needed. What would she do if she ran into Philip in Wilmington? Or Logan? If Charlotte could already tell, it wouldn't be long before everyone else could too. "How much is it?"

"Let me ask. I'll let you know tomorrow. I do know they're partial to teachers, so they'll work around your income and what you can afford."

"You have no idea how much moving here will help me."

Charlotte stood to leave.

"Oh, wait! I did need to ask you something." Addison wiggled herself free from the small desk. "I know we send food home on the weekends for a few children who need it. But what's the policy on keeping extra snacks in the room for children who aren't sent with anything?" Her eyes misted. "It rips me apart seeing those babies staring at the other children eating their snacks every day and they have nothing."

Warmth filled Charlotte's eyes. "What were you thinking?"

"Bringing in some bulk items to have on hand, like crackers and juice boxes. We could keep them in the closet. And have our assistant stick a treat into their cubby before snack."

"That's a great idea."

"Do you think Mrs. Andrews will be all right with it?"

"Oh, yes. Most definitely." The light in Charlotte's eyes brightened. "In fact, we could get all the classes do this."

"In my past experience, there wasn't extra money in the budget for something like this, so I would buy the snacks myself."

"You're probably right."

Things would be tighter when Addison moved into her own place, had her own bills, but it would be worth setting some extra aside for her children who needed it.

"I even think a few of our parents may be willing to donate some items too. I wish I had something to give to my student today that never has a snack packed."

Addison reached into the closet and grabbed a few packs of cheese crackers. "Here, take these for now."

Charlotte took the packages with a smirk. "Look at you being sneaky. You are amazing, Addison."

"I was planning to talk to Mrs. Andrews today. Just wanted your opinion since you've been here awhile." Addison joined her at the door. "And thank you for your concern. You're so sweet to check on me."

"I'll let you prepare for your class, but I'm here if you ever need to talk." Charlotte leaned her head against Addison's shoulder the same way Casey used to do. "You'll be a wonderful mother, Addison. I can tell by how much you love these children."

The effect of Charlotte's words lingered long after she left, and even into the following weeks as Addison packed her things to move into the rental house.

"I'm ready," she said to Aunt Brenda on a cool October morning, as she loaded her last few bags into the car. "I can't wait for you to see it. You're going to love it."

Aunt Brenda cleared her throat. "I'm sure I will, honey."

"It's fully furnished, and it even has a back porch. You know how much I love sitting on the porch."

"Yes, I know."

"I'll be back. It will be less stressful without the drive. And it's only until after the baby comes." She hugged her aunt from behind.

There was some excitement, but it was mostly worry. All the confident talk was just as much for herself as it was for her aunt. "Besides, I'll visit some weekends when I can, and you can visit me too."

Aunt Brenda frowned. "I'm trying to be happy about this, I really am. It's a good thing for you. You'll do great, honey. But if you need anything, you call me. And don't forget to call me when you get there."

"I won't."

Addison drove the hour drive the last time for a while. But something about leaving Logan permanently behind, opened the fresh wound of her broken heart.

And now that she was alone settled inside the house, she waited for that certain surge of peace.

It didn't come.

The next two months crawled by and the cold weather arrived, mimicking her mood. Addison worked busily on the last-minute details for the Christmas play the elementary students would perform tonight. They had a total of eighty-three kindergarteners and needed every teacher to pull this off.

Addison was in charge of the music. She'd play the piano and help the third through fifth grade boys and girls with their solos and choir pieces. It had given her something to think about—something other than Logan. She hadn't seen or spoke to him in months, but she thought of him constantly.

"Miss Morgan?"

Addison swiveled on the keyboard stool at the sound of the soft voice. "Yes, Cassidy."

"Are you having a baby?"

Addison covered her mouth. "What?"

"You look like my mom. She's having a boy."

Addison couldn't speak. She only stared at the precious child who waited for an answer.

"Addison Morgan." Taylor called from across the room and she sighed in relief.

She pulled the child into a hug. "I'm so happy for you. How exciting it will be to have a baby brother!" She pulled her blouse away from her midsection as she strode across the auditorium to her friend.

Addison pulled Taylor into a hug. "Hey, you made it."

"I wouldn't miss this for the world. And you look good." Taylor gave her a crooked grin. "How're you feeling?"

"Today's a good day."

They walked away arm in arm, Taylor filling her in about how nothing had changed in Wilmington, and how she hadn't seen or heard anything from Philip and there was no news about Logan or his family either.

"You should call him."

"I'm not calling him," Addison told her, though not a single day had passed that she hadn't considered it.

"When are you coming home?"

"I'll be home for Christmas, but I have to be careful. I can't take a chance of running into Philip." The menacing thought wormed into the hollow of her mind.

Taylor frowned as if sensing her sadness. "Nothing's been the same without you."

"I'm sure you're so busy with what's-his-name, you haven't missed me a bit."

Taylor placed her left hand on her arm. "His name is Michael and even though he's perfect, I've missed you like crazy."

Addison's mouth hung open, the diamond sparkling on Taylor's finger almost blinding her. "You're engaged? When did this happen?"

"Last night. You should know you would be the first to know."

"Oh, Taylor, I'm so happy for you."

"You can have this too." That calming smile of Taylor's expanded. "And I still believe it will be with Logan."

"You're not going to do this again, are you?"

"It's not fair what Philip did to you. But I know God wants happiness for you. Look how far you've come? You're so strong and I'm so proud of you."

"Thank you, Taylor. I could've never made it through this time without him or you."

The cold wind whipped through Logan's hair when he opened the door.

"Hey, li'l bro. You ready to bust this joint?"

Logan clasped his brother's shoulder. "Are you ever going to grow up?"

"Not if I don't have to."

In the parking lot below, Logan searched for Nathan's car.

"Where'd you park?" Logan turned to find Nathan standing in front of a black Mustang. Nathan hit the automatic car lock button and the head lights flashed. "You didn't."

"I did. Climb in." Nathan opened the door and slid onto the black leather seat. "What are you waiting for? I'm not opening the door for you."

He did a thorough scan before climbing in. The scent of leather filled the small space and Logan rubbed his fingers against the soft material and sighed.

"It was love at first sight."

Logan flinched as if physically slapped. Did everything have to remind him of Addison? "Why did you have to get all the good luck in this family?"

"Me? You're the lucky one. If you'd just let me explain."

Logan opened the car door. "Don't or I'll get out."

"Okay, okay. Don't be so touchy."

Logan slammed the door harder than he'd intended, his emotions raging. "Not one word about her, Nathan."

Defeated, Nathan hung his head. "How's Ami? Does she like her classes?"

"I don't know. She never talks to me anymore."

Nathan smirked and set the car in reverse. He floored the gas, squealing out of the parking lot, throwing Logan's head back. A rebuke was on the tip of his tongue, but he fought the urge and stayed silent.

A mile down the road, Nathan punched him in the shoulder. "You got the tickets, right?"

Logan lifted the wallet from his khaki's and slipped two square cards from the pocket. "One for you and one for me."

Nathan howled. "Friday night football."

On the first day of Christmas break, Addison drove the short distance to Charlotte Avery's house after getting the news, a week ago, that she'd had her baby.

There was something nerve-wracking about visiting a mother who'd had a baby, a mother who could keep her baby, a mother who didn't have to hide her pregnancy. Especially when nothing about her own pregnancy was certain.

A great part of her hesitancy was her fear that seeing Charlotte's child would somehow make her feel even closer to the one she carried. Make her want to keep her baby instead of giving to another family who couldn't conceive one of their own.

She pulled into the driveway, past the mailbox still decorated with limp pink ribbons.

Charlotte's husband answered the door, and a rush of warm air from inside mingled with the icy air surrounding her. "Come on in. It's freezing out there."

"Thank you." Addison walked into the living room and set her wrapped gift on the table before removing her heavy coat and gloves.

Charlotte didn't say anything; she only smiled, the kind of smile that brightened her whole face.

The infant, bundled in her mother's arms, made a soft sucking sound as she searched for her tiny fingers.

Addison took a seat on the couch next to Charlotte, leaned closer, and tilted forward to get a better look at her tiny face. Charlotte twisted slightly, placing the baby into Addison's unsteady arms.

"She's so beautiful, so perfect," Addison said as tears she'd hadn't known were there dripped onto the pink blanket. The baby's gentle coos strengthened in volume as her mouth opened a fraction. Addison's short burst of laughter blended with the sob at the back of her throat. "I'm so happy for you."

Addison placed a soft kiss on the infant's warm head; her scent, so soft and sweet, was something she'd never forget.

While Addison attempted to amuse the baby with various expressions, Charlotte retrieved the gift from the table. Charlotte carefully tore away the pink wrap adorned with a gray elephant and, lifting the box lid, she pulled out the tiny dress. "Aw, it's beautiful."

Addison smiled, when truthfully, shopping for Charlotte's baby had been one of the hardest things she'd ever done. Mourning the loss of her baby had begun months ago, the moment it was confirmed. Then shopping for things, she would never be able to buy for her own baby deepened her grief with a sharpness she never expected.

"Have you thought of any names yet?"

The question stiffened Addison's shoulders again. Even though the answer hung on the tip of her tongue for weeks now. *Sophia Rose.* The name had come to her hours after the nurse accidentely told her the sex of her baby during an ultrasound.

Charlotte held the dress up for several seconds before folding it gently and placing it on top of the box. "I hope you have a girl, because I can share so many things with you. You may not have to buy anything."

Clearing her throat, Addison scrambled to maintain her smile, when it took everything within her not to burst into a harsh, blubbering cry. It was only then that she'd realized how much she wanted to keep the baby growing inside her.

Addison arrived back at her small rental house just as the first flurries fell. Within two hours, snow covered everything, creating a white wonderland with the usual traffic ceasing. Addison somberly listened, over the next few mornings, to the sound of children playing and laughing as they sledded down narrow sidewalks. Their voices were filled with joy at being given the gift of a white Christmas.

Addison herself would normally be thrilled to see a snowfall like this, but the condition of her own heart was dreary and gray. It dangled over her like a black cloud, stripping the joy from any circumstance. The snowfall had stolen her gift of being able to go home a few days. Phone calls, texts and FaceTime would never compare to warm hugs and face-to-face conversations.

When Addison was finally able to return to school a week later, she hoped the shadow of gloom dangling over her would dissipate. She prayed being around her children would drown out the whispers of her broken heart. It had been the loneliest Christmas of her life. And it wasn't until yesterday that the temperature had warmed up enough to melt the icy roads just in time for school to resume as scheduled.

"Addison Morgan?" someone called as she stepped from her car.

She stared at the young man facing her. Was she supposed to know him? "Yes?"

"I'm McKenzie Richards. I'm taking Mrs. Avery's kindergarten class while she's out on maternity leave." He offered his hand.

"Oh, but I was expecting a…"

"A woman to take her place. Don't worry, you're not the first one."

She pulled at her shirt smiling sheepishly. "I'm sorry. It's nice to meet you."

"So, this is your first year?" His voice was loud and enthusiastic.

Addison reached down to lift the box of books. "Yes, my first year."

A crooked grin filled his lips. "I saw you on campus. UNC Wilmington, right?"

"Yes." Her surprise at them graduating from the same school leaked into her voice. "You graduated this year? Or last year since it's the new year?" She laughed.

"Last year."

"Okay." She gave him a sideways glance and smiled and so did he.

"Here, let me." He lifted the awkwardly shaped box effortlessly from her hands. "Where to?"

"To my room, but I can manage."

He shook his head. "Lead the way. I don't mind at all."

She reached her classroom and opened the door, allowing him to pass through. "I really appreciate your help."

"A pregnant lady should never have to carry anything when a capable man is anywhere nearby."

He glanced at her ring finger and Addison felt the heat rushing up her neck. "Thank you again, Mr. Richards, for your help."

He took a step toward the door. "It was no trouble at all and please call me McKenzie."

Addison's mind whirled. Something about him seemed oddly familiar.

He returned a moment later, clinging to a folder. "Oh, I've spoken with Charlotte and she gave me her outline. Could you walk me through it? She said you worked out the details together."

"Of course."

His deep brown eyes studied her every move as he slid a chair next to her desk.

"You'll go through the schedule as planned out."

"Do you follow this schedule as well?"

"Yes, and we go to break and lunch at the same time."

"Great, so if I have any questions, I'll be able to ask you." He paused, leaning back. "I must admit, I'm a little nervous. Me against twenty-two five-year-olds. It seems a bit overwhelming."

"Yes, but you'll have Miss Davis assisting you. She's great."

"Well, Addison ..." He propped his elbows on the table and leaned forward. "Is it okay if I call you that?"

"Yes, of course."

"You've been a great help to me. I don't know how I'll ever be able to repay you."

A nervous laugh fell from her lips. "Don't be silly. We all have to help each other occasionally. You just watch, I'll be asking you for help before you know it."

"I'll be looking forward to it."

She stood as children filtered in and placed coats and lunchboxes in their cubbies. "Class starts in a few minutes, but we can finish at lunch. If you have any questions or need anything—"

"Thank you, Addison. I'll see you at lunch."

At the end of the day, Addison started her car and the song playing on the radio caused an audible gasp to slip from her throat. Why did her mind insist on returning to thoughts of Logan over and over throughout the day? Her heart was still breaking as if she had just seen him yesterday.

It occurred to her that there was little comfort in being the one to end things even when it was for the right reasons. Instead, the pain seemed deeper, more irrational. She caught herself having unspoken arguments with herself more than once that maybe she'd made a mistake. But then her sensible self would always win.

Logan had probably moved on and never even thought of her anymore. She glanced at the clock on the dashboard, another full lonely evening stretching out before her.

If only she could forget him.

41

The first few weeks of the new year brought more cold weather with long dreary days. With each kick, the baby grew stronger as she weakened in her determination to give this baby to another family. And by the end of January, there was no hiding her pregnancy from anyone.

Addison hadn't been to Aunt Brenda's house since before Christmas and couldn't wait any longer to see her. Even though she was taking a huge risk, she took off on her trek to Wilmington the first weekend of February after a long, exhausting day of school. Five minutes before she reached her aunt's house, her phone rang. Aunt Brenda had forgotten the dressing and asked if she would mind picking some up.

The grocery store was nearly empty this time of day. It was a good thing. Addison was ready to get to the warmth and comfort of Aunt Brenda's and was in no mood for running into anyone she might know.

After making the quick purchase, she looked both ways before crossing the parking lot. She hurried to reach her car, when a familiar voice called her name. "Addison?"

Panicked, she picked up her stride, hoping her pursuer would realize he had been mistaken in his recognition and leave her alone.

"Hey, Addison, wait up." The sound of his voice drew closer and she could no longer ignore the familiarity. Little could be done now so she turned. "McKenzie, what in the world are you doing here?"

He took the last few steps, closing the gap between them. "I'm visiting a friend this weekend. What about you?"

"My aunt lives here. I'm visiting too."

"I'm so glad I ran into you." He took her bag. "I was hoping to talk to you after school, but you got out of there so fast."

"Yeah, trying to avoid the five o'clock traffic." She kept walking, dodging a vehicle backing out. Taking her bag from him, she dropped it onto her back seat. "What did you want to talk about?"

"The Valentine's party is Wednesday and I wondered if maybe"—he took a step closer—"you and I could work together on the preparations. Maybe have dinner and discuss the plans or whatever."

Addison leaned against the car. "I already have plans for dinner, and my best friend will want the rest of my time. But sure, we can do that. It will make things easier. We'll get together Monday. I've already sent a treat list home with the kids."

"Yeah, me too. Okay, I'll see you Monday then." He reached across, opening her door. "Take care and be careful in this storm."

"Thanks, McKenzie, you too."

───────────

Logan had stood motionless at the end of the aisle as the young woman grabbed a bottle of salad dressing. She had glanced over her shoulder after making her purchase and in that one moment his world rocked on its axis.

It was her.

With slow steps he walked through the automatic doors, his heart wrenching in agony. She had to be at least seven months pregnant. Why hadn't she told him? Was it Philip's? Suddenly the last time he saw her, the night he found her at Nathan's, came rushing back. No, it couldn't be Nathan's.

No.

The sky darkened and a flash of lightening lit the clouds.

A conceited smile filled the guy's face, the guy she'd been talking to, when he turned to run across the parking lot and reached his car just before the skies opened.

Rain fell from the heavens, drenching Logan within seconds.

Unable to move, he stared as Addison's white Camry backed out of the parking space and turned in his direction. She drove slowly, her windshield wipers clearing the heavy raindrops away. She reached the end of the row in front of him and she stopped.

Their eyes met and hers widened before she drove slowly toward the exit and out of his view.

Addison parked in Aunt Brenda's driveway, her hands trembling. *How could I drive away and leave him standing there?* His shocked look could only mean one thing. He hadn't known.

Pulling herself together she collected her bag, walked inside, and collapsed in her aunt's arms. "What's wrong?"

"I saw him."

"Who?"

"Logan. He saw me. He was just standing there in the pouring rain, staring at me." Seeing him made her want to go to him, to selfishly soothe her aching heart. Addison sat on the couch, lowering her head. "He didn't know."

"What do you mean, he didn't know?"

"That I'm pregnant. I never told him." This revelation had somehow given her hope. Made her forget why she had done such a foolish thing as giving him up.

Aunt Brenda sat in the recliner across from her, resting her fingers against her knees. "Was Nathan supposed to tell Logan?"

"No, but I thought he would." Just as quickly as the hope had taken root, it decomposed. "He isn't going to understand why I never said anything. I can only imagine what he must be thinking."

"I'm wondering the same thing myself."

Heat flushed Addison's cheeks. "I couldn't take that chance. I had more to consider than just myself. With Logan being a cop, he wouldn't understand why I didn't press charges." Had she been wrong all along. "If Philip knew this baby was his ... well, what if he tries to take the baby?"

"Maybe you should call Logan and explain? I have a feeling he would understand."

Addison slumped into the couch.

"Why don't you rest for a bit while I finish dinner." Aunt Brenda walked into the kitchen as Addison carried her overnight bag to the bedroom.

Overwhelmed with emotion, she heaved air into her lungs as she curled onto her side in the middle of her bed and stared at the walls of a bedroom that no longer belonged to her. She was haunted by the fact that she belonged nowhere. Not with her mama, not living here with her aunt, not in Jacksonville in a rented house hiding her pregnancy from the world.

But what troubled her most of all, she didn't want her baby to ever feel alone and unwanted, or that she didn't belong. Addison imagined all the ways she could give this baby a wonderful life. Be the kind of mother that would make her daughter feel secure and loved. She would be nothing like her mama had been for her.

There was only one thing her and her mama had in common, her mama carrying another man's baby because of her infidelity. And Addison carrying Philip's baby, even though it wasn't the easiest choice.

With an image of Charlotte's baby girl merging with the baby living inside her, Addison drifted into a restless sleep.

Logan had called Nathan as soon as he reached his truck. "I need to talk to you now. I'm coming to Raleigh."

"Did you want me to meet you at Mom's?"

"No, the ride will do me good. I'm on the way." He pressed end, not giving Nathan a chance to object.

Two hours later, Logan dropped his coat in the corner of the room and stood across from his brother. "I saw her. Today."

Nathan's eyes brightened. "Addison? Where? Did you talk to her?"

"No, I didn't talk to her. What am I supposed to say to her? 'Wow, you're pregnant'?" Nathan's expression showed no hint of surprise. "You knew?"

Nathan wandered across the room toward him. "It wasn't my place to tell you."

"Is it yours?"

Nathan's face twisted in anguish. "Logan, how could you even say that? After all we've been through."

"I don't know what to think." Logan shook his head and sat on the sofa. "Why didn't she just tell me the truth?"

"The truth?" Nathan walked toward him. "What would you have said to her? Would you have stood by her?"

"I don't know. I don't know anything. I'm so confused."

Nathan sat in the space next to him. "She doesn't think she deserves you."

Logan buried his face in his hands, staring blankly at his fingertips.

"Talk to her, Logan. She needs your friendship."

"She doesn't want my friendship. She wanted yours. She came here to you, instead of me."

"Quit being so stubborn. She had nothing to lose with me. With you, she faced losing everything."

"She didn't lose me; she tossed me out like I was nothing to her. Twice."

"You don't understand."

Logan clenched his fists. "And I suppose you do? Of course, you do. She confided in you. I knew she still had feelings for Philip and was having a hard time getting over him, but I would've never thought she would—"

"Look at you." There was a steely edge to Nathan's voice. "You always jump to conclusions and react before hearing the whole story. I saw her here in Raleigh … at the mall. She was crying and I knew something had happened. She'd come to see her mom, but her mom already had plans and didn't have time for her. I just happened to be in the right place at the right time for Addison during a very vulnerable time."

Logan fell back against the sofa, staring down at his hands. "I knew she was dating Philip, but she told me it was over between them. She was still seeing him behind my back." Logan stood and scuffled his feet. "Why do I even care?"

"Because you love her."

"Well, apparently my love wasn't enough for her. She wanted that jerk instead."

"You're wrong. It wasn't like that."

"She was still with Philip while we were supposed to be dating."

Nathan threw his hands up in the air. "Do you really believe she would do that to you? Are you so self-absorbed in your pity over what Carrie did to you that you can't trust anyone? After all these years you fall for the most beautiful, caring, girl you will ever have the opportunity to love and you are throwing it all away because of your jealousy."

"I'm not jealous. She's pregnant, with Philip's baby. Are you telling me she got pregnant before we started dating? No, you can't. I've done the math a hundred different ways. And it all ends up with the same sum. She got pregnant while we were together. Unless I'm way off with my calculations from how pregnant she looks."

Nathan closed his eyes. "The baby's due in March."

Logan counted the months on his fingers and flinched. He turned to leave. He knew it. There was nothing else to say.

"Where are you going?"

Logan crossed the room and grabbed his jacket. "I'm leaving."

"Are you going to talk to her?"

Logan pressed his lip into a thin line fighting to gain control. "You can't be serious. What am I supposed to say, congratulations? I hope you and Philip will be happy together."

"She isn't with Philip."

"Is that supposed to make me feel better? Nothing you've said changes anything."

Nathan clutched the edge of the table and leaned forward. "Then why did you come here? If it bothers you so much that she's pregnant, why are you here? Because you wanted to make sure it isn't mine."

"Are you trying to push me?"

"I'm trying to help you understand that you can't jump to conclusions and act on them. You should talk to her. Don't let her go, Logan. Fight for her."

"I tried. She didn't give me a choice. But none of that matters now."

Nathan rubbed his jaw, studying him with weary eyes. "So, I guess she did the right thing not talking to you. It would have devastated her if you'd said any of this to her."

"It doesn't matter what I would've said to her."

Nathan slammed his fist against the coffee table. The gesture reminded him of Dad. "It matters more than you think, because it would have driven her even deeper into despair if she'd told you the truth."

"What truth? That she cheated on me, or that she's sorry she got caught?"

"No," his voice lowered in defeat, "that Philip raped her."

Addison spent the rest of the weekend unable to remove the image of Logan's face, the sorrow in his eyes. She'd tossed and turned every night, dreaming of Logan standing in the rain staring at her, begging her to stop. She had hoped he would call and demand an explanation, but even as she drove back to Jacksonville Sunday night he still hadn't.

And she knew he never would.

Logan was a part of her past and that was where he would stay. As bad as she wanted to go to him and beg his forgiveness, what good would it do? Nothing would change the fact that she was carrying Philip's baby, a baby that wasn't conceived out of love.

Early the next morning, she reached for her phone and called in for a sub to take her place. She couldn't face anyone. Not today.

Settled on her decision and relieved to have a few more hours to herself, she climbed under the covers and buried her head in the pillow and cried until her head ached.

At noon, she shuffled to the kitchen to the coffee maker. Maybe a strong cup of coffee would make her feel better. The cold winter air filled the house and she snuggled on the couch with her coffee and blanket.

After several hours of watching reruns, she turned off the television. The cold wind howled outside, and she stared through the front window as a school bus stopped just up the block. Children bundled up in coats and scarves wobbled toward their homes. Fresh tears blurred her vision as she thought of the child she carried inside.

It's not fair, God. She spoke through the windowpane, her hot breath fogging it instantly. With her sweatshirt, she made a circle, erasing the evidence. A gray Silverado crept by her house, the tinted windows exactly as those of Logan's truck. She leaned back but quickly changed her mind, wanting to see the truck so similar to his. But when she looked again, the truck was gone.

It couldn't have been him, he was working in Wilmington, but her heart pounded for an hour after seeing the familiar truck. She wanted to climb in her car and drive back to Wilmington, to go straight to Logan and confess her undying love. But she couldn't.

She would leave Logan and his family alone. She'd caused them enough pain. Mrs. Tant, Ami, and Nathan, even Mr. Tant, had all been so wonderful to her, accepted her as part of their family. And she wanted her memories of their time together to remain untainted by the ugliness hovering over her.

Addison returned to school on Tuesday glad for the normal routine.

"We missed you yesterday."

Addison glanced up to see McKenzie walking toward her. "I wasn't feeling good. Did anything exciting happen in my absence?"

He took a seat in one of the student's chairs facing her. "No, but I'm glad you're feeling better."

"Yeah, me too. So how far behind am I?"

"You're not behind at all. I took your papers home last night and graded them for you and I've got some ideas for the party tomorrow. See what you think." He pulled a piece of paper from a manila envelope and handed it across the desk to her.

"Wow, you did all this?"

"Actually, Mrs. Thompson let me look at her list of games and I jotted down what I thought would work for us."

"This looks good to me. Let me make a copy for tomorrow."

"That one is yours to keep." He walked around the desk, closing the distance between them. "Were you feeling unwell because of your pregnancy?"

Addison blushed at his bluntness. "Not exactly. It was probably just a bug."

"If there's anything I can do, let me know." He turned and winked.

"Thanks, I will." She hoped she didn't seem rude, but his question stirred unwanted feelings. Feelings she couldn't deal with right now.

She stood against the brick building as her class ran toward the playground. Keeping her eyes on the small girls climbing the monkey bars, she set her things on the bench and rubbed her arms. The last of the snow had melted, but the icy air remained.

Addison glanced at her assistant, Mrs. Baker. "We won't be out here long."

"I now it's freezing. I thought it would have warmed up by now. It was supposed to reach the mid-fifties by noon. Are you feeling better?"

"Yes, thank you."

A soft voice caught her attention. "Miss Morgan?"

"Yes, Amelia?"

"My nose is burning."

Addison laughed. "It's a little too cool to be out here today. Why don't you stand here while I call the others and we'll go in and play a game instead?"

"Yes, ma'am."

After her class formed a single-file line, they headed inside and she worked to get the excited children, full of energy, to settle down.

"Okay, class. It's a little too cold to play outside, so Amelia," she said glancing at the blue-eyed girl, "and I have decided to play a game inside."

The boys and girls formed a circle on the carpet for their game and Addison pointed to David, who sat quietly. "We're going to play basketball with our sight words. David, you will go first. When you name a word correctly, you get to shoot this ball to the basket. If you make it, you go again. Ready?"

The game continued through their thirty-minute recess break and she smiled at each child as they took a turn.

"Okay class, let's return to our seats and take out your readers."

Mrs. Baker returned from the teacher's lounge and handed Addison a chocolate éclair one of the teachers had made."Oh no, you don't. You know I'm trying to watch what I eat."

Mrs. Baker smirked. "Really, Addison. You look fabulous. That baby's hungry too, sugar."

A pang of regret filled her. "This isn't exactly healthy food for the baby."

"Is anything ever really healthy? Come on, you look so sad. I thought this would cheer you up."

Addison took the wrapped glazed dough drizzled with chocolate. "Thank you. It was very sweet of you."

Mrs. Baker slipped her arm through Addison's. "You know, if you ever need to talk, I'm a really good listener."

She smiled and took a small bite, washing it down with her bottled water. "I know you are. Hey, this is really good."

"I know."

Mrs. Baker turned her attention back to the class as Addison called for Derek to come to the front to read.

While leading the rest of the children through their reading time, Addison pulled apart the valentines she'd bought for the children and signed her name on each one. After dropping a few pieces of candy in each bag, she tied them and placed them in a basket to pass out during the party scheduled for tomorrow. She should've done this yesterday, but after seeing Logan Friday standing in the rain, she couldn't bring herself to look at the little cards containing words of friendship—words of love.

After giving homework instructions, she read a valentine's story to her class, ignoring the smoldering ache of her heart.

43

Logan pulled into the school parking lot and sat there for ten minutes before he climbed from his truck. He had taken all weekend to think through every detail of how he wanted to handle this.

It had taken all his strength to keep from finding Philip and beating him to a pulp for what he had done to Addison. Instead, he had made a decision. He would fight for Addison Morgan.

There was no better day than Valentine's Day to start his quest. He loved her with all his heart and would stick by her no matter what. And he was ready to show her just how much he meant that.

After signing in, Logan got directions to Addison's room from one of the ladies working in the office. "They're scheduled to be in the auditorium, but you may catch her before she takes her class." She wrote down the directions to the auditorium just in case. "Are you a parent?"

"No, a good friend. Thank you so much."

Minutes later, Logan stood across from Addison's classroom as she read a story to her class from a wooden stool. She propped the book over her protruding belly and the sight took him by surprise.

Logan took a step back into an alcove, hiding as children exited from a classroom across the hall. Kids talked and snickered among themselves as they made a formal line on the other side of Addison's doorway.

The teacher, a tall young man not much older than him, walked to Addison's door and stood there silently watching her. After a moment, he approached her and she smiled, her eyes embarrassed. It wasn't until the teacher walked from the room that he recognized him from the grocery store parking lot on Friday afternoon.

What was he doing in Wilmington, if he worked here?

Logan pulled the vase filled with daisies closer against his chest. Logan hoped Addison waited until her class filed from the room and would follow behind them, but that wasn't what happened. She walked side by side with the other teacher in between both classes. They talked and laughed, and he carried her things.

Hot anger ripped a jagged hole through his chest. He thought of Nathan's words of advice.

Don't jump to conclusions. Don't act on what you think you see. Wait for an explanation.

That all sounded good, but right now watching the two of them walking side by side, talking in hushed whispers, that advice didn't make him feel better. Calm down. They work together, that's all. He wasn't going to give up that easily.

He followed a safe distance behind and waited until everyone had entered the auditorium before he slipped in through the side door. He searched every corner for Addison but didn't see her. Anywhere.

"May I help you?"

Logan turned to find the teacher from across the hall, looking down on him. Of course, he was taller. Regaining his composure, he straightened. It didn't matter if the simple act didn't increase his height, it made him feel better. "I'm here to see Addison. Addison Morgan."

"Logan?" The sound of her soft voice from behind him calmed every jealous emotion in one instant.

He turned slowly, taking in her blue-violet eyes, mesmerized by the warm glow in her cheeks.

She turned to the other teacher. "I'll be right back." She took Logan's arm, and he obliged. Her soft grip could have pulled him anywhere at that moment. They reached the hall before she stopped and faced him. "What are you doing here?"

He cleared his dry throat and handed her the vase. "Happy Valentine's Day."

Her head tilted to one side. She kept her gaze locked on the flowers, and he immediately regretted not going after her, for giving up so easy.

"You came all the way here."

"I wanted to see you." He couldn't say the words he wanted to say out loud, and the silence was deafening. "I would've called, but I was scared you wouldn't talk to me."

"You were scared I wouldn't talk to you?" Her gaze fell to the flowers again and her frown deepened.

"Not after I saw you that day at the grocery store."

"I'm sorry, I should've stopped. I—" He brushed his fingers against her cheek, encouraging her to look at him. A sheen of moisture filled her eyes as she looked from him to the flowers. "I've hated myself that I left you standing there every minute since."

From the moment Nathan had told him the truth, he'd wanted to hold her. She was standing here in front of him and he couldn't resist. He wrapped her into his free arm, relishing the feel of her body leaning into his. "It's so good to see you. Happy Valentine's Day." They stood there in the darkened hallway, holding to each other.

Reluctantly, he let her go and, though each step hurt, he backed away. "I should let you get back to your class."

"Thank you, Logan." The underlying tone in her voice told him all he needed to know. She was glad he'd come.

"I'll see you later?" he asked, hoping, begging for some sign that he would be welcomed if he showed up again.

"Okay." Her soft whisper resonated through the deepest corners of his mind.

Addison wanted to run after Logan's retreating form but stopped herself. He reached the double doors at the end of the hall and turned with a final wave. Her skin still tingled from where he had touched her. Lifting trembling fingers to her parted lips, she slowly entered her classroom, inhaling the scent of the perfect white daisies staring up at her.

After setting the vase on her desk, she wiped at her fresh tears and surveyed her makeup before walking back to the auditorium.

He came. The reality of his presence brought on such an exhilarating rush of emotions, she walked down the hall as if gliding on a cloud.

Several of the other teachers stopped her when she entered the room. "Who was that?"

A nervous laugh escaped her lips. "A friend of mine."

"A very nice-looking friend." Miss Davis, her assistant, said, pinching her cheeks. She winked at Addison. "Valentine's Day makes me crazy."

Mrs. Baker smirked. "Don't let her fool you. Everything makes her crazy, especially a good-looking man."

"Thank you for covering for me."

Addison laughed, unable to contain the joy filling her as she glanced at McKenzie Richards. He stood across the room with both of their classes, his lips tightly pressed together. She walked toward the children gathered at one of the games.

"Could he be the reason you're bursting with joy?" He didn't wait for her to answer. "He's a lucky guy." The friendliness in his voice didn't match his eyes. They were darker, sunken. "Hey, I didn't mean anything by that. I'm sorry." His voice was softer, yet his disappointment remained.

Her emotions were raw due to seeing Logan after all these months, having him show up here, on Valentine's Day. "No, it's okay. Excuse me."

Addison breathed a sigh of relief at the end of the day when she had a moment alone in her classroom. She held her hand against her pounding chest.

As she grabbed her belongings, a note card fell to the table. She pulled it free, eager to see the note Logan had written her, hating herself she hadn't noticed it earlier. The small card was covered with tiny writing, leaving no space empty.

We came to know each other by accident, but now that I know you, I can't bear to lose you. My family loves you, and Ami adores you. Please don't let my mistakes keep you from being a part of our lives. We're having a cookout this weekend and we're grilling cheeseburgers. Please come and spend the day with us. The fun will start at three. It won't be the same without you. Yours always, Logan

44

Logan paced back and forth, willing the time to move faster. Two-thirty. This Saturday had been the longest day of his life. Would she come? What if she didn't? How would he survive the rest of the day if she didn't? Was he crazy for inviting her?

"Logan, can you grab the other tablecloth from the coat closet?"

He walked mechanically, each step light yet nervous. It was a mistake to ask her to come. He needed to explain to Mom.

The familiar chime rumbled above him and his blood quickened through his veins.

Standing only inches from the front door, he opened it slowly to find Addison standing on the other side, facing in the opposite direction.

She turned her cautious eyes to meet his. "Hi."

"Hi." A cool breeze blew in from outside and he moved to the side so she could enter. "I'm so glad you came." She stepped past him and he inhaled the familiar scent of her. "Addison, I haven't—"

Mom met them in the foyer and pulled Addison into an embrace. "It's so good to see you. We've missed you so much." Mom pulled back and regarded her just as she'd done him and his siblings so many times. "Logan, don't forget the tablecloth."

Mom reacted to Addison as if she'd known about the pregnancy all along. Had she? Had Nathan told her? Then he caught the brief shock in Ami's expression as she joined them.

Over the next hour, Logan watched from a distance as his sister and Mom claimed all of Addison's attention.

"Why don't you sneak off with her?" Nathan said, breaking his trance.

"What do you mean?"

"Take her somewhere. You don't have to stay here. You'll never get her alone with them hogging her."

Logan shrugged. "Maybe she doesn't want to be alone with me."

"You won't know unless you ask." Nathan walked away, leaving him standing by the fence. His gaze moved back to the porch toward Addison. She was no longer talking but still standing by his mom and sister.

Then, as if reading his thoughts, Mom and Ami walked inside.

He climbed the porch steps and moved into the space next to her. "It's chilly out here." Her lips curved into a slight smile, giving him the courage to continue. "How's teaching going?"

"Good."

"Will you ride with me?"

She glanced at him, her eyes full of questions. "What?"

"Can we go somewhere? Just you and me?"

"Now? But what about—"

Without thinking, Logan took her hand, opened the back door, and told his family, "We'll be back."

Logan led her around the house, and he didn't stop until they reached his truck.

"Where are we going?"

"I wanted to show you something."

Addison tilted her head. For a moment, he worried he was moving too fast. It was crazy to be here with her. He had been crazy for inviting her, her for accepting. His heart pulsated to a faltering beat.

"Logan?"

285

As he looked into her eyes, he relished the wonder of standing here with her after all these months.

"Before we leave, can I say something?"

For a heartbeat he panicked, afraid she had changed her mind. "Of course."

"I'm sorry. For everything. You have been—" Emotion cracked her voice.

He reached for her hand, wrapping his fingers around hers.

"I don't deserve your kindness."

He opened and closed his mouth before forming his words. "I want to be your friend." As her striking eyes met his, he knew his heart could never adjust to being just friends.

"After everything that's happened. I just don't know how—"

He took a step closer. "It's easy. You came today."

"It wasn't easy coming here."

"Why not?"

"Look at me," she said with lower volume. "Your family—"

"My family adores you." Carefully, Logan pulled her against him, and he savored the comfort of her wrapped inside his arms. The roundness of her stomach, the baby growing inside of her, had created a barrier between them. And if he wasn't careful, it could separate them forever. It was written all over her hesitation of joining him. "I've been wanting to show you something."

Her eyes softened, relaxed. "Okay."

They drove in silence, the faint sound of the radio playing in the small space between them. If he brought up the subject of her baby, he'd no doubt make her uncomfortable but didn't want her to think he didn't care. Especially under the circumstances that caused her pregnancy. "How are you feeling?"

She smiled and he remembered the first days of their relationship, when they were only beginning to get to know each other.

"Pretty good."

He switched the stereo to media and played one of the songs that they had danced to from his playlist.

"I like this song," she told him.

The simple action had the desired effect. Logan parked his truck in a space by the water. He shut off his engine, and they listened to the song while watching the ducks play on the water's edge. "Maybe we could dance to it again sometime."

Logan ignored the twinge of hurt when Addison didn't reply immediately.

Neither spoke for a long time, then Logan twisted in his seat.

Addison watched him. Her blue-violet eyes sparkled in the sunlight reflecting off the water. "Philip was at Ami's débuette dance."

"I know."

Delicate lines formed between her eyebrows. "You saw him?"

"When you were dancing with Nathan."

She held his gaze for another moment before her focus drifted to the water stretched out before them. "He stopped me when I was coming from the bathroom. I should've told you. I should've been honest with you about the way he treated me."

The truth punched him hard in the gut. He knew how Philip treated her. And he did nothing to prevent it. Just stood by and watched Philip use her, hurt her.

"Philip was waiting for me the night you picked me up from the restaurant. The same night we went to Mr. Baker's." Tears spilled freely onto her cheeks. "He was already so jealous of you. Had warned me not to see you anymore. When you drove away, he grabbed me and he"—she glanced down as she ran a hand over her belly— "he forced himself on me."

Nathan had told him the basics. And for days outrage had flared through Logan's veins. He had wanted to track down Philip—make him pay for his cruel, brutal act against Addison. How could anyone hurt her?

But seeing the pain in her eyes, feeling the devastation that moment had caused her as she relived that night stole his ability to speak or even move.

"I wasn't honest with you or Philip. If only I'd told the truth, none of this would've happened."

"It wasn't your fault." His anger crumbled into affection as she seemed to consider his words. Surely, she didn't believe she was at fault.

He leaned closer and lifted her chin. Opening her eyes, she met his gaze. "Addison, there are things I should've done differently too, but none of this is your fault."

She nibbled her lip and resumed her gaze across the water. Logan sensed her grief and paused for a few moments not wanting to push her too fast. "When you pressed charges—?"

Her shoulders stiffened. "I didn't. And I can't. Philip can't see me like this." Her chin dipped. "He can never know about the baby."

Logan's anger escalated. Philip didn't know about the baby? The only thing keeping him from arguing was the sadness, the evident battle in her eyes.

Before he could say anything more, Addison broke the silence with a deep inhale. "That's the reason I left, Logan. I knew you wouldn't understand that or me choosing to carry the baby."

The realization of her admission pierced him straight through the heart. Their last conversation came rushing back, stealing his breath. *The one thing Carrie knew I couldn't live with ... her having another man's baby.*

He needed to clarify but she needed his support more than simple words of promise.

He leaned forward and took her pinky in his need to touch her, to be closer, to somehow comfort her in this moment.

She had been hurt enough.

———

Remaining unaffected by Logan Tant was going to be more of a challenge than Addison had thought. The subtle change in the atmosphere between them made her stomach flutter.

"Can I ask you something?" The shift in his voice was unmistakable. "Can I see you again? Not because you're my sister's friend, but because you want to see me—because you want to be with me?"

His question inflated her admiration of him. Conflicting thoughts danced through her mind, each one desperate for control. "I would really like that?"

He gently brought her fingers to his lips. "Come on. I want to show you something."

What was she doing here? But as her pulse thumped through her veins, the explanation came to her. He'd come to see her. On Valentine's Day. It was incredibly romantic—bringing her flowers, inviting her here today. The one thing she would've never anticipated, much less believed. Heaven knew how much she wanted this, wanted him.

Still, she had to use her brain when it came to her heart.

Ten minutes later, he turned into a driveway and parked the truck. Confused, she studied the small house. Its black shutters complemented the gray siding. Why had he brought her here?

Logan twisted in his seat, facing her. "I bought this house."

Addison leaned forward, getting a better look. "Really? You bought this?"

"I've been thinking about it for a while. I was throwing my money away on rent, and let's just say it was time I moved out on my own."

"Wow, I'm so happy for you," she told him, though it felt as if her world was crumbling all around her.

He turned toward her. Leaving one hand on the steering wheel, he placed the other on her shoulder. "Do you want to go inside?"

"Can we?"

He climbed from the truck and walked around to help her down. He must have read her hesitation. "It's mine," he said with a laugh.

He unlocked the front door and led her inside, the scent of fresh paint and new carpet tickling the back of her throat and she coughed.

"Are the fumes too much for you?" he asked, glancing at the roundness of her belly before his gaze claimed hers.

Her cheeks burned. "No, I love the smell of paint."

"Let's open a window just in case."

She stared at the empty off-white walls, frustrated that she couldn't fully enjoy this moment with him—not with her heart shouting the impossibility of it all.

This was too much. The way he talked to her, the familiarity of his

289

touch. As if no time had passed between them. It wasn't real. Every-thing had changed and nothing would ever be the same.

He didn't seem to notice her unease and led her on a tour through the rest of the house.

"When will you move in?"

"I'm not sure, but I hope by the end of the month."

Regret filled her. Could-have-been thoughts spiraled through her mind with each step through the house, seeing the kitchen, his bedroom, the spare room for future children. Her heart broke a thou-sand times over.

"You don't like it?"

Addison, consumed in her loss, was caught by surprise at his ques-tion. "It's perfect." Her throat thickened and she looked down at her hands. "You'll be so happy here."

She smiled, fighting the tears burning the backs of her eyelids. Unable to speak, she walked toward the kitchen. Clearing her throat, she turned to find Logan leaning against the wall his gaze locked on her. "What?"

"There's one more thing I wanted to show you."

He led her through the back door, and cool, fresh air hit her in the face, slamming her thoughts back to reality.

He took her hands into his and Matthew 6:27 came to her. *Can anyone of you by worrying add a single hour to your life?* In that moment, Addison decided to quit choking out her precious time with Logan. Because a single hour may be all they have together.

The patio had no furniture or flowers adorning it, but she could imagine all the colors bringing this area to life. She glanced down at the cobblestoned walkway leading to a storage building. "This is great, Logan. I'm really happy for you."

"Can I visit you in Jacksonville?"

"What?"

"I want to come see you." He fell silent for a moment, his gaze never leaving hers. "Will it be all right to visit you?"

Yes," she replied without hesitation, though her hopeful expecta-tions would most certainly get shattered.

But she was even more certain, for now, she was willing to take the risk.

A ddison stood at her desk the following Thursday afternoon studying the writing papers she intended to file for the parent-teacher conference at the end of the school year.

McKenzie cleared his throat. "Hi, can I come in?"

Addison glanced up at him briefly. "Of course." She grabbed a paper she had set to the side. "Does this one belong to you? I can't make out this name."

Addison started to hand it to him, but McKenzie was closer than she'd thought, and she hit him in the face. "Oh, I'm so sorry." She covered her mouth with her hand. "Did I hurt you?"

He sat on the edge of her desk. "Only a little, but if you have dinner with me tonight, we'll forget the whole thing."

Addison laughed, shaking her head. "Is everything a joke to you?"

"Only if you want it to be."

Addison looked at him. "Did you need something?"

McKenzie didn't blink. "I wanted to tell you something, but I didn't want you to take it the wrong way."

Her eyes crinkled. What could he have to say? Would it hurt her feelings? "Okay."

"Do you promise?"

She laughed and leaned her thigh against the desk. McKenzie was never this serious. "I promise not to take whatever you tell me the wrong way."

He stepped closer. "You are the most beautiful woman I have ever laid my eyes on."

Addison scrunched her mouth. "Stop it."

She started to turn away, but he caught her arm and pulled her against him. Before she realized what was happening, he was kissing her. Stunned, she stumbled back.

Regret filled his eyes. "Addison, you must know how I feel."

"I'm sorry if I gave you that idea, but I—"

"You didn't. But I needed you to know how I feel." He glanced at her belly. "You need someone who will love you the way you deserve to be loved—someone who will love your baby girl as their own." A subtle accusation edged his tone.

She stepped behind the desk, separating them. "My baby girl?"

"I've heard you call the baby her several times. It doesn't matter as long as it's healthy though, right?"

"McKenzie, you're a wonderful guy and I like you a lot, but I can't do this."

"It's your friend that visited Valentine's Day, isn't it?"

The mention of Logan caused her hands to tremble. She didn't want him to see her weakness—

"I just don't understand. If I were him, I'd be by your side every day. I wouldn't be able to go weeks without seeing you. I wouldn't be able to stand one day."

McKenzie's words lingered through her mind. There was so much he didn't know about her history with Logan. Logan had kept his distance, and she had respected his desire to take things slow. He had probably come to his senses as soon as she left Wilmington. "I need to go. I'll see you tomorrow, okay?"

"No hard feelings?" His tone was confident.

"Of course not." She kept her voice even and without emotion.

He left the room and she leaned against the desk, dazed. *What in the world?*

Logan drove down US17, his chest aching with emptiness. How could this be happening again?

After witnessing Addison in an intimate conversation with her teacher-friend, he had walked away. A deep gnawing in the darkest recesses of his mind shouted at him. *Don't leave her. She needs you. You need her.* But he couldn't stop. With his head down, he had exited the school and mechanically walked toward his truck, the teddy bear still stuffed in his jacket. It would give him a reason to see her at least one more time. He needed time to sort things through. Each mile drove them farther apart from each other, his heart aching with each length of space.

Ami met him at the door when he arrived at his parents' house. "What're you doing here? I thought you were going to Jacksonville."

"I changed my mind," Logan lied, unable to bear telling Ami he'd seen Addison kissing someone else.

"Well, you're taking me tomorrow when you go. Or I'll drive myself. You can't keep her away from me, no matter how stupid you act about her. You act like you don't even care. Is it because of the baby? Are you so disappointed that she's pregnant, you can't forgive her?"

"Ami, that's enough," Mom told her, keeping her stance against the kitchen counter.

"Well, he can't keep her from me. She was my friend first," Ami fumed, leaving him stunned.

Ami stormed up the stairs and he turned to Mom. She was waiting patiently for him to say something, and when he didn't, she spoke. "Logan, I understand this is very hard on you. You didn't ask for this, but neither did she. Do you know what she plans to do?"

"I never asked her."

Mom took a seat at the kitchen table and patted the chair next to her. He took the seat reluctantly.

"I believe she's scared out of her mind. Try to see it from her point

294

of view. If you love her, you should find out what it is she's planning to do, so you can prepare yourself for that."

"I wanted to ask, but the time never seemed right."

She said nothing, waiting for him to continue.

"I did go to Jacksonville. I was going to surprise her. When I reached her classroom, she was talking to a teacher. A male teacher. He made her laugh a few times and then they kissed."

Mom kept her eyes on the table but squeezed her hands together. "I don't understand. You think she's been seeing him?"

His chest tightened at hearing the words. "I don't know. I saw them together here in Wilmington too."

"But wouldn't she have said something to you? I assumed you two had a nice time together Saturday. How did you leave things?"

"I asked her if I could visit and she said yes. But I didn't tell her I was coming today."

"I see." Mom shook her head. "Do you really believe Addison would lead you along if she was in love with someone else?"

"I don't know what to think."

Mom took his hand and squeezed it. "Maybe you should ask her. Maybe you are mistaken in what you saw. Either way, I believe Addison would be honest with you."

Mom stood and left him sitting there, left his mind racing in a million different directions.

They definitely shared a kiss. But from where he was standing, it was hard to make out Addison's response, her reaction. She could've been the instigator and had even enjoyed the kiss.

But maybe, just maybe, she hadn't.

46

An empty flutter filled Addison's stomach as she pulled onto her street. She searched for Logan's truck, hoping to find it parked on the curb by her house. A cold, sharp wave of affliction rushed through her when she reached her place and its empty driveway.

After two hours of working through papers her students had finished today, she wandered into the kitchen. At the grocery store yesterday, she'd stocked up on ingredients for a few recipes in case Logan showed up. She had hoped he would come today, though he'd never said when or if he'd come for sure. Only asked if he could.

Addison pulled the ingredients from the pantry for the green chile chicken and rice soup. After cooking and shredding the boneless chicken breast, she dropped a tablespoon of oil into a large frying pan.

Adding chopped onions to the pan, she sautéed them for five minutes, then added a clove of garlic. She moved through the motions mechanically, fighting against her disappointment. Stirring slowly, she poured some chicken broth, tomatoes, green chiles, the shredded chicken, rice, and seasonings into the pan. She turned the eye down to simmer.

Her cell phone vibrated. She'd forgotten to turn the ringer back on.

What if Logan had called and she'd missed it? She checked her notifications. Aunt Brenda had called.

She'd call her back in a few minutes.

Five minutes later, she ladled some soup into a small bowl and topped it with chopped cilantro, diced avocado, and the juice from a fresh lime.

After she ate, she took a shower and settled onto the couch to return Aunt Brenda's call and catch up with all that had been going on in Wilmington.

Aunt Brenda was on her way to the mountains for a long weekend. Then Taylor called while they were talking, and she opted to end the call with Aunt Brenda. Addison was anxious to tell Taylor about the incident with McKenzie, how each day this week she had hoped Logan would come, how she still worried Philip would find out.

Taylor and Michael had dinner plans, but she offered to cancel and drive to Jacksonville.

"No, you go, have a good time with your fiancé. I'm fine."

Addison grabbed her journal and Bible from the table. She read her devotion for today and the answer came over her slowly. She wasn't in control of this situation. God had a plan for her and would protect her baby. She jotted down another verse in her journal next to her memories with Logan on Saturday.

Jeremiah 29:11 For I know the plans I have for you declares the Lord, plans to prosper you and not harm you, plans to give you hope and a future.

Who could blame Logan for being cautious? Addison had pushed Logan away so many times, not trusting God in her circumstances.

Who was she to decide how Logan should react to what Philip had done? To her decision to not press charges? Why hadn't she been honest with him from the beginning?

McKenzie's kiss lingered in her memory. She wasn't attracted to him, but his kiss had brought an unexpected longing—a yearning to be loved, a yearning for Logan Tant.

Logan drove to his new house, his thoughts in a tangled web of confusion. He was going about this all wrong. He'd asked Addison if she wanted to see him, but he hadn't been completely honest about his intentions. And like his mom pointed out, he hadn't asked what her plans were. Did she plan to keep the baby or was she considering adoption? Was he willing to raise a baby that wasn't his own? A baby conceived from rape?

He walked through the living room, the empty space reinforcing his bleak mood. He should be at Addison's right now, sitting across from her, hearing about the children from her class—and even her favorite teacher friends.

His phone vibrated, interrupting his thoughts. He pressed the button and his heart skipped a beat at the words written across the small screen.

Hey, I was just thinking about you. I had so much fun spending time with you and your family last weekend. Hope to see you soon. Stay safe.

He read the message ten times, before the screen blacked out. He needed to think it through before he responded. He glanced at the time on his screen.

Six-thirty.

In one hour, he could be standing in front of her and would be able to find out once and for all where he stood.

No.

He should wait. Give it a few days. His thoughts were too sporadic tonight.

Addison pulled her wet hair into a knotty ponytail and collapsed onto the couch. The tightening in her stomach had increased in the last hour and sharp pains were now shooting across her middle.

Ten minutes later, vehicle lights shined through her front window and she scrambled to her feet, her pulse racing. She had received no response from Logan and that meant he was probably working, that it probably wasn't him.

The sun had already set, and the faint glow of the streetlight didn't help. Slowly she lifted one corner of the blind, hoping whoever was out there wouldn't see the shift. Even though she wasn't surprised, there was a moment of utter disappointment when she didn't find Logan's truck sitting in her driveway.

The driver had already left the car and was headed to her front porch. Maybe Taylor, but she always called first and she had talked to her earlier.

The soft knock startled her, though she'd been expecting it. "Who is it?" She placed a trembling hand behind her back.

"Addison, it's me. McKenzie."

McKenzie?

She clutched at her chest. What was he doing here? How did he know how to find her? She turned with a sweeping look at her living room. She glanced at her cell phone stuffed inside her purse, as her stomach tightened with another twinge.

After unlocking the door, she cracked it open. "Hey. What in the world are you doing here?"

He looked past her into the living room. "I felt so bad about what happened this afternoon. I didn't want you to feel uncomfortable tomorrow at school."

She opened the door a little more. "No, it's okay. Let's just pretend nothing happened. You're too much fun to work with for things to become weird between us." She tried to hide the pain she felt through her midsection, but her throat tightened, and her voice quavered.

He leaned against the frame and she swayed backward. "Does that mean I'm forgiven?"

"Yes, now go home, eat a big bowl of ice cream, and I'll see you in the morning." The quality of her words sounded fake even to her own ears.

"I was hoping we could talk. Can I come in?" There was an unmistakable pleasure in his expression.

Clearly, she had missed something.

Panic gripped the edges of her conscious awareness. "It's getting late, and I'm not feeling well. Can it wait until tomorrow?"

"It's about Philip." His usual teasing tone had disappeared. His voice was now loud and ominous.

She made eye contact with the man she had worked with for over a month and something in his expression made her skin crawl.

"Philip Baker in your class?" she asked him, keeping her tone even, unaffected, though she knew that wasn't the Philip he meant.

He leaned closer. "No, my cousin Philip. He's been so worried about you. When I told him we were working together, I promised him I would look after you. But then what I did today was so incredibly stupid."

Addison only heard bits and pieces of what McKenzie was saying. Her mind was racing in several different directions and she flinched as the pain across her middle deepened.

"I don't understand. I don't know who you're talking about."

"Of course, you do. As soon as he found out you were pregnant, he wanted me to look out for you. But then I went and fell in love with you." He pushed the door open.

She stumbled back, the door opening with her. A rush of unexpected dizziness slid across her vision as another sharp pain swept through her middle. She grabbed her stomach and screamed in agonizing pain. Suddenly, from behind McKenzie came another voice. It was male. She grabbed the wall to steady herself, but she was too late.

The room darkened as a wave of numbness washed over her and then there was nothing.

47

"Stay with me, Addison. Help's on the way." She had fainted, and Logan's lungs tightened in his chest.

"Logan?" Her heavy eyes searched his face.

"I'm here." He stroked her damp hair, pushing it from her face. "You're going to be okay."

Within minutes, the medics he'd called arrived and lifted Addison onto the gurney. Logan stood back, his body trembling in fear. *Please, God, let her be okay.*

"Are you her husband?"

Everything within him wanted to say yes. "No."

The EMS worker glanced at the teacher standing by his car.

"He's the husband?"

"No. I'm her boyfriend," Logan blurted.

"Are you following us, then?"

"Yes, I'm right behind you."

They lifted Addison inside the ambulance and the doors slammed behind them. Logan grabbed Addison's purse and locked her front door. Rushing to his truck, dread filled him. He glanced at the other teacher's somber look across the yard.

Logan's legs trembled as he sped onto the main highway, heading toward the hospital. Logan ran his fingers through his hair, his pulse thrashing in his ears. He hadn't heard the conversation between Addison and the teacher but seeing her standing there with him had inflicted a deep agonizing wound through his chest. Why was he there? Was she seeing him?

The drive took only ten minutes, but it felt like hours. *Please be with her, God. She's been through so much. Wrap your arms around her and protect her ... and the baby.*

Tears burned his eyes, as he struggled to stay focused. The ambulance's siren blared against the moonless night, vehicles pulling over, pedestrians staring as they sped by. Addison meant nothing to them, but she meant everything to him.

How would he ever survive if something happened to her? If God decided her time here was done?

Why did I wait so long?

Reaching the hospital, Logan fought his desire to park on the curb. Instead, he settled on a spot near the back and took off in a full run toward the emergency room.

Images of the night Ami was in the emergency room came rushing back. He had blamed Addison for Ami's accident. He had wanted to make her pay. And because of his stubbornness, he almost missed out on the best thing that had ever happened in his life.

"I'm here for Addison Morgan."

The blonde typed something into her keyboard and narrowed her eyes. "I don't have anyone listed by that name."

"They just brought her in on an ambulance."

"Are you family?"

"No, not exactly."

"I'm sorry. You'll have to wait out here."

"But she doesn't have anyone else here with her."

"Have a seat and I'll let you know as soon as I hear something."

He placed both hands on the counter. "But I need to see her."

"I'm sorry, sir. Unless you're a relative, I can't let you back there."

The girl scanned the screen, barely acknowledging his presence. "Thank you, next."

Defeated, Logan turned in a daze and met the eyes of the frazzled man behind him, and the man pushed by Logan, stepping closer to the counter. Addison was here somewhere in this building, but he couldn't get to her.

What am I supposed to do? Taylor! Logan ran through the automatic doors and reached his truck within minutes. It wouldn't be right to dig around in Addison's purse, but her phone was sticking out of a side pocket, so he didn't have to. He punched Taylor's name, her number appeared, and he pressed call. She answered on the second ring.

"No, Taylor, this is Logan. Addison's in the emergency room. She passed out. They brought her in, but they won't let me see her."

Logan waited while Taylor took in the news before he said more.

"I need to call her aunt."

"Yes." Taylor's high-pitched voice caused him to pull the phone away from his ear. "She's on the way to the mountains."

Logan's stomach lurched at her response. "I'll call her right now. What should I do until you get here?"

Taylor told him she had already started driving in the direction of the hospital. "I'll be there as soon as I can. Tell them you're her fiancé. In her condition, it'll work."

"I'm going back in. Call her phone when you get here. I'll keep it in my pocket."

He locked his truck and raced back to the front entrance and to the front desk. "Have you heard anything yet?"

"What was her name?"

"Addison Morgan," he told her, clinging to a small spark of hope. "Please let me see her. I'm the closest thing to family she has. I'm going to marry her."

The lady's eyes softened, and she pressed a button while giving quick directions to the internal waiting room. "I'll have one of the doctors meet you."

Logan didn't look back as he followed three glaringly white hallways until he reached the one he looked for. He paced back and forth, waiting for the doctor to appear. The seconds stretched into minutes and Logan finally sat, bowing his head between his knees.

"Addison Morgan?"

Logan jerked into a standing position and faced the doctor. "I'm her fiancé." He liked the sound of that. "What's wrong?"

"She's in labor. We're hoping to slow it down, but so far it's not working."

"How is she?"

"She should be fine. You did the right thing getting her here."

A wave of relief washed over him. "Can I see her?"

"Follow me."

Logan peeked into the room and got a full look at Addison. She was lying on the bed, tubes running from her arms and he shuddered. He strode across the room and stopped next to the bed.

He took her hand and she startled at the movement. "Logan," she mumbled, her eyes heavy. "You're here?"

"Of course, I am." He gently caressed the back of her hand and with his other brushed a stray strand of hair from her eyes. "I had to see for myself that you would be all right."

She nodded, her eyes drifting closed again. "They gave me something to help with the pain. It makes me sleepy."

He studied the machine. Her heart rate was being monitored, but so was the baby's. The steady rhythm calmed his nerves. He sat down softly on the mattress next to her, careful not to waken her, when she squeezed his hand. She pulled her body upward and her face twisted in pain.

"What is it? Should I call for help?"

"It's the baby. She's trying to come now."

She? Did Addison know it was a girl? She'd never talked about the baby, and neither had he. Addison was lying here in the emergency room because of the baby she carried … because of the baby's father. How did Addison feel about this baby? He had never asked her and now regretted it. What if she wanted to talk about it but didn't to protect his feelings?

"The doctor told me they were trying to slow the labor down."

"What if it doesn't work? What if the baby comes too soon—" She didn't finish her sentence as her face twisted in pain.

After it had passed, Logan responded to her question. "You can't think that way. God is in full control of this. You have to trust him." He squeezed her shoulder.

"I'm so scared."

Tears filled her eyes and he leaned closer into her. "I won't leave you."

The nurse entered and asked, "How are you feeling?"

"The pain has increased, and the contractions are stronger." She still squeezed his hand. "What does that mean?"

The nurse studied the machine. "It's too soon to tell. We're monitoring your contractions, so we'll just have to wait and see if they'll slow down or not."

"Okay."

Addison's soft tone, the way she showed respect as though she understood, though she didn't, deepened his love. The nurse left, leaving them alone once again. But his resolve to open his heart remained and he wanted to ask her now, before another moment escaped.

The vibration of Addison's phone startled him, and the ring tone rang out through the room. Addison's gaze darted around the room. "Is that my phone?"

"Yes." Logan pulled it from his pocket. "I grabbed it from your purse and called Taylor. They wouldn't let me come back here at first. She's on the way."

"Hello." He paused, keeping his eyes locked with Addison's. "No, she's awake now. The doctor said she was going to be okay." He handed the phone to Addison.

He stepped to the window, looking through the darkened sky, grasping the reality of where they were. Why they were here.

"I'm in labor, but they're trying to slow it down. I'm thirty-four weeks, so if they can't, the baby should be fine as long as there are no other health issues. They'll have to keep the baby a few days longer," she said, her voice breaking, "I don't know. They have me on a monitor." Addison paused, taking a deep breath.

Logan listened to the one-way conversation. The unmistakable concern in Addison's voice tortured him. He waited until she ended the call before he approached her.

"Do you want me to go out so Taylor can come in?"

Her chin dipped to her chest. "You both can be back here with me. You don't have to stay though."

"I would like to—" He hesitated as the doctor entered the room.

He walked past Logan and stopped at the edge of the bed. "How are we feeling?"

"A little better. I haven't felt a contraction in a while."

"When was the last one?"

Addison glanced at the clock. "I don't remember."

Logan took a step forward. "It's been four minutes."

Within the next few hours, they admitted her to a labor and delivery room. She was in labor, but stable. Taylor helped Addison get settled into the bed, while Logan waited outside in the hallway. He called his mom.

"She's going to have the baby tonight? Oh, Logan. I'm so glad you decided to go to her. We'll be there in a little while."

"You don't have to come, it's already so late."

"Yes, we do, especially if her aunt's out of town. She's like family to us."

Taylor stepped out when a nurse entered Addison's room and he ended the call.

"Thank God she's going to be okay." Taylor said. "I'm so glad you were there. What happened?"

Logan remembered the teacher. He hadn't followed them to the hospital. "I went to her house. One of the teachers she works with was standing on the porch talking to her."

"McKenzie?"

Hearing Taylor mention the teacher's name as if Addison had told her all about him nauseated him. "Are they seeing each other?"

Taylor's eyes crinkled under her frown. "What?"

"I saw them together this afternoon." He turned, the memory slamming into his consciousness as if it were happening all over again.

"What do you mean you saw them together?" Taylor had taken a step closer. There was a certain determination in her voice. "Today?"

He was hesitant to put his thoughts into words. "I found them kissing in her classroom—"

Taylor's smile was replaced by an incredulous look. "Wait. You were there? She didn't tell me that."

The nurse left the room and told them they could go back inside. He started to walk through the door when Taylor grabbed his arm.

"They weren't kissing, Logan. McKenzie kissed her, but it wasn't something Addison wanted. And no, they're not dating. She's in love with you. She has been for a long time."

Taylor walked past him, leaving him to gather his thoughts.

Addison waited patiently for Logan and Taylor to return. This baby was coming tonight, and she wasn't prepared to face the decision she'd been dreading all these months. She wanted to love this baby, to be the kind of mother she'd always longed to have. But how?

"Logan, were you at my house?" she asked when he entered.

"Yes, I got there around seven-thirty."

"I remember seeing you, but I thought maybe I was dreaming." Addison stared at him in wonder. "Did you see McKenzie?"

His eyes swept the room, his facial expression blank. "Yes." He did not react until his gaze reached hers.

Unspoken questions filled her mind and in that moment the memory of McKenzie's words came rushing back. "Did he say anything to you?"

Logan shook his head. "No, I never spoke to him."

She leaned against the propped-up pillows. "He said something about Philip. I thought he was talking about one of the students, but then he said, 'No, my cousin Philip.'"

"Philip's cousin?"

"He said he graduated from UNCW too."

Logan's detached stare broke her heart, but then, as if someone switched places with him, his gaze filled with a combination of love and protection. "Did he say anything else?"

"No, I don't remember anything after that."

"Did you tell McKenzie about Philip?" Taylor sat on the bed next to her.

"No. He said Philip knows I'm pregnant."

Logan stood by the chair in the corner and stared through the window. She turned to Taylor, who was watching him also. The epidural had eased her pain and she now only felt the hardening of her middle.

Her doctor entered the room. "How're you feeling?"

"Good. I'm beginning to feel pressure."

"That means it's getting close. Let me check you to see how much progress we've made."

Taylor stood next to her bed holding her hand. Logan returned to the window while the doctor did his examination. Her heart ached with yearning at the sight of him standing here in her hospital room. She loved him. Desperately.

"It's time. I'll be back shortly." He closed the door behind him.

Logan suddenly stood next to her. She never saw him move from the window.

Taylor's eyes widened. "It's almost time. Do you want me to stay in here with you?"

"Yes, thank you for coming, Taylor."

Taylor squeezed her hand. "Girl, you know I wouldn't miss this for anything."

Addison looked at Logan standing on her other side as her contraction relaxed. He had come to see her. She'd been hoping he would all day and now despite everything that had happened, he was here.

His smile, when it finally reached his lips, revealed a depth of emotion she hadn't seen before.

"I'm glad you came."

"Me too." Logan took her pinky in his. "I'm going to step out. I'll be right down the hall in the waiting room."

"Thank you for coming. For being here."

He stepped outside but within seconds reopened the door. "Aunt Brenda's here."

Addison's tears flowed freely down her cheeks. "How did you—"

"Logan called me." Aunt Brenda kissed her on the forehead. "And it looks as if I made it just in time."

The doctor entered seconds later. "Are we ready to have that baby?"

As agreements were lifted into the room around her, Addison whimpered. All those months of fears were finally coming to a head.

Now that the time was here, she longed for her mama to hug her tight and tell her everything would be all right. Addison's chin trembled. Thinking about her mama always made her sad. Made her wish things could go back to the way things were before daddy had died. Made her worry she wouldn't be a good mama.

Made her want to believe she would be.

4 8

One hour later, Logan stared in awe at the baby girl Addison held in her arms. Countless emotions fought for their place in his heart.

Addison had been so brave and had given birth to this baby when it would have been so easy to take a different route.

The admiration and respect Logan felt for this young woman caused a longing in ways he hadn't known possible.

Logan sat on the edge of Addison's bed, his gaze drawn to the softness of the baby's cheeks, her tiny lips, her squinting eyes.

A nurse entered carrying some paperwork. "I'll need you to fill these out when you can," she said, placing the clipboard on a nearby table.

He glanced at Addison and found her cheeks wet with tears. Their gazes met and he read her heart. Would she put Philip as the father on the birth certificate? Would she leave it blank? For the first time, Logan wished he was this baby's father.

"I'll need to take the baby now," the nurse continued, coming for the child bundled so tight Logan could barely see her face.

Wonder enhanced Addison's beautiful features as the nurse reached for the baby. A sob escaped Addison's throat and the sound ripped through another layer of his heart as the nurse left the room with the baby. He had never seen so much love in an expression in his entire life —or how one could grieve so rapidly.

"Why don't we go downstairs for a coffee, Taylor, and give these two a few minutes alone?" Addison's aunt said.

Aunt Brenda and Taylor followed the nurse into the hall and closed the door behind them.

"She's so beautiful." Addison turned her head slightly into her pillow and let her tears fall. "I love her, Logan. How am I going to let her go?"

Logan's commitment and desire strengthened. "You don't have to."

Addison lifted her wet lashes to him. "What?"

"You don't have to give her up." Logan searched Addison's eyes, raw and tormented and painfully beautiful. He had never felt more connected to anyone than he did to Addison in that moment. "You don't have to do anything you don't want to."

"But—"

"I love you, Addison." He sat down next to her and took her hand. "I want to marry you." Battling a swell of emotion, he continued, "I want to spend the rest of my life with you and I promise to love you both forever."

Addison stared into his eyes, drawing him closer. "Logan, are you sure? What if you change your mind? What if—"

"There will always be what-ifs. But I want to share all my what-ifs with you. I'm committing to you and your baby right now, Addison."

Addison reached up and swept a shaky finger through his hair. "I love you so much."

"Does that mean yes?"

"Yes, that means yes."

He wrapped his arms around her. Absorbing her yes, his mind raced thinking of all the ways his life would forever be changed from this moment on.

He pulled away from her only when his cell phone vibrated against his leg. He glanced at the message written across the screen. *We're here. Tell Addison we're praying.*

"Do you feel up to having company?"

Addison wiped the tears from her cheeks and sat up a little as the tiny lines on her forehead crinkled. "What do you mean?"

"My mom and Ami are in the waiting room."

Her eyes widened, her expression astonished. "They're here?"

"I'll go get them. I'll be right back."

People were scattered throughout the waiting room, but he found his mom and Ami easily. Mom stood when he stepped toward her, and he fell into her arms. Unexpected tears welled in his eyes.

Taking his hands, she pulled away. "What's wrong? Is Addison okay?"

"She's fine. The baby and Addison—I've never seen anything more beautiful in all my life."

Mom squeezed his hands. "The baby has already come?" A wave of relief leaked into her voice.

"Can we see her?" Ami asked.

"Of course."

He wasn't sure what he'd expected, but the profound happiness in Mom's eyes filled a jagged hole in the core of his soul.

Mom's shoulders lifted with excitement. "Oh, Logan. Take us to her." His mom held so much love for Addison.

Ami followed behind, and he slowed to keep pace with her.

"She'll be so happy to see you."

She glanced up, sorrow filling her eyes. "I'm sorry, Logan, for being so hard on you." She slipped her arm beneath his. "Please forgive me."

He stopped and wrapped his sister in his arms there in the hospital hallway. "I love you." He pulled away and looked into her eyes. "You were right all along, you know."

A half sob, half giggle fell from her lips. "I know."

He stepped backward and pointed the way to Addison's room. "You go ahead. I need a few minutes." His mom and sister walked away, and he sat and studied the square pattern of the waiting room carpet as he said a prayer of thanks.

A few days later, Addison was near tears as she sat in the cool leather seat beside Logan, her mind unable to comprehend all the changes she'd faced over the last few days. She had given birth to a baby girl and was taking her home. She'd accepted a marriage proposal from Logan, and the three of the them would be a family. A real family. Sophia was secure in the car seat behind her, but Addison kept peeking over her shoulder unable to keep her eyes off her.

She was so beautiful—so perfect.

When Logan started the truck, Addison forced herself into her seat-belt and stared through the passenger window as the world sped by in a blur. It was hard to sit still for the ten-minute ride with the baby sleeping right behind her. "There's so much to do. I need to call Principal Andrews. I have to move my things out of the house in Jacksonville." She shot Logan a quick glance. "I need to call Charlotte."

"Don't worry. We will have plenty of help." Logan pressed his lips to her temple after he parked the truck. "But first we have to get the nursery ready for Sophia."

Logan's voice caressed her as he spoke Sophia's name. Addison followed Logan as he carried Sophia's baby seat up the stairs of her aunt's porch. All at once, a current of emotion surged through her, baring her pent-up feelings. The happiness, the desire, the love she felt for Logan.

Shutting the door, she turned to face him. "Thank you for everything."

Logan set the carrier, holding her sleeping baby, on the floor next to where they stood and gently took her hands into his. When he pulled her against his chest, she savored the feel of being in his arms again. The woodsy scent of his cologne filled the space between them and a wave of burning desire washed over her. She had longed for the feel of his lips against hers for months and she pulled back to look at him.

Reaching up onto her tiptoes, she closed the space, connecting her smiling mouth to his, melting into him as he devoured her with a passionate kiss. Control of her emotions had long abandoned her as the kiss ended and she snuggled into his embrace.

"I'm home." The door burst open, breaking the moment.

Logan rushed across the room to take the grocery bags from her aunt. The tenderness and loyalty he had shown in the last few days played over in her mind as Addison watched him from where she stood. He had stayed at the hospital, even though Aunt Brenda had offered to stay with her instead. And he stayed awake with her every time the nurse brought her the baby throughout the night.

Smiling as Logan walked outside to gather more groceries from Aunt Brenda's car, she thought to herself, *I'm going to marry him.*

"This came," Aunt Brenda said with apprehension.

Addison took the envelope from her aunt as she walked outside to help Logan. It was addressed to her from New Hampshire with Philip's name listed in the return address.

Not until Aunt Brenda had closed the door behind her did Addison sit on the floor beside Sophia and open the envelope from Philip, her hands trembling.

Addison,

I know I'm the last person you want or expected to hear from, but I needed to do this, for you and myself.

I'm not writing to give you excuses, but to ask your forgiveness for my behavior and the awful things I've done to you.

I have been in a very bad place for a very long time and only added to it with the drugs and alcohol.

Six months ago, I checked into a rehab center to get clean, and while I was there, I met a young man who told me about a place called His Mansion in New Hampshire. I sent in an application and they accepted me into their program. I have been here for three months, and my life is already changing for the good.

I know there's nothing I can do to take back the pain I caused you, from the very first time I hurt you to the last time when I did the unthinkable.

Because of my actions, I can't expect your forgiveness, but I still need to apologize.

Even though I don't deserve a second thought where the baby you're carrying is concerned, I know you, Addison, and you will want to do the right thing.

Addison cleared her throat, fighting the wave of raw emotions taking root in her chest. Years of memories unfolded, and she pictured Philip the first time she'd met him; the young carefree boy who had taken her hand and led her down the sandy beach the very first time. His eyes sparkled with delight.

I don't know what your plans are when the baby comes, but I want you to know I will not interfere with whatever choice you make.

I have no right to that baby anyway, not after what I did to you, but am willing to provide for the child. You will never have to worry about me showing up or interfering in your life or the child's life or changing my mind.

Thank you, Addison, for giving the baby a chance. I can't imagine how hard that must have been for you. I think about that child every day, every moment, and how lucky he or she was to be carried by you.

Take care,

Philip

Addison exhaled finally able to let go of the anxiety she'd dwelled in for months. And as Logan returned inside, his eyes sought her out and beamed when they connected with hers.

. . .

A few short weeks later, Addison walked along the path at her new home. Admiring the cherry trees blossoming in their driveway by the crooked fence, a peace washed over her.

As if she was looking through a lens, the last year came into view with remarkable transparency. A glimpse of how every moment was knitted together from beginning to end and had brought her to this very moment of pure happiness.

There was no other place she would rather be, now or ever.

Nearing the back porch of their new home, she walked inside and through the kitchen, now stocked with a few groceries. As she headed into the living room, she ran a lone finger across the slick wood of their kitchen table. Navigating through the living room, and then the short hallway leading to the nursery, she found him.

Logan stood leaning against the crib, watching Sophia sleep. Quietly, Addison moved into the space next to him.

Looking up from Sophia's precious face, Logan's gaze met hers. Addison returned his look, a look that united them on a deeper level than any words could say.

There had been no time to wait for a beautiful wedding that took months to plan. They took only the short span of a few days to gather their family and friends to witness a once-in-a-lifetime love as the two of them became one.

After years of a strained relationship with her mom and stepdad, the presence of Sophia had brought them together like nothing else could. And her mom for the first time since Addison could remember, looked as if she were truly happy. Addison missed her sister and always would, but God was a God of blessings. He had given her the beautiful gift of a wonderful sister-in-law.

Their short, simple wedding came a few days after bringing home a beautiful baby girl. A home where Sophia would have a mommy and daddy who would forever love her with all their hearts. Sophia also had grandparents, a great aunt, an Uncle Nathan and an Aunt Ami who were already head-over-heels in love with her.

Gazing at Sophia as she slept soundly, Addison thanked God for the precious gift before her. For a man who loved her so much, he had been willing to turn his world upside down for her and her new baby.

So much pain had led her to this place, pain that had left her heart shattered, but God had taken her shattered heart and, in its place, had given her a family, a beautiful, unshattered treasure.

THE END

ABOUT THE AUTHOR

Cindy Patterson believes in life changing fiction and happily ever afters that start with Jesus. Her passions include Jesus, her husband, and her family. She's an ordinary girl wanting to do extraordinary things for Christ. In her stories, she loves to give glimpses of how God can use brokenness and make them whole. Her favorite pastimes are spending time with her family, reading, and writing. She reads a lot, drinks too much coffee, and wishes she had more time to write. She loves to connect with her readers and you can find her at cindypattersonbks.com.

ACKNOWLEDGMENTS

Dreams in my world are vivid. Thank you to everyone who encouraged, blessed, and helped make this dream a reality. Every time you ask me when will the next book will be out, it's a huge boost of confirmation. Saying thank you doesn't seem like enough.

Every single reader is so valuable. You are the reason I'm on this wild and crazy and exciting journey and you make every moment worthwhile. I wouldn't be here without you.

Thank you to my husband, Rocky, for being so supportive as I spend countless hours on the computer and for always believing in me.

My children Tyler, Zachary, and Brooklyn for loving me through it all.

My editor, Charlene Patterson, for answering all my questions and excusing the weird way I put question marks in the wrong place, even though I know the difference between a statement and question. April, thank you for helping to make this baby shine.

My critique partners who labored over chapter after chapter. I've learned so much from each and every one of you.

And most importantly, thank you, Jesus, for without you, none of this would be possible.

ALSO BY CINDY PATTERSON

Chasing Paradise

Broken Butterfly

Thank you so much for reading Shattered Treasure. I hope you enjoyed it and will tell your friends and family.

Please consider leaving a review on Amazon, Barnes & Nobles, and Goodreads. Reviews are so very helpful to Authors. Every single one of them are appreciated more than you can possibly know.

Cindy Patterson

CPSIA information can be obtained
at www.ICGtesting.com
Printed in the USA
LVHW092139101219
640116LV00007B/41/P

9 781646 690411